Being Modern in Japan
Culture and Society from the 1910s to the 1930s

Published in North America by
University of Hawai'i Press
2840 Kolowalu Street
Honolulu, Hawai'i 96822

First Published in Australia by
Fine Arts Press
42 Chandos Street
St. Leonards Sydney
NSW 2065 Australia

Printed in Singapore

Library of Congress Cataloging-in-Publication Data

The CIP application for this book has been submitted.

ISBN 0-8248-2360-5

Cover Image: *Yorozu Tetsugorō, Nude Beauty, 1912, oil on canvas, National Museum of Modern Art, Tokyo*
Designer: Lee McLachlan
Printer: Kyodo Printing Co.

Being Modern in Japan
Culture and Society from the 1910s to the 1930s

Editors

Elise K. Tipton and John Clark

UNIVERSITY OF HAWAI'I PRESS
HONOLULU

Contents

Acknowledgments

We would like to express our appreciation to various institutions that have provided support for this book in different phases of its development. Most of the papers in this volume originated in a symposium held at the Art Gallery of New South Wales, Sydney, Australia from late July to early August 1998 on the theme of 'Modernism, Modernity and the Modern: Japanese Culture and Society in the 1920s and 1930s'. The symposium coincided with the Art Gallery's exhibition 'Modern Boy Modern Girl: Modernity in Japanese Art, 1910–1935'. The Japan Foundation provided magnificent support for both the symposium and exhibition. In addition, we welcomed support from the School of Asian Studies and Faculty of Arts at the University of Sydney. The present volume represents a number of the papers from the symposium, revised and expanded from the original presentations. The editors also asked Professor Vera Mackie, who had been present at the symposium, to provide an overview of the final collection of essays. Leon Paroissien has been a constant supporter of the project, and we appreciate his efforts in securing Japan Foundation support for the publication of the volume.

A note on Japanese names

Japanese names appear in customary Japanese order, namely surname first, except in certain English works where Western name order is followed.

Introduction

Elise K. Tipton and John Clark

The volume before you examines the meaning of "modern" as reflected in the relationship between culture and society in Japan from the 1910s to the early 1930s. This was an era when the forced Westernization of the Meiji period (1868–1912) had been superseded. During the Meiji period modernization was equated with Westernization, and it was promoted in no uncertain terms by both nongovernmental and governmental elites. But being state-driven, this Westernization had a clear political agenda — achievement of "a rich country, strong army" to gain a position of equality with the Western powers. Although not necessarily agreeing on specific issues, leaders in the private as well as public sector advanced their views in the context of a shared national goal.

After World War I a second wave of Westernization swept over Japan, and by the mid-1920s "*modanizumu*" became the catchword of the times. "*Modan*" this and "*modan*" that repeatedly cropped up in the titles of newspaper and magazine articles and advertisements of the period. But although this flood of new Western ideas and practices has sometimes been compared to the Westernization of the early Meiji period, this time it was less state-led and no longer focused on the national, political goal. Moreover, Japanese receptivity to Western concepts in the Taishō (1912–26) and early Shōwa (1926–37) periods derived from indigenous developments. While modernization based on Western models still had its faddish or imitative aspects, it was no longer simply derived from attraction to the Western as a status symbol of up-to-dateness. Indeed, during the past two decades historians have emphasized the indigenous roots of Japanese modernization in the Meiji period and the ways in which Western models were selectively borrowed and adapted to Japanese needs and conditions. The same emphases must be made regarding Western influences in the 1910s to 1930s; modernization cannot merely be equated with an unreflective Westernization. In this sense, there was nothing inauthentic in the experience of being modern in the Taishō and early Shōwa periods.

At the same time, being modern did not have the same meaning or evoke the same responses from all Japanese. We should include an emphasis on the depth and breadth of the penetration of new Western concepts and of the process of modernization among Japanese at various levels of society and in regions throughout the country. The fruits of mass education and the development of mass media enabled an unprecedented level of communication and dissemination of ideas and images of the modern, even to villages in remote parts of Japan. Attendance levels in primary schools reached close to 100 percent by the beginning of the 1910s. The consequent expansion of the reading public provided the market for commercially oriented newspapers and magazines. Technological advances enabled the print industry to develop unprecedented mass circulations and also created new media of popular culture such as the movie industry. Though never commercialized, the new media of radio, which began broadcasting in 1925, provided yet another channel for diffusion of knowledge of the new and modern, besides being in itself a representative of the latest in modern technology. These new or expanded industries appealed to the growing literate public. In the cities they increasingly targeted the new middle class of salaried white-collar workers in both private enterprises and government offices, but rural dwellers were neither isolated nor ignorant of the latest developments either in Japan or foreign countries, even if they could not yet fully participate in them. Images of "modern life" projected by these industries of entertainment and consumption not only created new material wants, but also offered alternative life choices and role models which did not always support the officially sanctioned ones. Being modern therefore provoked a wide range of responses from ordinary Japanese as well as from social and political commentators, artists, writers, and government officials.

The chapters in this volume are all concerned with questioning discrete properties of Japanese modernity, but, in addition, they may be of wide relevance elsewhere in Asia, Europe, and North America. Moreover, we have deliberately chosen contributions which attempt to supply new insights based on considerable research into Japanese modernity. Readers may recognize aspects of Japanese modernity presented in these chapters as different from the modernity with which they are familiar, but they will also find aspects which resonate with their own knowledge and experience. Questions raised will therefore be relevant to issues about modernity elsewhere, even though they are concerned with the specificities of defining what being modern meant in Japan during the 1910s to 1930s.

For example, is modernity in Japanese art characterized by the simultaneity of certain aesthetic concerns with those of other modernisms as much as the adoption of a common formal language (Mizusawa)? Did Japanese visual representation become modern at the end of the Meiji period in the early 1910s, or did it have to wait until the emergence of a more broadly mass society during the late 1920s (Clark)?

Does modern art rely on the institutional provision of a new kind of art audience, and how is this established (Omuka)? What new forms of design were required for a modern Japanese lifestyle (Kashiwagi)? How was a concept of art articulated through commercial design, and a new role for the designer (Weisenfeld)? How does the notion of culture change with variation in the structures of domestic housing to accommodate it (Sand)? What new forms of entertainment and sites of leisure became part of a modern lifestyle (Tipton)? In what ways did new opportunities and images of women subvert or support the official ideology of female domesticity and submissiveness (Sato)? How did literature reflect the increasing stratification and diversification of Japanese society (Aoyama)? Reacting negatively to these changes in Japanese values and social behavior, how did government officials and conservatives try to restore unity and harmony (Wilson)?

Japanese modern art of the 1910s and 1920s is frequently misconceived as derivative, a view which may too easily recognize only the transfer of European modernist forms of discourse like Fauvism, Expressionism or Futurism, and not see the way these were varied and developed by their articulation in Japan. The work of Yorozu Tetsugorō is an example of this kind of interaction. Mizusawa Tsutomu carefully demonstrates Yorozu's debts to various European artists, but he also shows how Yorozu's preoccupation with the deformation of the human body and its contortion in dance or circus cabaret corresponded almost uncannily with that of Kirchner in Germany, an artist whom he never met and of whose work he could have known very little. Japanese art discourses here demonstrate a simultaneity of aesthetic participation in similar subjects and formal issues which we find elsewhere in modern art.

It is also often supposed that the high art of formal modernism follows the invention of an avant-garde, and later is succeeded by its spread to a mass audience through commercial graphics and design. However, John Clark has carefully analyzed the graphic illustration styles of the generalist magazine *Taiyō* (The Sun) from 1885 to 1928 and discovered that many features formally associated with modernist visual representation can be found in this magazine almost at the same time as the advent of modernism in high art. These features include the shift from verbal to visual reinforcement of an advertising message and the collagist overlaying of different photographic images to provide a synthetic view from multiple perspectives to the reader. In addition, the use of illustrations without a frame for short story narratives facilitated a verbal–visual montage in a way parallel to cinema. Although the circulation of *Taiyō* never reached the scale of mass magazines in the 1920s, it does point to the much wider penetration of modernist representation and to a time much earlier than might be thought through a straightforward developmental account.

But modern art does not arrive in an institutional vacuum. It needs an audience, and that audience has to be formed. Omuka Toshiharu's chapter patiently outlines the way an official or quasi-official salon exhibition structure developed in Japan, and demonstrates the participation in this by different kinds of publics. He also shows the kinds of preparation for the viewing of modern art found through non-professional art training magazines, especially the water-color movement in Japan. In today's world, where fashion is no longer the parasite on art it was until the 1960s, and where art has often taken to acting as the simulacrum of fashion, his chapter is a timely reminder that there is much more to the early institutionaliza-tion of modernity in art than the display of "modern" forms in exhibition spaces.

Nevertheless, modern art does not remain the exclusive preserve of artists and the new audiences of its exhibition spaces. It is also linked to new images of life. The ability to concretize and distribute these new images through objects, Kashiwagi Hiroshi demonstrates, is reciprocally privileging for the designer. Lifestyle becomes an object in itself, to be redesigned and articulated through a new range of concepts and objects. These allow for a fascinating series of syntheses between culturally defined habits, and Kashiwagi shows how the use of "Western" furniture in Japan was related to new notions of the lives which would be led with it.

The figure of the designer, the intellectual knower and fabricator of new visual representations through domestically consumable objects, reappears in Gennifer Weisenfeld's discussion of commercial art. Here the central phenomenon of graphic mediation reappears for new designs and manifests a new status for the designer, who is now seen on the same level as an artist. This role for the designer is made feasible by the production of models of graphic art and the circulation of images of objects in the 1920s on a hitherto unparalleled scale. Of course, a "Japanist" argu-ment would point to the earlier historical existence of general cultural entrepre-neurs with their "invented" designs like Sen no Rikyū in the late sixteenth century. While undoubtedly models could be cited in an early twentieth-century Japan fascinated with linkages to its own first mass consumer urban society in Edo of the eighteenth and early nineteenth centuries, such designers were in a quite different position from the Bauhaus-trained or -influenced designers of the later 1920s and early 1930s. Early twentieth-century designers were catering for a mass market through the wide circulation of products, or images of them, and Weisenfeld demonstrates how intrinsically modern they were.

When we look at specifically 1920s and 1930s Japanese design and house styles, we see how they anticipate, often in considerable detail, the mass consump-tion and housing forms of the 1960s and 1970s. On another level this historical shift reinforces the wider historical perspective that Japanese modernity was deflected by the onset of military ultranationalism. The potential for a mass, liber-ating, consumer-oriented modernism can be inconvenient for historical views which see the Japanese militarism of the late 1930s as necessarily concomitant with that modernism, rather than simply having deflected or perverted it. Perhaps no firm historical reply to this problem will be possible, and we may look between the gaps of broader social phenomena for where modernity actually lies. For as Jordan Sand demonstrates, there is evidence that notions of dwelling and culture were in contest in the two aesthetics he identifies for the "culture house." He identifies a transgressive undercurrent which tended to destabilize established categories for "home" and "lifestyle," ones which could be the subject of "play" from within the other hegemonic discourses of wealth or gender.

Themes of transgression and contestation recur in the chapters by Elise Tipton, Barbara Sato and Tomoko Aoyama. The growing number of white-collar, middle-class consumers of "culture houses" also sought new forms of leisure and entertainment to define their "modern" lifestyle. Tipton examines the development of modern life in "the streets" of the city, or more specifically, in the cafés, which were regarded as extensions of the streets. Here, ordinary Japanese could actually participate in the modern life and not merely view images of it. Tipton finds that while the modern continued to be associated with Western, though increasingly American rather than European, lifestyles, what was often regarded as *the* symbol of the modern — the café — was unlike either its American or European counter-parts in many ways. Its menu, architecture, and decor were Western-inspired, but the post-Kantō earthquake developments in size, lavishness, and service took Japanese cafés far from the dimly lit intellectual salons of Europe. The distinctive-ness of the Japanese café suggests the autonomous development of a Japanese modernity even as Western images of modernity flooded in. But despite this Japanese distinctiveness, critics of modernity focused on its foreign inspiration. Other commentators extolled it. In the diversity of commentaries on the café we can discern the contradictory nature of responses to modernity itself. Seen as liberating to some, to others it represented selfish decadence and perversity.

And at the center of such controversies was "the new woman" of the early 1920s and, even more threatening, "the modern girl" of the late 1920s and early 1930s. The café waitress, whose beauty and eroticism became increasingly com-modified for a mass clientele in the early 1930s, was a modern girl. In a less obvi-ous way, but also potentially threatening to the ideology of female submissiveness and passivity, so were readers of the new popular women's magazines, as shown by Sato, or wives who decorated the "culture houses" which were their new domain, as Sand suggests. The commercially oriented women's magazines of the 1920s targeted women as consumers, offering images of an independent as well as affluent lifestyle, at the same time as they encouraged women to be efficient household managers and savers. "Family" articles, including both "practical" and "fashionable" ones, showed housewives how they might bring rationalism and modern efficiency into their households. But they showed them at the same time how they could make themselves into modern beauties with instructions on the latest fashions, hairstyles, accessories, and cosmetics. Although these articles did not really refashion a new role for women in society, they presented a new perspective on everyday life. In addition, the innovative inclusion of readers' letters and "confessional" articles opened up a new channel for communication with women outside the sphere of their day-to-day contact, a channel through which they learned about other women's problems (often similar to their own) and gained information and support for thinking about change.

At the same time as the modern girl and, to a lesser extent, the modern house-wife threatened the gender divisions of Japanese society, the expanding working classes questioned the inequalities resulting from industrial capitalist development. Aoyama reveals in her original study how food in literature of the 1920s serves as a signifier of the increasing diversification and divisions in Japanese society; it was a significant component in the new literary genres and movements of the period. Differences of class underlay one type of division, prominent not only in proletari-an literature, but also in other types of texts written from the viewpoint of the elites, such as Shiga Naoya's celebrated short story "Kozô no kamisama" (The Errand Boy's God, 1920) and Kawabata Yasunari's "Izu no odoriko" (The Izu Dancer, 1926). In Kawabata's story as well as others, food and drink also mark gen-der divisions. Usually it is taken for granted that women prepare and serve food, a symbol of women's subordination to men. But in Nakamoto Takako's "Suzumushi no mesu" (Female Bell-Cricket, 1929) and Tanizaki Jun'ichirô's *Chijin no ai* (A Fool's Love, 1924–25), the female protagonists gain power over their male admirers by taking food from them. They epitomize the threatening aspects of the "modern girl" portrayed by much of the media during the late 1920s and 1930s. Besides act-ing as a marker of gender and class divisions, food in addition highlights differ-ences in social relations and ethical values. Aoyama examines the way eating scenes provide the vehicle for revealing problematic relations among family members, and how being eaten recurs as an allegorical motif in a wide range of texts from the 1920s. In Hagiwara Sakutarô's poetry and many texts by Tanizaki, food is also used to represent the cultural division between Japan and the West. Although the rela-tion between the eater and food is not always destructive, across all genres of litera-ture Aoyama finds the awareness of social division and the desire or curiosity to transgress or destroy boundaries.

Government officials and conservative scholars and social commentators viewed these developments of the 1920s with growing concern and hostility. The early 1930s saw not only heightened criticism of materialistic consumption, the pursuit of erotic pleasures, and other individualistic tendencies, but more proactive efforts to reunite the Japanese people not only to maintain domestic peace and order, but also to support the state's increasingly expansionary foreign policies. As Sandra Wilson shows, these included efforts to rewrite the Japanese past which gave Japan's modern wars — especially the Sino-Japanese War of 1894–95, the Russo-Japanese War of 1904–05, and World War I — a prominent place in the narrative. In fact, she argues, the "official" versions of these wars were crucial in constructing a "pedigree of modernity."

The concern of the state with daily life, with the practices and spaces of modernity, is a major theme of Vera Mackie's overview of the chapters in the volume. As she notes, the new practices of work, leisure, and home life constituted individuals into new groupings with new identities — "new selves" — which were marked by gender, class, and race. The state played a part in introducing men into practices of modernity by conscripting them into military service and modern warfare, and in linking women to the nation's military ventures through development of the modern nursing profession and women's patriotic organizations. It denounced the expressed sexuality of modern women, such as café waitresses and the nude women in modern art, and repressed the politicized bodies of suffragists and labor activists. As a counterweight, it supported the new modern "housewife" in her efforts to be a frugal and efficient household manager and carer of children. But despite its efforts, the state did not achieve full control. Among the spaces of modernity, the factory and the streets became those of conflict and resistance as well as leisure and consumption, and even the new modern home involved challenges to existing institutions of the family and gender roles as well as aspirations for a more comfortable standard of living.

During the 1920s both the practices and spaces of modernity changed in their meaning or took on multiple meanings, but by the early 1930s Japan was widely perceived by Japanese themselves as "modern." The ability to wage war with advanced military technology was to become one indicator of this modernity, and perception of this capability as a positive and justifiable undertaking, a "modern" thing to do, at both elite and popular levels, has suggestive implications for understanding popular support for war at the end of the decade. However, as the chapters in this volume show, being modern in Japan raised many other issues outside politics and foreign policy and remained a subject of contestation unresolved by the advent of war.

Fig. 1 *Yorozu Tetsugorō*, Nude with Parasol, *1913, oil on canvas, The Museum of Modern Art, Kamakura*

CHAPTER ONE

The Artists Start to Dance
The Changing Image of the Body in Art of the Taishō Period

Mizusawa Tsutomu

What happened to Japanese artists during the Taishō period in the deepest layer of their consciousness? They furiously struggled to get free from the feudal restrictions of the Meiji period which still existed. Some exceptional artists were able to break through and keep pace with almost all the modernist developments in Europe and the United States. But if they were not satisfied with merely imitating or copying the latest artistic trends of modernism, they were able to find something original and creative through their efforts. In order to become real modernists, they had to confront something that could not be a substitute for European modernism. This was the paradoxical situation for Japanese artists after the Taishō period: the conditions which allowed them to become real modernists in Japan inevitably demanded that they face something which could hardly be modernized in Japan. It was in this context that "the body" showed its most crucial aspect in the history of modern art in Japan.

Fig. 2 *Kuroda Seiki,* Emotion, *1898, oil on canvas, Tokyo National Institute of Cultural Properties*

When Yorozu Tetsugorō presented one of his most famous paintings, *Nude with Parasol* (Fig. 1) for the second Fusain Group show which was held in Tokyo in 1913, he obviously intended to do more than merely criticize the academic image of Westernized nudity seen in the 1898 painting *Emotion*, the left wing from the triptych *Knowledge, Sense, Emotion* by Kuroda Seiki (Fig. 2). Yorozu also wanted to

Fig. 3 *Yorozu Tetsugorō, Nude Beauty, 1912, oil on canvas, National Museum of Modern Art, Tokyo*

confront the audience with a non-idealized or real human body of a Japanese woman. As a result, this female body came to have a kind of poignant humor. The more conventional the motif itself,[1] the more poignantly and ironically this body should have shocked the Japanese audience. At least in the early Taishō period they ordinarily expected to appreciate such values as the harmonious proportion, fluent and smooth outline, and brilliant and healthy color of the female body in a painting with a title like *Nude with Parasol*. But in the end they responded to this provocative painting with total ignorance.

Yorozu graduated from the Tokyo School of Fine Arts in 1912 when he submitted a large oil painting entitled *Nude Beauty* as a graduation work (Fig. 3). At that time Yorozu was strongly influenced by Post-Impressionism, Fauvism, Expressionism, and even Cubo-Futurism. We can find such diversity in his style as early as 1912. It might be said that Yorozu in 1912 was placed in a strikingly similar artistic position to that of Otto Dix in the same year. The German art historian Dietrich Schubert pointed out clearly that the work of the young Dix, who could manage to paint in various styles at the same time, should be characterized as *Stilpluralismus* (stylistic pluralism).[2]

But whatever diversity Yorozu's works at that time did show us, we must not overlook the fact that he had never abandoned motifs indigenous to his own culture. In the case of *Nude Beauty*, Yorozu decisively refused to justify the nudity of the model by setting her in Westernized surroundings. The figure wears the red *koshimaki*, which is traditional Japanese female underwear. The background is probably a northern Japanese landscape with typical Japanese red pine trees, possibly like the landscape around his small home-town of Tsuchizawa in Iwate Prefecture.[3]

Thirteen years later Yorozu commented on this work as follows:

> *This painting was strongly inspired by the works of van Gogh and Matisse. I depicted a half-nude beauty wearing red underwear. She is lying on glaring green grass. And her arrogant face is looking down at us.*[4]

This "beauty" is "looking down at" the beholder and at Yorozu himself as well. Although his *Self-portrait with a Cloud* (Fig. 4), again of 1912, is much smaller than *Nude Beauty*, these two paintings could be treated as a kind of pair, the models for the

Fig. 4 Yorozu Tetsugorō, Self-portrait with a Cloud, *1912, oil on canvas, Iwate Prefecture Museum*

Fig. 5 *Ludwig Ernst Kirchner,* Dancing Woman, *1911, polychrome wood sculpture, Stedelijk Museum, Amsterdam*

paintings being Yorozu himself and his wife. But a remarkable contrast between these works may be found in the psychological tension which these two figures evoke. While the arrogant "beauty" has been filled with the brutal and mysterious energy of a victor, the miserably haggard Yorozu of the self-portrait is looking at nothing but his own interior state as a defeated person. The different meaning of the pink cloud in each work is undeniable. The cloud in *Nude Beauty*, while slightly threatening in character, also seems to strengthen the rhythmical articulation of the beauty's body and to radiate the same primitive energy as the prehistoric nature in the background. In the self-portrait, the cloud is hovering menacingly above the artist, who is in despair. Here the cloud becomes an obsessive being without any kind of liveliness.

If we go back to "the body," we can find another important aspect in these two paintings. The posture of the figure in *Nude Beauty* is strikingly similar to that of a polychrome wood sculpture, *Dancing Woman*, which was made in Dresden by Ludwig Ernst Kirchner in 1911, just before he moved to Berlin (Fig. 5). Probably a couple of years later, in the late 1910s, Yorozu became much more aware of Kirchner's works through art magazines and books. But the astonishing similarity of posture in these two works must be purely coincidental, because Yorozu had already begun to prepare a first study drawing for this graduation work as early as the autumn of 1911. By means of the expressively powerful articulation of the body, including such a detail as the forcibly bent right hand, *Nude Beauty* and *Dancing Woman* managed to create a completely new visual language which was impregnated with a primitive and uncultivated Nietzschian vitalism.

When one of Yorozu's teachers at the Tokyo School of Fine Arts, the oil painter Fujishima Takeji, tried to grade this painting, he could not understand its revolutionary nature and gave it a very low mark. It is said that Fujishima was particularly dissatisfied with the way the painting related the body to its surrounding space. Fujishima, a great Symbolist, accused his student of irrational treatment of the pictorial space. He said: "It's my honest impression that this woman could not appear to be lying on the grass at all." But, ironically, does not this statement itself precisely point out the very nature of the body depicted by his rebellious student? In other words, *Nude Beauty* is no longer indulging in a *fin-de-siècle* Symbolist dream. Now she is going to start to dance in an Expressionist manner, just like Kirchner's vital wood sculpture. But in contrast, in the case of *Self-portrait with a Cloud*, the artist was so heavily emaciated by his desperate solitude that he seems to stand without any support, like a bodiless ghost.

In 1913 Yorozu frequently visited the Asakusa district in Tokyo which, before World War II, was the city's most popular and famous downtown amusement center. He was deeply attracted by the performances of Egawa-Ichiza, a traditional Japanese acrobatic troupe. Inspired by one of the troupe's programs, Yorozu painted a small but strongly impressive oil painting entitled *Karuwaza* (Acrobatics, Fig. 6).

Decisively departing from the academic linear perspective, the artist made use of intentionally distorted space as a visual means to concentrate the viewer's attention on the superhuman performance on the stage. But at the same time, this unusually high-positioned viewpoint necessarily creates a kind of psychological distance between the acrobats and the viewer of the painting. As a result, the viewer cannot really share in the imaginary excitement which the extraordinary performance would have caused among the audience. Here again we encounter the poignant humor that is a hallmark of this painter.

Fig. 6 *Yorozu Tetsugorō*, Karuwaza (Acrobatics), *1913, oil on canvas, location unknown*

Fig. 7 *Ludwig Ernst Kirchner,* Japanese Acrobats, *1912, woodcut, Buchheim Collection*

Another interesting work by Kirchner is his *Japanese Acrobats* (Fig. 7). Kirchner, too, had been inspired by the Japanese acrobatic troupe Yokota-Ichiza, which had started its European tour in Russia as early as 1904 and arrived in Berlin in 1912.[5] Kirchner probably attended one of their performances in Berlin, and made his black-and-white woodcut of the subject in 1912.

It is astonishing that, without any kind of personal contact, these two artists almost simultaneously picked up the same motif and, moreover, reached the same quality of image regarding the human body, even though they were as far apart as Berlin and Tokyo.

We must look closely at the way in which these artists dealt with the body of an acrobat standing upside-down, or at a moment which looked like upside-down. While Yorozu depicted a man (or woman) in motion being rolled around in a big barrel, Kirchner paid much more attention to the rigid geometrical construction of the human bodies. (By that time Kirchner had become interested in Cubism.) But both were able to suggest the totally emancipated energy of the body through a detour, such as the depiction of the rigorously disciplined bodies of Japanese acrobats, with all their agony and anxiety. In other words, Yorozu and Kirchner coincidentally groped for a lost circuit that would lead us to the hidden power of the body without any reference to the rules of academic pictoriality.

In this context, one of Yorozu's woodcuts, probably made in 1913, now appears in a different light. There is no extant artist's proof of *Tight-rope* (Fig. 8), and the original woodblock belongs to the collection of Iwate Prefectural Museum. It shows a tight-rope walker lying on a thin rope, playing with a parasol by skillfully using his feet. One should remember that Friedrich Nietzsche frequently compared his image of the superman with a brave tight-rope walker balancing on the rope stretched between the past and the future. In Taishō Japan the name of Nietzsche was as popular among young intellectuals as were those of Ruskin or Tolstoy.

Fig. 8 *Yorozu Tetsugorō,* Tight-rope, *c. 1913, woodblock, Iwate Prefectural Museum*

Fig. 9 Yorozu Tetsugorô,
Diving, c. 1913–14, oil on panel
(verso of Fig. 8), Iwate Prefectural
Museum

If we turn the woodblock over, on its back unexpectedly appears a small oil painting called *Diving* (Fig. 9) which depicts primitive, naked people cheerfully diving and dancing with orgiastic gestures. There is no doubt that this uncultivated nature looks very similar to the background landscape in *Nude Beauty*. It is rather difficult to determine the precise date of this painting, but it could have been made from the end of 1913 to September of the next year when Yorozu decided to leave Tokyo with his family for his native town of Tsuchizawa in order to concentrate on working as an artist. He was to spend about one-and-a-half years in this culturally isolated and tiny town, where he made a large number of truly experimental works.

His famous text, "Tetsujin Dokugo," was written in one of the sketchbooks from this Tsuchizawa period:

> *Together with me a barbarian started to walk. We need not any kind of knowledge. We see what we can see. We hear what we can hear. We eat what we can eat. Then we walk, sleep, and paint. That's all. We should say that Futurism and Cubism were nothing but products of artificial civilization. They must be superficial because they are based on civilization. The primitive man unites with nature itself as one.*
>
> *We need not try to copy nature any more. We should express the nature within us. If I draw a circle, I do it only because I want to do so. There is no other reason.*[6]

Diving looks like it was a kind of illustration for this text. It clearly visualizes "the nature within" the artist. Yorozu also emphasizes the possibility of impregnating a human body with emancipated and pure natural power through dancing. We must not forget that Yorozu always dealt with the body as a dynamic field of potential powers even when he adopted the manner of Analytical Cubism, as in his work *Man* (Fig. 10).

We need take only a few steps further to be conscious of our own body as a means to "express the nature within us." From the viewpoint of the history of ideas it looks by no means accidental that the composer Yamada Kôsaku started to dance in Tokyo

Fig. 10 Yorozu Tetsugorô, Man, 1925, oil on panel, Iwate Prefectural Museum

almost at the same time as Yorozu retreated to his native town. A photograph was taken at the time, probably in the garden of Yamada's house in Akasaka in 1915 or 1916 (Fig. 11). It is also known that the painter Fujita Tsuguji (Tsuguharu) and his friend Kawashima Riichirô started to take lessons in dance in the style of Isadora Duncan, at the private school "Academia" in Paris, as early as about 1913.[7]

The image of the dancing Murayama Tomoyoshi (Fig. 12), which was used as an illustration in his first one-man show catalog in Tokyo in 1923, is no doubt the most important historical token of the radically changing image of the artist as a body. Already in the early Taishô period the academic restrictions on the representation of the body had been broken down and the deepest layer of physical consciousness had been exploited and exposed by the unprecedented efforts of an artist such as Yorozu.

Fig. 11 *Photographer unknown, Yamada Kōsaku dancing in his garden, about 1915–16, photograph, private collection*

Fig. 12 *Photographer unknown, Murayama Tomoyoshi dancing, c. 1922–23, printed photograph, private collection*
Fig. 13 *Photographer unknown, Dance, 1924, photograph, location unknown*

One might dare to say that the small work *Diving* by Yorozu had already foreshadowed the strong indigenous group-performance works by the Mavoists at the end of the Taishō period (Fig. 13).

Notes

1   It was Nabei Katsuyuki, one of Yorozu's friends, who later recalled that Yorozu had suggested using this typical Impressionist motif during their school days at the Tokyo School of Fine Arts. See Nabei Katsuyuki, *Kanchūbōjin*, Tokyo, Asahi Shimbunsha, 1953, pp. 83–4.

2   Dietrich Schubert, "Rezeptions-und Stilpluralismus in den frühen Selbstbildnissen von Otto Dix," in W. Hager and N. Knopp (eds), *Beiträge zum Problem des Stilpluralismus*, Munich, Prestel Verlag, 1977, pp. 203–24.

3   Arikawa Ikuo, curator of Miyagi Prefectural Museum, has pointed out that this landscape could be a suburb of Tokyo because at the beginning of the Taishō period one could see faraway mountains covered with snow even from the center of Tokyo. "Yorozu Tetsugorō 'ratai bijin' no gendaisei," in *Jibun no shizen o motometa gaka Yorozu Tetsugorō*, Tokyo, Chōritsu.

4   Yorozu Tetsugorō, "Watashi no rirekisho," *Chūō bijutsu*, November 1925.

5   "at this period Sawada Yutaka, one of the Yokota-Ichiza acrobats, became famous for his performance of *atama tōritsu* (upside-down acrobat on his head). He could stand upside-down only on his head, balancing with his arms and without any other means of support." See Ōshima Mikio, *Umi wo watatta sākasu gēnin — Kosumoporitan Sawada Yutaka no shōgai*, Tokyo, Heibonsha, 1993, p. 72.

6   Yorozu Tetsugorō, "Tetsujin Dokugo," in *Tetsujin garon*, revised edition, Tokyo, Chūō Kōron Bijutsu Shuppan, 1985, p. 59.

7   Unno Hiroshi, "Senkyūhyakunijūnendai no mōdo to butō," in *Senkyūhyakunijūnendai no Pari yori — Kawashima Riichirō, Goncharova, Larionov*, Tokyo, Shiseidō, 1995, pp. 19–20.

Chapter Two

Indices of Modernity
Changes in Popular Reprographic Representation[1]

John Clark

Introduction

The reasonably familiar ways of constructing modernity in Japanese art include those which see it *horizontally* in chronological terms of a simple tripartite periodization, and *vertically* in structural terms of a stratification of art activity.

To take periodization first, the familiar view holds that modernity in art began with the Meiji Restoration of 1868 and a Japanese response to the "West" which relativized existing Japanese discourses over many fields. That is, such discourses were forced to lose their hitherto unquestioned or "natural" legitimacy by their constrained comparison with an external "other." In a second period from around 1906, modern art discourses were then reconstituted in terms of greater artistic freedom and self-expressiveness: Japan's victories in its first two modern wars of 1894–95 and 1904–05 had solidified the state, popular self-consciousness, and the institutional legitimacy of a newly educated professional class as interpreters of the "new" and the "Japanese."[2] This was broadly followed by a third period from after the earthquake in 1923 to the full-blown domination of all areas of social life by ultra-nationalist militarism from around 1936.

The third period is also that of modernism, a reflexive understanding of modernity, where the past is not simply relativized by current practice, but relativization itself becomes part of the subject of art practice. Japanese modernism has two faces. One is the intellectual tendency toward rationalism of the West and mechanization — that is, rational thought applied to everyday life which puts value on machine civilization which was brought about by mechanized industry and represented by the Ford system. Another is the "modern girl" (*moga*) and what were taken as her symbols, the liberation of everyday customs, which were brought in through Western, and particularly American, movies.[3]

This position holds that changes in life and customs were followed by changes in art. Modernism in urban customs detonated modernism in art, literature, and culture. Whilst these schemed a revolt or treason against modernism in customs, in fact they came into being with modernism in customs as their condition. An intellectual current was born where the world was made ungraspable in the pre-existing system of inter-pretations and beliefs. The tentatives of new art and literature appeared one after another and themselves became an unfamiliar message.[4]

But in fact, artistic modernism — as a position distinct from "the modern" as defined above — seems to have been increasingly understood in many parts of the Japanese art world from the late 1910s when it was institutionalized in exhibition and art group practices. Its advent in Japan was masked by the 1910s also being the period when many Euramerican forms of artistic modernism arrived in Japan and achieved prominence in the art world. But Japanese modernism in art is neither coterminous nor even wholly contemporary with the arrival in Japan of these specifically Euramerican art styles. Japanese modernism in art can be more accurately seen as pre-ceding, or only accompanied in parallel by, the widespread adoption of "Western" dress and social mores by women, as well as the penetration of the products of mass consumer technology into many areas of urban life. Modernism in Japanese art did not depend on modernist social customs or mass-media technology for its advent, however much it was connected with these for its later reception and diffusion.

The vertical stratification of art practice and institutions often posits a gradation between a burgeoning and more institutionalized practice of "fine art" from the 1890s, in late Meiji, as against increasingly modern styles in mass graphics or popular fash-ions in dress and other customs from the mid-1920s in late Taishō. It assumes that, with the transition from the late Meiji to early Taishō periods around 1912 as temporal threshold, modernity at the institutional top of the art world — defined as a fine art practice by art school graduates — was accompanied at the base by popular illustra-tion in mass graphics.[5] This was increasingly done by non-certificated illustrators who were reflective of or responsive to those at the top. These vertical relations may theor-etically be seen to have privileged origination at the fine arts level, or, when conversely seen from the bottom, to have legitimated fine art practice because it had emerged from an increasingly differentiated and only informally institutionalized craft or graphic practice at the mass level. Between fine art and "popular art" there existed various kinds of mediation. These included the circulation of artists as producers who might paint for a government salon as well as illustrate for a newspaper, a magazine, or a book. They also comprised differentiation of various coteries of place and later of ideological sympathy. These can be seen in the formation of coteries for creative graphics (that is, artist-produced and identified), and in various types of avant-gardism formed around art practices and attitudes to form, as well as the splitting of these tendencies during the late 1920s into more clearly marked formalist or socially oriented groupings involved in proletarian art.

Horizontal and vertical constructions of the transitions in the late Meiji art world have elided another interpretive position: the horizontal stages of relativization, expressiveness, and reflexivity in art practice may have coincided. The incorporation of reflexivity into art practice might be seen as always nascent within relativization itself. Thus, artworks or other cultural representations on the Euramerican periphery, such as Japan's in late Meiji, may be conceptualized as intrinsically postmodern from the onset of their relativization by contact with the Euramerican center. Relative cultural distance from dominant discourses may have in certain situations allowed selective, even eclectic and putatively "postmodern," quotation from "modern" Euramerican discourses without total absorption into their structure of hegemony.[6] In the vertical relations of art practice, originations in craft production, in mass graphics, or in popular art at the base, would take precedence over the fine arts superstructure.

This chapter uses such a perspective to question more precisely the conditions for transition to modernity. Even if modernity is found in visual expressions in late Meiji and among a quite broad intellectual stratum, it appeared without the presence of a mass consumer society integrated by communication of objects, ideas, and visual representations on a large scale. Mass communications and collective dreams only seem to have broken with the Japanese past after the earthquake in 1923.[7] This chapter will look at a rather special kind of graphic expression in an encyclopedic knowledge magazine before that. It examines the creation of the possibility of the modern, not its broader social working out which came later.

The problem of what is modernist will be investigated here through one aspect of its pre-history in the modern. The investigation begins with the processes of new reprographic technology, and is followed by inquiry into the new graphic styles they brought, the new definitions of the graphic art producer which turned artists into illustrators, the definition of graphic styles by reference to one magazine, *Taiyō*, the creation of a new kind of decorated space through consumer advertisement, the process of allegorizing reality through certain types of photographic representation of the real, and, finally, the new constructions of a transition to modernism through new kinds of self-reference found in mass media.

Processes: New reprographic technology

For the Japanese reprographic industry, the first and modern relativization of its practice came with the introduction of new technology in the Meiji period. The oft-lamented decline and passing away of *ukiyo-e* in fact historically masks the entire restructuring of reprographics and printing in general with new techniques from Europe and the United States. This change occurred on such a scale that one may unhesitatingly call it a revolution. It involved the widespread acceptance of lithography after 1874,[8] the spread in parallel of copperplate intaglio printing for bookplate illustrations from the same period until the early 1900s, the introduction and use of end grain woodblock printing for mass-circulation magazines from 1887 to about 1905, the development of a large range of planometric aluminum and zincplate lithographic processes from the 1880s through the 1890s, the adjustment of photographic colotype printing to various metal plate and even luxury end grain woodblock processes in the 1890s, and the development of three-color chromolithography by 1902. This was the base on which offset lithography developed in Japan from 1914, the use of the HB (Huebner and Bleistein) polychromatic flat-plate process from 1920, and photogravure printing in newspapers from 1922.[9] Technological improvement made it possible for the print run of the profusely illustrated, mass-circulation *Shufu no tomo* (The Housewife's Companion) to start at around 800,000 copies a month in 1917, and reach 1,200,000 copies a month by 1934.

This development occurred against the background of the increase in daily newspaper circulation. The volume, increase, and rate of increase of such newspaper circulation gives us a crude but probable index for the scale of other kinds of social circulation. The daily sales of the *Tōkyō asahi shimbun* increased from 47,642 in 1896, to 125,630 in 1912, to 289,464 in 1923, to 431,811 in 1926, and to 1,011,190 in 1936.[10] Against the base of 1896 this gives annual average increases in circulation of 10.2 percent for 1896–1912, 31.3 percent for 1912–23, 99.6 percent for 1923–26, and 121.7 percent for 1926–36. The percentage increases of 10.2 percent, 31.3 percent, 99.6 percent, and 121.7 percent for these four periods mean that the speed of social circulation was three, nine, and twelve times faster in the three periods after 1912.

But the changes in reprographic technology (further detailed in the Appendix) resulted not only in the improvement of the quality of images and in the possible volumes of print runs, but they also involved a qualitatively different relation between the original of an illustration and the final printed version. If lithographed and later offset- and chromo-lithography allowed for a more direct relation between the artist of an image and the printed state, it was a relation which was still dependent on technical interaction with the printer but of a more precise kind than hitherto. However, with the advent of various photographic techniques, the artist was simply the provider of the original image, the graphic effect of which depended entirely on the printer's manipulation of photomechanical processes. Here lies an undiscussed conundrum, for as the control of the final image lay in the hands of the printer, so with the advance in technology, and particularly with the advent of the HB process and photogravure, the intervention of the printer changed radically toward realization of the graphic potential of an original image or toward the reproductive felicity of a final print. This meant that the role of the printer changed from a necessary intervention in the graphic process to merely a sufficient control over final outcomes. Thus, from the 1920s, but even identifiably from around 1903 with chromolithography, the image finally produced lost its absolute dependence on intervening graphic qualities and became closer to that produced by the artist. The status of the reprographic image changed

Fig. 1 *Nomura Shigeyoshi (studied with Yamamoto Hōsui and later died in France), lithograph published by Gengendō, 1882*

from one having significance in its own right due to the intervention and therefore relativization of the visual effects on an original image, to an indexical replica of the original. Inasmuch as the latter position implied an awareness of the now removed graphic intervention, it is modernist. But it also made possible a nostalgia for the original — and for past images presumed to be in the same series as the original — which turned the image reproduced into an allegorical reference of its original.

Of course, a paradox remained, for at the same time as more faithfully mimetic technology made it the printer's task to increase the directness of the internal (or indexical) relation to the original, so the technology also freed the printer — as designer — to externally (or iconically) manipulate the original image in ways impossible earlier. The full possibility of this secondary intervention at the compositional stage, one which is structurally analogous to the reflexivity in modernism itself, only came to full potential in advertising graphics of the late 1920s, as will be discussed shortly.

This technological situation also came at the time when people began to look back on the residues of Edo culture which they had experienced during the 1880s.[11] Thus, if we look for the moment of shift from modernity to modernism in visual representation it can surely be found in the relation to an original which the reprographic technology made possible, even before the end of the Meiji period in 1912. That is, this moment lay *before* the rise of the modernism premised on a degree of mass consumerism and the greater mass-media penetration throughout the population which actually came into being a full ten years later in the mid-1920s.

Graphic styles I: The image of women

Some indication of this shift may be found in the imagery of women in popular illustrations and posters, in figures which overlay the long-standing habit since the late seventeenth century of picturing courtesans in *bijin-ga*. In the 1880s are seen lithographed figures of women which face the frontal plane of the image as in a portrait photograph, but avert their eyes from the viewer's gaze (Fig. 1). By around the turn of the century in some images by art school-trained artists the figure of the woman is set further back with a spectacle of plenty before her (Fig. 2). Indeed, such certificated artists seem to play with the ambiguity of directness in placing the figure of the woman

Fig. 2 Okada Saburōsuke, advertising poster, c. 1897

— be she wife, geisha, or musician — just far enough away in the visual field from the viewer to allow consumption of a spectacle.[12] With the absorption of broadly *art nouveau* mannerisms from 1906 onward the figure now appears as if lost in her own reverie (Fig. 3), one which allows her to luxuriate in the atmosphere of wealth displayed for the viewer in some posters for the clothing store Mitsukoshi, for example. By around the end of Meiji in 1912 a much more vernacular group figuration is displayed for a consumption which is public (Fig. 4). This was about the time when bottled beer was being purchased by peasants in the countryside, and slightly later around 1919 when department stores started to have bargain days to appeal to a middle-class consumer stratum who had come in groups from some distance.[13] In the 1920s this consciousness of the consuming group is reversed toward a privatized erotic pleasure, one which mimics the self-conscious use of the most advanced reprographic technology then available in photogravure (Fig. 5). The 1910s had already seen the emergence of the luxury print, in some cases using more than thirty litho plates. By the 1930s the consciousness of luxury technical effect was extended via plate camera HB-process images in the manner of movie stars and to elaborate gravure printing. Designers were themselves very conscious of the thematizing of technology, as the poster designer Kôno Takashi wrote in 1930:

> *The total result in producing movie posters depends on the printing, and the design ultimately just exists as a suggestion towards this purpose. Our work has to be satisfied with absolutely being controlled in the end by the mechanism. Put another way, don't we know the pleasure of fully bringing out the functions of superb machines?*[14]

This attitude by the designers was also behind the images in propaganda magazines

Fig. 3 Fujishima Takeji, illustration, c. 1890s, lithograph, from Shimaya, 1939, p. 765

Fig. 4 *Hiraoka Gompachirō, poster for Mitsukoshi Gofukuten, 1913*

Fig. 5 *Poster for Akadama Port Wine by Kawaguchi Photo Studio, 1922*

like *Nippon* for overseas consumption, for which Kôno later worked. In some cases this display of luxuriant technical effect was intended to absorb the viewer, as Yamano Ayao, who also later worked for *Nippon*, wrote:

> *The powerful point in cosmetic advertisements is to put into the advertisement an atmosphere which responds to women's desire for beauty, to their yearnings and longings. Women do not "read" advertisements. Women sense their own fantasy of beauty in them.*[15]

Both the displayed pleasure in technical effect and the absorption of the viewer by its allure were soon extended to an appropriation of the exotic other in figures from the Asian mainland, particularly in images for cosmetic posters where the target audience was Chinese women.

Producers: Artists into illustrators and designers

The history of modern Japanese prints is normally constructed as the rise to autonomous status of the specialized graphic artist and the prints which are drawn — and have blocks or plates made and printed — by the same producer. But this trajectory does not by itself allow us to understand the interrelations between types of graphic artist and the types of work they produce. One may more precisely typify primarily graphic artists against types of work since the 1890s as follows:

I.   Craftsman printers who had received some kind of atelier technical apprenticeship but who had no formal art school training: Okumura Masako, Yamamoto Kanae, anonymous artisans.

II. Photographers and photographic technicians who adjusted the look of photographed material for luxury or mass-circulation printed matter in which photographs appear: Ogawa Isshin, anonymous technicians.

III. Art school-trained fine artists, some of whom came from among print artisans such as Yamamoto Kanae, some of whom did illustration as a secondary activity to "fine art" painting or sculpture and who left printing to a technician like Kuroda Seiki, Fujishima Takeji, or Aoki Shigeru (Fig. 6).

IV. Professional illustrators, sometimes with art school or professional art studio training, who worked for books, magazines, and also did commercial posters: Takehisa Yumeji, Hashiguchi Goyô.

V.   Artists who were the producers of signature prints. These fall into three subtypes: those associated with the Creative Print Movement for a period, such as Onchi Koshirô or Yamamoto Kanae; those working in neo-Japonaiserie manners, such as Itô Shinsui and Hashiguchi Goyô; and those who extolled a new humanist sympathy with the urban dispossessed, such as Ono Tadashige.

VI. Avant-garde artists who occasionally engaged in graphic expression as a type of formal exploration: Murayama Tomoyoshi, Okada Tatsuo.

VII. Commercial design illustrators who came from a technical school design training background: Maeda Mitsugu, Yamana Ayao, Kôno Takashi.

Fig. 6 *Illustrations for the poems of Arishima Ariake by Aoki Shigeru using end grain blocks cut by Yamamoto Kanae, 1905*

This typification — which could readily be refined and corrected — has one obvious property: it does not conceptualize artists who make graphic images as unique or autonomous producers. They are clearly imbricated in their own training background, in the kind of market for which they work partially or wholly, and are involved with different kinds of reprographic technology, some of which they control directly, from some of which they are very distant. This typification also indicates that if there is a shift from modern to modernist art practice, it may coincide with increasing reflexivity in (repro)graphic art itself, where the makers of signature prints are discriminated from producers of illustrations for mass-circulation graphics. That is, differences in the type of graphic artwork produced are in some way a function of role specialization among producers between types V–VII.

The formation of these artists itself, particularly those of type VII, seems to hang on several changes in Japanese art education in schools and technical colleges since the 1890s. At the primary and middle-school level there was a gradual shift away from copy drawing after textbook models with the rise of the free art movement led by Yamamoto Kanae who had returned from Europe via Russia in 1917. The Ministry of Education introduced free drawing into education in 1919, and in 1922 crayons replaced pencils in drawing classes.[16] Moreover, drawing textbooks which prior to 1920 had been laid out vertically were from 1925 laid out horizontally, with Japanese language being read horizontally from the left.[17] The new textbooks also included design exercises with lettering and logos.[18] This change reflected existing developments in graphic styles and in the layout of advertisements but also popularized them further, to the extent that by the late 1920s horizontal writing from the left with all manner of script variations for emotional effect was common in Japanese advertisements.

Furthermore, by the 1890s design departments were being founded at many vocational technical colleges,[19] but their establishment was followed only shortly thereafter by the growth of a movie industry, particularly in the 1910s. This industry itself produced a demand for many kinds of ancillary design and set workers, so the poster and billboard designers for movies were often found in technical college graduates working on the edges of that industry, and had not necessarily come from art school. For example, in 1924 Yamada Shinkichi, who was then twenty years old and had no design training to speak of, became the poster artist for the first Japanese cinema built in concrete at Shōchikuza in Ōsaka.

Graphic styles II: *Taiyō* as index

The brief examination of printing technology, arts styles, and artist types above equips us now to see the kind of graphics used in one magazine in a much clearer context. The magazine *Taiyō* was published from 1895 to 1928, and conveniently spread from the late Meiji, through Taishō to the early Shōwa periods. Its material allows approach from both art historical and social historical perspectives and provides a longitudinal glimpse through a unified source of some of the variations from the horizontal and vertical constructions of the Japanese modern indicated at the beginning of this chapter. Because of *Taiyō*'s longevity, and parenthetically because it did not make a particular production value of employing new graphic styles, it may prove to be a check of some of the hypotheses about the moment of modern/modernism.

Taiyō was a new kind of magazine in late Meiji Japan formed from the amalgamation of five earlier magazines.[20] It was published by Hakubunkan and, following in the success of the same publisher's *Nisshin sensō jikki* (Record of the Sino-Japanese War), it was fully illustrated with end grain woodblock illustrations, followed very shortly by photo-lithographs. *Taiyō* began with a claimed monthly circulation of 280,000 to increase advertising revenues, when it was in fact about 90,000–100,000 per month.[21] When it closed in 1928[22] its circulation had declined to 10,000 a month at a time when the popular magazine *Kingu* had a monthly circulation of 300,000, and the two other rather more specialized "serious" magazines, *Kaizō* and *Chūō kōron,* had circulations of 100,000 and 20,000 respectively.[23]

The rather encyclopedic character of its articles has led some scholars to use it as a register of shifting opinions in Meiji and Taishō Japan, since it seems to have moved away from a rather old-fashioned moralistic style of editorial to a closer questioning of reported facts. Indeed, the encyclopedic content and the division of the layout by subject units was made possible by the abandonment of a "unified" or integrative thought system applied from above which seems to typify intellectual tendencies in late Meiji.[24] The magazine was mostly read by local officials and students throughout Japan and began at a time when newspapers were at last penetrating into the middle class in smaller cities, as opposed to having been confined to three large cities and trading ports. But of great interest for the purposes of analysis here is that *Taiyō* involved a new way of reading.

For the world of reading of small textbooks by repetition until fluent, in the tradition of the old reading aloud of *on* sounds (the Sinified sound for a character, rather than its syllabic Japanese *kana* sound), it was a completely new way of receiving magazine text. This meant the move away from the stage where a small amount of information was received orally via the whole body by repeated repetition, to a more modern reading habit which would receive a large volume of information visually and simultaneously.[25]

The readership of *Taiyō* may have begun to break up as early as just after the Russo-Japanese War in 1904–05 with the spread of middle-school education and advanced differentiation in its readers, gradually rendering it impossible for an encyclopedic magazine to satisfy all of them. Some of its more serious or intellectual readers moved to specialized magazines like *Kaizō* (published from 1919) and *Chūō kōron* (from 1899 the successor to *Hansei zasshi* from 1887) which were not so extensively illustrated and did not have to aim for large sales.

There is, however, a link to some kinds of urban consumerism through the close links between Hakubukan and the department store Mitsukoshi, whose house journal *Shikō* it published. Moreover, when Hakubunkan became a limited stock company in 1917, its links with serious writers were cut and in later Taishō it began to publish translated detective stories as well as give over its creative writing columns to popular novels.[26] Thus *Taiyō* may be considered overall as a media source which embodied a conservative modernity to be bypassed by the increased massification of consumerism and mass media in the late 1920s.

Let me now see if it is possible to characterize broadly the graphic styles employed in *Taiyō*, taking graphic style in a wider sense to include formal regularities in both script and image presentation, as well as in their interrelation. These appear to fall into five general types:

1. naive or conventional realism, the snapshot of the world as a thing-in-itself (1895–1900);[27]
2. a display which is only a step forward from naïve realism, which betokens legitimacy by simple presentation, including that of the magazine itself through the outside cover page (1900–05);
3. an up-to-dateness by stylistic display in the fashion of the times, beginning with *art nouveau* — interestingly in some illustrations this very quickly approaches a formal modernism of the Euramerican kind (1906–09 to about 1920);
4. a tendency toward *moderne* abstraction forms and self-conscious layout, paralleled by obvious use of photographic collage, probably derived from film (from about 1920 to 1926); and
5. the beginnings of a formal modernism, even possibly already showing the conscious impact of *art deco* in cover layouts and in advertising graphics (1926–27).

The periodizations are in parentheses because they are more or less notional, but the following rather simplistic observation cannot be escaped. The moment of transition from the relativization implicit in the "modern" to the self-consciousness which is in practice characteristic of the "modernist" is found surprisingly early, around 1909–10. It corresponds rather accurately with the onset of formal modernism in fine art practice. But it is also around ten years before the mass consumerism and rise of mass media in the 1920s which is associated with Japanese modernism, as it is usually understood by Japanese scholars. If such a conservative journal as *Taiyō* can show these changes so clearly, then Japanese modernism as a broad social phenomenon was led by relatively exclusive media which used various kinds of new reprographic technology. That is, it was not social phenomena which led the media. In this transitory moment, the intriguing intervening variable of fine arts practice as a kind of leader in stylistic consciousness is introduced by the figure of *art nouveau* style around 1905–10, and then by a *moderne* style we call *art deco* later in the 1920s. Thus it is not necessarily the transfer of any given style which creates a moment in the trajectory of modern into modernism. But the opportunity provided by such transfer may be a sufficient condition to abstract and concentrate such a style, and usually in terms of existing local preferences.

The decorated space: Consumption advertisement

Late Meiji readers from the 1890s inhabited a new kind of modern visual space defined for them by the relativization implied in assimilating "Western" objects, ideas, and visual styles themselves. This relativization as a new visual style had quite a long history, since aspects of Western visual styles had been absorbed into popular cultural expressions by the 1740s, and operated as the site of a popular discourse. But the scale and extension of this relativization had reached a quite different level in the Meiji era, to the extent that by the advent of *Taiyō* in 1895, quite clear distinctions from previous visualizations in popular advertising were to be seen. The former were often designed with asymmetrical open fields and a kind of fluid graphism in the texts which followed the dynamic nature of the image. But later Meiji advertising in the 1890s was often symmetrically arranged, with a single image articulated in a separate space from the text (Fig. 7).

This difference also has unforeseen implications. There is first the application of a border to a text in a symmetrical field-definition with advertising text within it, say up to 1900. Then shortly afterwards, in 1904, this was followed by the provision in some advertisements of the figure of an absent or supposed spectator which is implied by

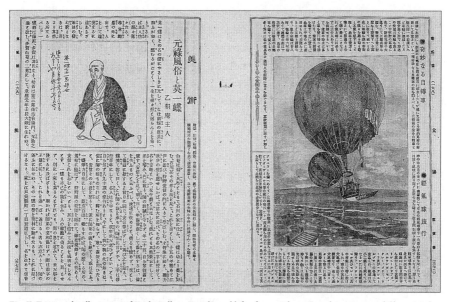

Fig. 7 Taiyō, right: illustration of "Light Balloon Travel"; and left: of an article on Genroku customs and (the painter) Hanabusa Itchō, vol. 1, no. 2, M28/1895/2/5

framed space (Fig. 8). It would seem that the surrounding border receives the sanction of the text it encloses in 1909,[28] but by 1915 — if we can take non-*Taiyō* advertising material for the same department store as comparable — the text-image relation of late Meiji is reversed, and from early Taishō the visual sanctions the text. Indeed, it may have been the awareness of the large European *art nouveau*-style poster — such as those of Alphonse Mucha which were published in Japan from 1900 — which allowed a switch in the perceived relation between text and image.

Another way in which the relation of the viewer to the text changed between the 1890s and the late 1920s is in the way in which the hypothetical obtaining of the advertised product is positioned for the viewer. In some advertisements during the 1890s the object is often shown as desirable by the visual replication of its packaging, whereas by the late 1920s the object is suggested by the visually suggested desirability of obtaining it. The former is object-oriented, the latter feeling- or satisfaction-oriented. This interpretation would tend to support the general understanding of modernity and modernism in that the former concerns some objects (artworks now) in their perceived space of relationship with other objects (artworks then). The latter concerns the perception of this relationship and even the consciousness of making works defined relationally, or as in this case, seizing a desire in a circle design around a glass, in a choice between beer (for men) and soda (for women and children).

One can also compare advertisements from around 1895 which place the desired object at the top of an enclosed field, with advertisements from 1899 which use a similar enclosing field, but which include a fantasy angel-figure and not the object itself

(Fig. 9). True, these figures are mobilized for intangible products like creosote-based lung medicine, and illustration by an image of a bottle might have been a little uninspiring, but the inclusion of the angel-like figure, as in a poster by Sugiura Hisui seventeen years later, points to the contrast between seizable objects and a sensed or felt world which may be seized, in the second case via a borrowed allegorical fantasy. When we begin to examine closely what is implied about the way images are viewed by these early modern advertisements we see that it is already implicit in the way objects or feelings about them are positioned to sight at the very beginning of the consumer society. The advent of these phenomena do not accompany the huge leaps in scale we see from the late 1920s.

Fig. 8 Advertisement for Mitsui Gofukuten, vol. 10, no. 1, M37/1904/1/1, Taiyō.

Fig. 9 Taiyō (illustration in the manner of Yamamoto Hōsui), advertisement for creosote-based lung complaint medicine, Kintooru, produced by Oki Ltd, vol. 3, no. 1, M32/1899/ 1/1

Thus, when we see the delineated objects of progress in high-class consumer goods from abroad advertised in the early 1900s, followed by advertisements for much more mundane and Japanese-made objects in the early 1920s, such as tooth-paste, they should be seen as occupying the same visual space with different styles and structures of their distributions. They are not different spaces, one identifiably "modern" and the other "modernist," but are extensions in both directions of the same phenomenon. The objects brought by foreign progress and now made Japanese by advertisement, the consumable good and the expensive vehicle for a fantasy emula-tion of lifestyle, are not so far removed from one another in the functions of their world of visual representation.

The allegory of the real

Materially desired objects were not the only subjects which served as visual represent-ations. The real world was itself positioned in representation by mimetically

Fig. 10 Taiyō, *anti-Japanese demonstration over Shandong in Beijing of December 7, 1909 (17 days earlier), vol. 16,
no. 1, M42/1909/12/24*

conceived images which cognitively stood for that world, or connoted an emotional reaction to it. In the sense that these images caused associations of an automatic kind, they were also indexical links to the world. We might also ask, what were the properties of the medium in which this representation took place and which revealed or made interpretable those cognitions or emotional reactions? In what way were representations of the real shown as allegories for a parallel set of propositions, usually about social values, via the way they were presented?[29]

To begin with, we may classify those subjects shown which were indications of the real: portraits of statesmen and other public figures, ruler portraits, photojournalism of current events and — although the inclusion is problematical — landscapes. The world could be known through photographs of eminent people. Statesmen such as Ōkuma Shigenobu could be shown in rigid poses with their family, standing for some notion of stability of the family and the state. The rigidity and uprightness of such poses is an allegory for unchanging values in a situation of change.[30] The allegory of progress or excellence in the image was reinforced by the technologically advanced methods of photoengraving used to print them. Nine years later such portraits came to have an element of informality and thus a hint at the contemporary man of affairs in the casual pose of the hands and the slightly jaunty angle with which both heads face the camera.[31] By around 1906 these images are printed from a zinc photolithograph and the grayness of tone gives an indirect air of up-to-dateness.

A detailed understanding of any given allegorical use of photographs requires considerable knowledge of a period and the uses to which images are put, or the emotions they may provoke in a given context. For example, photographs of Itô Hirobumi and Ôkuma Shigenobu were scheduled among the series of "Twelve Great Men of Meiji" which were selected from various professional categories by votes from readers and were published in the March 1899 issue of Taiyô. The photograph of Ôkuma and Itô sitting together which was shown in that issue provoked rumors of a change in the political world because the two were thought to be antipathetic.[32]

But the style of photograph could hint at many other values beside political ones. Taiyô includes some industrial and urban landscape depictions which point to a dynamic of progress.[33] These images are separated from each other by square borders, a technical effect which monumentalizes the property of making the manufacturing process and their engineer controller. These are to be compared, perhaps, with the photojournalism images which appear from the early 1900s, in particular the images of strikes in Britain in 1909. These overlap in a visually significant manner which creates an overall representation, despite the fact that each image retains its own identity within the whole. Here is the beginning of collage effects through the properties of the reprographic medium as an allegory for the dynamic of events, or history writ large. A property of visual representation which is usually given on the one hand to Cubism in the 1910s, or on the other to movie montage in the late 1920s, is thus found earlier in photojournalism.

Even single-framed images can suggest historical allegory, depending on the placement of figures within the frame. What better way to show the city as a crowded place full of uncontrollable social forces than through hinting at the fearfulness of the awakened Chinese urban masses (Fig. 10)? These are shown gathered in a 1909 demonstration before Tiananmen against Japanese pressures on Shandong. This may be contrasted with photographs which show the city as still, majestic, untroubled, and permanent, in views of cities like London without crowds.[34]

Allegories even exist in references between images. In particular, they are often found between propaganda images which are not strictly mimetic but claim to embellish the

Fig. 11 Taiyô, Taishô Emperor, vol. 21, no. 1, T3/1914/12/28

meaning of the real world. Here one may contrast the dumb, inarticulate prestige shown by the rather sketchy, almost unfinished, portrait of the Taishō Emperor in 1914 (Fig. 11) with the very violence of the social upheaval itself in the explicitly hostile propaganda image of *The Bolshevik* in 1919 (Fig. 12). New reprographic technology, especially mass-production chromolithography in Japan since 1902, allowed the transfer of images into a mass domain almost as they stood. Thus the allegory of unspoken prestige, or of unspeakable violence, could be transferred directly to a mass domain, and since both images were now co-present, they could serve as co-polarities for a political or social life presumed to stand between them.

Finally, landscape could be used as a sublime allegory for some super-ordinary place of peace. One can see this in the frequent uses of famous places photographed in Japan and abroad, as in *Dusk in the Adirondack Mountains, New York State*,[35] or in *Country Scene in Summer*, after a painting of 1895 by Asai Chū which was published in 1897.[36] Such allegories of elegiac repose are only modern in that their sublimity is made available via the photographic technique which seized it and the lithographic technology which allowed its reproduction. But it is interesting how this feature of technology is largely overlooked if interpretation concentrates on the image itself, or on

Fig. 12 Taiyō, The Bolshevik, *vol. 26, no. 7, T9/1920/6/15*

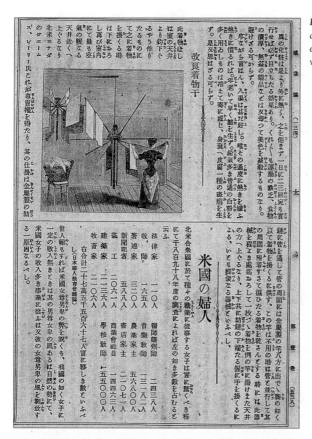

Fig. 13 Taiyō, *improved clothes dryer with statistics of women in employment in the United States, vol. 1, no. 3, M28/1895/3/5*

the lack of questioning of the world which the supposed naturalism of the visual style encompasses. Allegories of the real belong to a visual world which it would appear is unrelativized and which attempts to replace with modern means its habits of viewing from the past. But the technology makes those habits untraditional and incapable of silent motivations because the viewer knows they have been subject to a definite choice for reproduction, even as they may also be well aware that their presentation is conditioned by the reprographic means employed. In other words, the basic condition of modernity is met in that all presentation is known via the medium to be a representation. That the selection is conservative or replicative of earlier viewing habits cannot alter this implicit and necessarily modern relativization.

Modernist transitions: New media, new self-reference

Having recognized that modernity may be conservative but modern nonetheless, and almost despite itself, one must also recognize that certain genres of reprographic subject matter are in themselves modern and, further, may imply a characteristically modernist reflexivity.

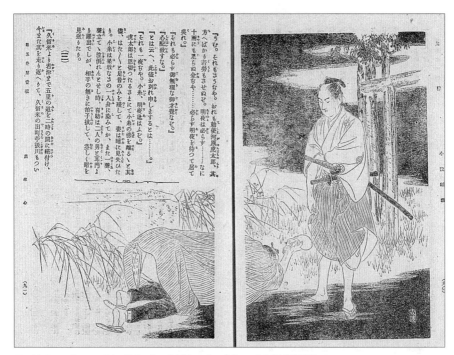

Fig. 14 Taiyō, *Samurai Tale, "Dekigokoro", lithograph, vol. 5, no. 1, M32/1899/1/1*

The encyclopedic quality of *Taiyō* also includes articles directed at women and includes what one might call a modern bifurcation between representations of a new internalized or domestic domain of everyday life, and the representation of the external romance of foreign places. The switch to the latter might be seen as implicitly modernist, accompanied as it is sometimes by far more effective use of the same reprographic technology after the slightly earlier enclosed end grain wood engravings. The same women's page in 1895 includes an illustration of an improved clothes dryer, patented by the Canadian James Rayley, the reader is told, together with details of women in employment in the United States in the 1890s[37] (Fig. 13). But the enclosed style of this illustration is to be compared with the open style of illustrations interleaved slightly with text. Here begins that interaction between image and text which we might think of as characteristically modernist yet is already implied in such layouts from the late 1890s.

Text could enclose instructional illustration, as in 1899 descriptions of the stages of Tea Ceremony etiquette, but the graphics became meaningful entities in their own right alongside the written instructions.[38] The enclosed image was never dispensed with, but the function of the frame changed toward instantiating an image which encapsulated meaning. It is found in the satirical illustrations at the end of the 1920s where the ground within the frame is almost completely stripped away to give prominence to the gestures within, some of which are of social types being parodied.[39]

The interleaving of text and image can also be seen in the collective fantasy space of the serialized novel and seems independent of the reprographic technology used, whether it was in a simple lithograph in 1899 (Fig. 14) or offset lithography later in 1924.[40] The reprographic technology — because it can manipulate text–image relations — almost requires that the possibility of their mutual segmentation be foregrounded.

Not only are text and image mixed, but image styles are also mixed. This can often be seen in explanatory or expostulatory texts dealing with science, such as the combination of different image types on two adjoining pages.[41] There is a kind of logic of combination in play by this time, one which seems to have begun by the late 1910s, and seen in a commentary on military expenditures of various countries shown in a collaged image of battleships in 1919 (Fig. 15). It is perhaps too easy to see this as a logic of free image quotation of even a latently postmodernist kind, but it is certainly significant

Fig. 15 Taiyô, *military expenditures expressed through collaged image of battleships, vol. 26, no. 2,* T8/1919/12/27

Fig. 16 Tokyo Pakku, *no. 2,*
Spring 1936, cover illustration by Ono Saseo

that such collaging effects had become habitual to mass-circulation media by the end of the 1910s. The image space of even quite conservative modern magazines was freed up long before the advent of more modernist magazines. Indeed, the latter seem to show a return to the allegorical mode of nameable types but nameless individuals (Fig. 16) which cover the front pages of mass-circulation magazines in the early 1930s. The nameless figure of the masses is now the allegorical figure for a future world to which all march, by way of a detour back, as it were, through the unrelativized legitimacy of a world from before the modern.

Brief conclusions

There is an in-built tendency in the scientistic bias of modern thought itself to construct the transition from the modern to the modernist along teleological lines. Sometimes the rationality of ends in historical processes derives from a developmental model of change in cultural phenomena where these are dependent on changes in the scale and type of social, economic, technological, or more broadly structural processes. Other teleologies suppose that changes in mass-media technologies drive transformations or produce various *aporia* in cultural conceptions and practices, particularly the reflexiveness of the relation between formal styles and their contents which is made obvious to a mass audience by modern media technologies. However, one must not forget in passing that most specialized practitioners of visual representation, like painters and printers, knew this long before the advent of modern reprographic technology, at least when styles became separate from specific subjects.

One may simply and briefly conclude from an examination of the changes in the formal structure of images in the pages of *Taiyô*, their relation to texts, and the relation of both to putative viewers in Japan between 1895 and 1927, that changes in reprographic technology may be necessary (or primary) conditions for the change in visual representation from the modern to the modernist. One may also conclude that changes in the social structure and scale of their reception are only sufficient, but not necessary conditions for modernism.

Furthermore, a sufficient condition for the repositioning of the past characterized as modern is the advent of new visual technologies and also of new visual styles which allow existing visual discourses to be relativized, or to have their hitherto unquestioned or "natural" legitimacy brought into question. Modernism as a self-conscious embodiment of this relativization in new visual representations occurs almost simultaneously with modernity itself. Modernism's later social permeation via self-consciously adopted and manufactured styles on a mass scale may stand as a process of re-legitimizing what had once been relativized by modernity. But to understand that process would be another history.

Notes

(In the references to Taiyō below, M = Meiji, T = Taishō, S = Shōwa, with dates given as the Japanese calendar year/ Western calendar year/month/day.)

1   I would like to thank Suzuki Sadami for copies of materials on *Taiyō*, for the opportunity to present an earlier formulation of some of these ideas to the *Taiyō* study group at the International Research Center for Japanese Studies at Kyoto in 1996, and to the Center for making slides from *Taiyō* originals.

2   Such a view is implicit in Sōga Tetsuo (ed.), *Genshoku gendai Nihon no bijutsu*, vol. 11, *Hanga*, Tokyo, Shōgakkan, 1978, and in many of the essays in Aoki Shigeru (ed.), *Nihon no kindai bijutsu*, vol 12, *Hanga*, Tokyo, Ōtsuki Shoten, 1994.

3   Minami Hiroshi (ed.), "Nihon modanizumu: ero, guro, nansensu," *Gendai no esupuri*, no. 188, March 1983, p. 5.

4   Satō in ibid., p. 9.

5   This view would seem to underlie Ono's treatment of Meiji copperplates and lithographs in Ono Tadashige, *Hanga*, Tokyo, Iwanami Shoten, 1961, 1985.

6   I think such is one implication of Karatani Kōjin's re-periodization of Japanese modern history in "1970 nendai = Shōwa 45-nen — Kindai Nihon no Gensetsu Kūkan," Karatani Kōjin, *Shūen wo megutte*, Tokyo, Fukutake Shoten, 1990, pp. 9–44, where the years 22–45 of Meiji (1889–1912) are found to have a pattern of events correlative with the years 21–45 of Shōwa (1945–70). If the succession of periods is: modern, 1889–1912; modernist, 1912–45; modern, 1945–70; modernist, 1970–80s, with 1945 seen as the failure to go beyond the modern (and this issue was indeed debated by Japanese intellectuals in the late 1930s and 1940s), then what lies outside these periods comes into question. If Japan is in a postmodern situation in the 1980s, where we conventionally define the postmodern as freedom from the hegemony of master narratives, what was it in from 1869 to the 1880s, if not some analogue of this? Interestingly, the same tendency to eclectically quote in architectural styles rather than pursue dominant or "classic" styles, a feature later used to identify postmodernism in American architecture, is quite widely seen in Japanese buildings of the 1870s.

7   Based largely on analyses of literature, Suzuki Sadami, *Modan toshi no hyōgen*, Tokyo, Shirojisha, 1992, p. 237, has summarized the crisis of mentalities in the Japan of the 1920s as a problem of:
1. the lassitude caused by the standardization of the individual with the advance of capitalism and a decline in vitalist feeling with envelopment by material civilization;
2. the disruption of self-consciousness based on urban human relations in the period of formation of an urban mass society; and
3. the intellectual problem attacking the intellectual class, the prevalence of a fatalist view of the "fall of the intellectuals" with the permeation of socialist thought and a class view of society.
For an excellent survey of the intellectual issues of the 1920s and 1930s, see T. Najita and H.D. Harootunian, "Japanese Revolt Against the West: Political and Cultural Criticism in the Twentieth Century," in P. Duus (ed.), *The Cambridge History of Japan*, vol. 6, *The Twentieth Century*, Cambridge, Cambridge University Press, 1988.

8   See Ono Tadashige, *Sekibanga*, Tokyo, Bijutsu Shuppansha, 1967, 1976.

9   The clearest survey of these technical changes is in the later chapters of Shimaya Seiichi, *Nihon hanga hensen-shi*, Ōsaka, Ōsaka Shuppansha, 1939.

10   I take the Tokyo figures alone to give an indicative sequence for increases in the speed of social circulation and not of overall sales volumes. It will be recalled that *Asahi* was also published in Ōsaka where the sales were 585,294 in 1923, 782,709 in 1926, and 861,334 in 1936 respectively, so overall sales were roughly double those for Tokyo alone. See Yamamoto Taketoshi, *Kindai Nihon no shimbun dokushasō*, Hōsei Daigaku Shuppankai, 1981, Addendum Table 4, pp. 410–11.

11   Among texts written in the 1920s which look back nostalgically to Edo are: Abe Jirō, *Tokugawa jidai no geijutsu to shakai*, Tokyo, Kaizōsha, 1931; Kishida Ryūsei, *Shinko zaiku renga no michisuji*, 1927, republished in Sakai Tadayasu (ed.), *Kishida Ryūsei zuihitsushū*, Tokyo, Iwanami Shoten, 1996, pp. 29–40; partial translation in Jackie Menzies (ed.), *Modern Boy and Modern Girl*, Sydney, Art Gallery of New South Wales, 1998; Nagai Kafū, *Edo geijutsuron*, Tokyo, Shun'yōdō, 1920; Tanizaki Junichirō, "In'ei Raisan," *Keizai ōrai*, December 1933 and January 1934, reprinted in *Tanizaki Junichirō zenshu*, vol. 29, Tokyo, Chūō Kōronsha.

12   According to Suzuki Sadami, *Modan toshi no hyōgen*, Tokyo, Shirojisha, 1992, p. 152, the prototype modern educated woman is the love of the hero in the novel *Ukigumo* by Futabatei Shimei, published in 1894. He accepts the first appearance of the "modern girl" as occurring in the journal *Josei kaizō* (Women's Reform) of April 1923, in Kitazawa Chōgo's "Modan gāru no hyōgen — Nihon no imooto ni okuru tegami." There are many other indices pointing to the emergence of this distinct social phenomenon after 1923, including the change to Western-style dress for shop workers in Shirokiya Department Store in about 1924. High heels and a skirt were worn by stars for their film roles, such as Okada Yoshiko in about 1925, and the short-cut hairstyle for women emerged slightly later, being brought back to Japan by the Hollywood starlet May Ushiyama in 1926: Minami Hiroshi, *Taishō bunka*, Tokyo, Keisō Shobō, 1965, pp. 358, 366, 368.

13   See Minami, *Taishō bunka*, p. 253. Among other indicators of the spread of consumerism is the starting of the Association of Tokyo Consumer Unions in 1922. One base for the spread of urban consumerism is the speeding up of physical communications to new suburbs with the founding of the Tokyo Underground Railway Company in 1920 (the first subway opened in 1927), and private railways like Seibu in 1922 and Odakyū in 1923. See Minami, *Taishō bunka*, 1965, pp. 250, 254.

14   Kōno Takashi, "Eiga postaa no jissai, ichi," in *Kokusai eiga shimbun*, no. 39, May 1930. Cited by Kawabata in Mizusawa, 1998, p. 241.

15   Yamana Ayao, "Kesshōhin Kōkoku to sono bijin-e," in *Kōkokukai*, vol. 7, no. 1, January 1930. Cited by Kawabata Naomichi, "Modanizumu to shōgyōbijutsu," in Mizusawa Tsutomu (ed.), *Mobo Moga, 1910–1935 Ten*, Kamakura, Kanagawa Kenritsu Kindai Bijutsukan, 1998, p. 241.

16   A full description of various stages on the move from drawing models to free drawing and the use of the pencil, brush, and crayon in primary and secondary school education in Japan from late Meiji onwards can be found in Chapters 3–5 in Kaneko Kazuo, *Bijutsuka kyōiku (Dai 1,2,3 bu)*, Mitoshi, Kaneko Kazuo, 1987, 1989. I am grateful to Professor Kaneko for a copy of these most valuable research papers.

17   Kayano Yatsuka, *Kindai Nihon dezain bunkashi, 1868–1926*, Tokyo, Firumu Aato Sha, 1992, pp. 375, 390.

18   ibid., p. 389.

19   ibid., p. 387.

20   Nagamine Shigetoshi, "Meijiki 'Taiyō' no jūyō kōzō," Shuppan Kenkyū no. 21, [n.d.], pp. 34–6.

21   ibid., pp. 29–30.

22   Shikano Masanao, " 'Taiyō,' shu toshite Meijiki ni okeru," *Shisō*, no. 450, December 1961, p. 139, identifies five periods in the general position of *Taiyō*:

    I.   1895–1902, First period of Constitutionalism

    II.   Around 1902, Imperialism

    III.   1902–1910, Naturalism

    This was a period when any possible idea of a correlation between state development and individual prosperity came to an end, an idea which had been vaguely held until then: Shikano, p. 143.

    IV.   1910–17, Second period of Constitutionalism

    V.   1919–28, Mixed publication of different intellectual trends

    Shikano also notes that *Taiyō* almost entirely ignored socialism and Christianity, which were two currents of thought widely held among Taishō intellectuals. As reasons for the decline in circulation of *Taiyō*, he advances the publication of *ShinNihon* by Okuma Shigenobu in 1911, the publication of *Kaizō* in 1919, and the general loss of attractiveness of the magazine due to its worldly attitude of support for the status quo.

23   Nagamine, "Meijiki," p. 51. New media showed a very rapid penetration into many different strata of the population from the late Meiji into the early Taishō period (1910–20) among which the most astounding, certainly in urban areas, was movies. In 1917 a survey by the Ministry of Education revealed that at thirty-one schools surveyed in Tokyo, 98.7 percent of children above the fifth and sixth years of primary school (say, children around ten years and over) had seen a movie, and 50.8 percent went more than once a month: Minami, *Taishō bunka*, p. 236.

24   Nagamine, "Meijiki," p. 26.

25   ibid., p. 46.

26   Yamaguchi Masao, "Meiji shuppankai no hikari to yami: Hakubunkan no kōbō," [publishing details unknown], pp. 87–189.

27   The end grain woodblock process used for the first Taiyō illustrations may indeed have constrained this kind of realism even though the three illustrators mentioned in Taiyō, vol. 1, no. 1, 1895, p. 178, are the illustrators Takeuchi Keisen (ukiyo-e, 1861–1943), Tomioka Eisen (nihonga, 1864–1905), and Sakuma Bungo (nanga, 1868–1940). Also mentioned in this first edition are Gōta Kiyoshi (end grain block engraver), Ogawa Isshin (photographer, photoengraver), and Hori Kenkichi (zinc relief printing), indicating an interesting collaboration between up-to-the-minute reprographic technology and the conservative modernity of neo-traditionalist painting.

28   The December 26 Meiji 42 (1909), vol. 16, no. 1, issue of Taiyō gives the following as illustrators: Morita Tsunetomo (1881–1933), Hashimoto Hōsuke (1884–1953), Shimomura Izan (1865–1949), Ikeda Eiji, Uenoyama Kiyotsugu (1889–1968), Nabeii Katsuyuki (1884–1953), and Hata Teruo (1887–1945). As an example of the features content in Taiyō, this issue had articles on: "The Present Condition of the Former German Emperor," "London Rally in Great British Strike," "America of the Seas," "D'Annunzio's March on Fiume," "Mexican Sketches," and "Peking Anti-Japanese People's Meeting."

29   Because "realistic" imagery is actually functioning as part of a parallel and unspoken value-laden text, albeit not always a very coherently ordered one, its theme works against or even assumes a dominance over the image and the action it represents or records. Allegory violates the criterion of disinterestedness of the representation. See Chapter 7, "Value and Intention: The Limits of Allegory," in Angus Fletcher, Allegory: The Theory of a Symbolic Mode, Ithaca, Cornell University Press, 1964.

30   The photoengraving in Taiyō, vol. 1, no. 2, M281895/2/5, of Okuma Shigenobu and family, after a photograph by Ogawa Isshin, is an allegory of progress which also plays on the importance of this internationally recognized photographer's work. Ogawa had won a gold medal for photography at the Columbia Exposition in Chicago in 1893. See the biographical details in Taiyō, vol. 1, no. 1, 1895, p. 178.

31   As in the photographs of Okuma Shigenobu and Prince Itō (Hirobumi), Governor of Korea, in Taiyō, vol. 14, no. 15, M41/1906/11/15.

32   Tsubotani Zenshirō, Hakubunkan gojūnenshi, Tokyo, Hakubunkan, 1937, pp. 135–8.

33   Such as the still description in photographs of the Head Engineer Yoshida Tomoyoshi and the Kanegafuchi Spinning Factory in Taiyō, vol. 1, no. 4, M28/1895/4/5.

34   As in the view of De Keyser's Royal Hotel, view of St Paul's Cathedral from Blackfriars Bridge, Taiyō, vol. 1, no. 3, M28/1895/3/5.

35   See Taiyō, "Dusk in the Adirondack Mountains", New York State, vol. 14, no. 15, 41/1905/11/15.

36   See Taiyō, "Country Scene in Summer", after a painting of 1895 by Asai Chū, vol. 3, no. 9, M30/1897/5/5.

37   According to Taiyō, vol. 1, no. 3 of March 5, 1895, which also gives details of women in the United States in employment.

38   See Taiyō, "Tea Ceremony Etiquette," vol. 5, no. 1, M32/1899/3/1.

39   See Taiyō, social critique "Seigyū yoen" (The Young Bull Over-Salivates) by Mizushima Niou, vol. 31, no. 1, T13/1924/12/20.

40   See Taiyō, in a title which is equivalent to the "Story of the Heavy Drinker" by Mikami Otokiki, illustrator Ito Kikuzō, lithograph, vol. 31, no. 1, T13/1924/12/20.

41   On one page a filtration bottle is shown opposite a medical report on the relation between nervousness and the stomach in Taiyō, vol. 31, no. 1, T13/1924/12/20.

CHAPTER THREE

The Formation of the Audiences for Modern Art in Japan

Omuka Toshiharu

Who were the audiences for modern art in Japan? This is no easy problem to solve. Some aspects of the audiences for modern art in Japan have hardly been examined so far in art history. We have few reliable sources in this field and are without adequate methods to scan all the relevant texts. Thus this chapter will not be the last word on the subject, but rather a progress report. I should like to limit the scope of the chapter to the period after the inauguration of the official annual salon called Monbushō Bijutsu Tenrankai. Monbushō, the Ministry of Education, established the salon in 1907, and so it was first nicknamed Bunten. After 1919 it was reconstituted as the Teikoku Bijutsuin Tenrankai, Exhibition of the Imperial Academy of Fine Arts, and given a different nickname, Teiten. Bunten was a juried exhibition after the French salon. Its establishment in modern Japan stood as the last phase of modernization and reorganization of the whole art world, a policy that was promoted by the state after it established a national museum and the national art school in 1889.[1] The whole new system functioned from 1907 as a securely based art establishment.

But here we should not overlook the emergence of regular visitors to the annual event, in addition to its wide coverage by the popular press. Before Bunten, there were already annual exhibitions of two representative societies of Western-style painting, the Hakubakai (White Horse Society) and Taiheiyōgaki (Pacific Painting Society). There are no basic studies on visitors to their exhibitions, even though they made great contributions to the early cultivation of modern audiences for art.[2]

Bunten, however, inaugurated a new phase in the history of modern audiences as the number of visitors to each exhibition grew rapidly, reaching around 160,000 in 1912 and over 230,000 in 1916 at the tenth exhibition.[3] The whole population of Tokyo prefecture was then only 3.5 million, so if there were roughly 1.7 million adults, around one in eight of them must have seen it.

There is an obstacle to analyzing what these numbers meant because the masses of visitors were literally silent. We have only a handful of descriptions of them. In the

fall of 1925, Kon Wajiro and his colleague did unique field research on the daily attendance figures for visitors to exhibitions in the large historical park in Tokyo at Ueno,[4]
where the later Bunten and most Teiten exhibitions were held. Their results tell much
about what kind of people came to conservative exhibitions of established artists like
Teiten, or to the exhibitions of a modernistic society like Nikaten (Second Section
Exhibition), or to the yearly "Contemporary French Art" exhibition, or to the avant-
garde group show "Sankaten" (Third Section Exhibition). The figures suggest that it
was the conservative art among the major exhibitions which attracted the most visitors.
About 1100 visitors per hour attended the exhibitions, in a broad range of categories.
The Bijutsuin Tenrankai (Japan Art Academy exhibitions centered on anti-Bunten
Japanese-style painting, but later included some Japanified oil painting) were
crowded with 517 visitors per hour, especially rich middle-aged gentlemen, whereas
the French exhibit had 920 visitors per hour, and the modernistic Nika had 390,
including many students and especially female students. Lastly, the most radical
exhibition by Sanka attracted only thirty-nine visitors per hour, most of whom were
junior-high school students.

Kon's classification of the visitors is very helpful in examining the audiences: he
categorized these by male and female, profession and age (such as middle-aged and
young gentlemen, where "gentlemen" meant white-collar workers who had just
emerged as a new middle class in the Taishô period), wives, university students, workers, shopkeepers, and others. It was not so difficult to recognize each profession from
peoples clothes, as the fieldwork of Kon and others in popular streets in the center of
Tokyo had already clearly shown.[5]

Unfortunately, among these exhibitions it was only the state-run Teiten which
published the total number of visitors, who amounted to some 200,000 in 1925.
Further research can now only be done by patiently gathering various other materials.
Correspondence columns in art journals seem to be an important but neglected source
for further investigation into the nature of audiences for modern art. However, they may
not be completely representative of these audiences, since these correspondents must
have been different from the silent majority in that they actively sought publication of
their views. In addition, the editors must have selected letters according to certain
criteria. Nevertheless, in spite of these and other limitations, studies of such columns
must be relevant to the history and discourse of art. So far I have researched three
major journals from the 1910s and 1920s – Mizue (Water-color Painting), Chûô bijutsu
(Central Art), and Atorie (Atelier) – but the conclusions reached below are far from
definite.

In modern Japan between the Meiji and Taishô periods, a genre of generalist magazines called tôsho zasshi was most popular among youth. They accepted a surprisingly
large number of subjects for contributions, and hence a number of writers emerged
from such journals. For example, Bunsho sekai appeared in 1906, and its first editor

Fig. 1 Mizue, *cover*

was the famous realist novelist Tayama Katai. Together with correspondence, it published important texts by professional writers such as Futabatei Shimei's important piece "Yo ga genbun-itchi no yūrai" (Origins of My Unification of Spoken and Written Language). The magazine accepted not only texts but also so-called *komae* — that is, illustrations. A famous painter judged the best of those submitted and reproduced them with his commentary. Among the illustrators were future successful painters such as Tōgō Seiji, then a junior-high school student who made his debut in *Bunsho sekai* in 1914.[6]

Not all art journals provided the reader with such a column. The best example among the art journals from the 1900s to the 1920s was *Mizue* (Fig. 1), which Ōshita Tōjirō (Fig. 2) had started in 1905 to promote water-color painting, founding an association called Shunchōkai. However, for this period the art journal *Bijutsu shinpō* (Art News) is more reliable for art historians and had sophisticated contents written by famous writers and journalists, although it had no place for correspondence.

Mizue had a long life of some three generations and continued to appear well into the 1980s. It was already provided with a correspondence column from the second issue, which lasted continuously until 1931, the longest among the three magazines I have examined. Here is a list of such columns for *Mizue* (1905–92):[7]

- "Toi ni kotau" (a question-and-answer column), no. 2 (August 1905) – no. 243 (May 1925);
- "Yosegaki" (correspondence-like comments from the journal's writers), no. 2 (August 1905) – no. 114 (August 1914);
- "Dokusha no ryôbun" (The Readers' Domain), no. 5 (November 1905) – no. 103 (September 1913) and no. 169 (March 1919) – no. 212 (November 1922;
- "Tôkô" (Correspondence), no. 109 (March 1914) – no. 281 (July 1928); and
- "Dokusha kaidan" (Readers' Discussion), no. 311 (January 1931) – no. 316 (June 1931).

Chûô bijutsu (October 1915 – May 1929, August 1933 – December 1936) was published by a correspondence school for fine arts, the Nihon Bijutsu Gakuin, which had been established in 1913.[8] Before this publication, the school edited regular booklets for students in addition to textbooks for practice and thus the first number already had correspondence from students. Without doubt, it followed *Mizue* in its organization of reader-students. It ran "Dokusharan" (Readers'column) from issue no. 1 (October 1915) through to vol. 5, no. 9 (September 1919).

In contrast to the above, *Atorie* (February 1924 – present)[9] had nothing to do with education. This partly explains the rapid disappearance of its correspondence column, which was published as follows:

- "Dokusha no peiji" (Readers' page), vol. 1, no. 2 (March 1924) – vol. 3, no. 10 (October 1926); and
- "Kandanshitsu" (Conversation Room), vol. 4, no. 1 (January 1927) – vol. 5, no. 8 (August 1928).

As you can see, *Mizue* was the most active in cultivating a relationship with the reader. Early correspondents were very enthusiastic, and the 1906 issue no. 7, entitled "Readers' Number," consisted almost entirely of readers' letters. This was the age of *Shirakabaha* (White Birch Group), a group of writers who inspired non-political but idealistic youth movements all over the country.

Fig. 2 Ôshita Tôjirô

In schools there even appeared the popular expression "*Shirakaba kyôshi*" (Shirakaba teachers).

In contrast to *Bijutsu shinpô*, a quality magazine, *Mizue* in the early phase was a practical journal and was distributed principally among a limited circle of reader–students. *Mizue* magazine was closely related to the popularization and education of painting in water-colors, as an announcement for correspondence in its first issue read:

> *Those who hold workshops in school, or sketching groups who sketch or those who exchange postcard drawings, please inform us in as great detail as possible of your present circumstances.*
> *Please send us your correspondence on the following issues:*
> *Your first motivation in seeking to do water-colors;*
> *Your first impressions of sketching outside;*
> *Interesting events that you have encountered during sketching;*
> *Notable merits of drawing.*[10]

Mizue magazine prepared two columns for correspondence: one was the "Question and Answer" column, which was indispensable for propagation of water-color technique, and the other was the correspondence column. The "Question and Answer" column soon divided into two. One was more technical and dealt with such matters as drawing technique, name and quality of colors, names of stores for art materials, artists' addresses, art journal publishers and foreign booksellers, and practical details on how to exhibit one's work in the Bunten salon. The other column was "Dokusha no ryôbun" (The Readers' Domain), where questions were more general in character. For example, Gotô Kôgai, a frequent correspondent, asked a question about artists' incomes in no. 7, thinking that other people would also be interested in this subject. The editor replied as follows:

> *I do not know much about the case of Japanese-style painters. A Western-style painter, who teaches at junior high school, earns about 20 yen to 40 yen a month, according to the region where he lives, and where he belongs to a newspaper, he gets 25 yen to 50 or 60 yen, though both have no time to practice their art. If one draws by commission for a publishing house, the pay is relatively fair but this depends on one's popularity.*[11]

The answer informs us of the miserable economic situation of the typical Western-style painter, who could not gain a living as an independent professional and some-times had to move elsewhere to a prosperous city with a flourishing cultural life in order to elaborate his technique. Thus the column contains a lot of information about diverse aspects of the contemporary art world.

"The Readers' Domain" also contained notices of things for sale or exchange (these notices were later put in a separate section) and also letters on various topics often quite similar to those in the correspondence column. The ambiguous character of its contents is probably the main reason that the column was first suspended for five years between 1913 and 1919 and discontinued entirely early in 1922.

The correspondence column in *Mizue* was called *"Yosegaki,"* a public forum for the reader. The column clearly reflected the ideas of the editor, Ôshita Tôjirô, and included many of his own comments. The most important among these was his encouragement of the discovery or rediscovery of natural beauty. Ôshita must have been strongly influenced by Ruskin's view of nature and also by Shiga Shigetaka's nationalistic survey of the Japanese landscape.[12] This discovered landscape did not consist of certain historical sites with a particular visual and iconographical memory, but was a landscape held in common and hence accessible to Japanese people.

In "The Readers' Domain" of issue no. 17 in 1906, a correspondent asked what age-group constituted the major part of the associates of Shunchôkai, and the editor replied that many were around twenty years old. The magazine supported part of youth culture. We have good reason to suppose that most subscribers lived in smaller cities or in the countryside far from Tokyo or other major cities, where they found it hard to find places to learn how to paint in water-colors. In Tokyo there was an institute related to the Shunchôkai association, the Nihon Suisaigakai Kenkyûjo (Japan Water-color Society Research Institute), which was founded in 1907. *Mizue* magazine often publicized this school by carrying descriptions of classes and other activities such as its New Year party.

It is tempting to suppose that, encouraged by the magazine, youth who very probably had graduated from junior high school or normal school made their way into areas surrounding their native town or other places, not only on the island of Honshû but also in Taiwan and Korea. They looked for a good place to draw, with a paintbox especially designed for water-colors and a tripod. Then, on returning home, they sent works for critique by professionals of the magazine and sometimes mailed correspondence with it to the editor to provide the journal with information about the neighborhood and to communicate with friends via the column.

Texts, including articles by professional water-colorists and critics in the magazine, often appeared in the form of travel accounts. Some writers expressed views about the sources of their personal inspiration. For example, worship of nature appeared in one account under the initials "B.K." in Nagano Prefecture from no. 46 in 1909. B.K. wrote:

> It was only Mt. Myôko and I that stood in a dead winter field in the evening. My god was there at that moment when I faced the mountain. That moment when I listened to the evening solitude, was it real? Unexpectedly, inspiration penetrated my mind. I then got an intuition of nature.[13]

This passage suggests that the "I" or the artist's self played a great part in this experience. Self-expression became a key word for youth in this period.[14] One's art must be one's nature and so must be complete in itself without the need to expose oneself as a painter. The art of drawing could be a way of discipline. This position is closely related to the amateurism praised by *Mizue*, as we will see below.

A second major type of travel account is a guide to the best locations for sketching landscape in a given locality. The following was written by a certain Ryokuyō Midoriha, from Akita Prefecture, in no. 57, 1909:

> Lake Hachirogata is located in the northwest beach of the Prefecture [...] The lake is not deep but its landscape is great and everywhere you find a good place to sketch. Senshū Park is in the center of the city, on the site of Akita castle, and is famous for cherry blossoms and red leaves. Many ladies and gentlemen stop there to look in the best seasons. Strangers to this prefecture praise it as the best in the Tōhoku region.[15]

The editor commented that this kind of letter would be most welcome:

> The editor is grateful for this type of letter. Readers are kindly requested to present plainly famous and beautiful places of their own native places. It would be much better if you mention distances and transportation to the spot. Mr. Midoriha sent his correspondence with many postcards and for this I thank him very much.[16]

Another major theme of the correspondence column was views on art. This seems natural, as the magazine specialized in art, but we must take into account the fact that the circulation of the magazine was not open to general readers, but was limited to subscribers who shared a common ideal. Readers sometimes became excited and went to an extreme, expressing in their letters a kind of profession of love, or rather of faith, in art. A certain Shiroya Sei confessed his sincere worship for art in the March 1911 issue:

> I do not want a good profession or a precious treasure. In front of a canvas with a paintbrush, I forget appetite, bad association, and vanity and before a great landscape I am overwhelmed by the sublime and mystic beauty of nature. I would be grateful if I could forget myself and would not even fear starving to death.[17]

More moderate but common was the expression of frustration about the writer's remote location from the art life of the center. In no. 105, "Sankyaku dōjin" (Tripod hermit) introduced himself as "a commonplace official, living in the country."[18] The young man was anxious to seek a professional career against his father's will. In no. 150, the writer of "Mizu no awa" (Water bubble) in Fukushima Prefecture, who was graduating from junior high school, had to remain in his native town in order to succeed to the family business. He sent correspondence entitled "Farming or Art."[19]

Most *Mizue* correspondents were not professionals, although some would later become artists and critics, and they remained faithful to the amateurism advocated by Ōshita himself, and so were compelled to cling to the master's ideas. Ōshita publicly declared, in a contribution to the issue commemorating the fifth year of publication:

"I am always ready to give up the name of painter. I am satisfied with being an amateur."[20]

"Amateur" seems to be an exact designation of the reader–students *Mizue* intended to organize. One had to be just between a passive viewer and an active artist. To attain this aim, Ôshita systematically sought to propagate water-color painting. In addition to the magazine, he established art schools; first the Suisaiga Kôshûjo (School of Water-color) in 1906, and then the Nihon Suisaigakai Kenkyûjo (Japan Water-color Society Research Institute) in 1907, which founded branches first in Yokohama and then in other cities. He and his colleagues often held workshops in various places in Japan. These resulted in the formation of an exhibition society, Nihon Suisaigakai (Japan Water-color Society), in 1913. Thus, students who joined the society and the school, as well as readers who subscribed to the magazine, were systematically united in an organization or in organized education. Thanks to its cultivation all over the country through correspondence, workshops, and other means, this organization contributed greatly to the formation of the audience for modern art in Japan.

Now I would like to turn to the other two art journals, *Atorie* and *Chûô bijutsu*. Correspondence in the former is in general of little interest, partly because the magazine had no specific distribution circuit with enthusiastic reader–students like the latter, and partly because the column was open to any kind of letter. In other words, it lacked a core focus to attract the attention of various readers. Thus in the October 1926 issue, the editor frankly complained about the inactive correspondence column, and demanded that readers write more on new experiments in technique or old artworks in their locality, and present the circumstances of their painting, in addition to contributing humorous letters about their own interests.[21] *Atorie* published many of these in its first numbers. For example, Miki Tadao, a frequent correspondent in Osaka, wrote his first letter under the initials "S.M." in the January 1925 issue and entitled "Gadan Kyûshô-roku" (Tragi-comedy of the Painting Establishment), in which he mocked two popular artists, Umehara Ryûzaburô and Yasui Sôtarô, as "two silent stars, but silent only in speech."[22]

The correspondence column in *Atorie* did not last long and received contributions from few future artists or critics. One exception was Ei Kyû, the future experimental artist, who was then still an art student in Tokyo and who disclosed his disdain for the modern art movement.[23] Another was Iwamatsu Jun, the future proletarian artist, who discussed caricature for people in Japan.[24] Another was Hasegawa Toshiyuki, a legendary painter. The column was barely active, in contrast to the other pages of the magazine.

The correspondence column of the first numbers of *Chûô bijutsu* was very confusing and diverse in its content. However, it was quite interesting in its active exchanges of opinion about this new publication, which had changed from being a supplement to the regular textbooks previously provided by the correspondence school. Some of the student–readers felt they were losing their forum as well as their privilege to communicate with each other in the sincere intention of learning to draw. The correspondence column was open to the reader in general; it was not only for a limited circle of associates. A reader called "Banjii" in Kumamoto Prefecture deplored in no. 4, 1916, that associates in the period of the previous supplementary booklet were happy and belonged to a kind of large family.[25] The editor did not seem to exclude correspondents who did not support the new editorial policy. After all, as announced in the June 1916 issue, the correspondence school had been forced to republish the supplementary issue to the textbook every three months.

Second, in the *Chūō bijutsu* we find a few rare issues which carry a small number of letters written by women, although they were soon to be suppressed by the strong opposition of male correspondents and male editors. Incidentally, *Mizue* also eliminated women's correspondence. But in *Chūō bijutsu* no. 31, 1907, for example, one photograph of a workshop in Osaka tells a rather different story, for it shows four female students.[26] In fact, women's letters in *Chūō bijutsu* were distinguished by their characteristic means of expression and clichés. No. 4, 1916, contained as many as six letters from women. In the next issue, Tsubouchi Naoko from Maizuru stated that she lived in a lonely part of the countryside and asked for friendship as follows: "Dear sisters and brothers! Please count this lonely child among your close friends forever and ever."[27] In no. 6, 1916, she repeated the same expression, with "Dear sisters and brothers! I am a lonely child."[28] This kind of plea did not fail to irritate male readers. Fujishima Shūchō in Shimonoseki, in the same no. 6 issue, very much deplored the fact that he felt like he was reading a women's or girls' magazine.[29] Thus, issue no. 10 eliminated women's correspondence, although a few frequent correspondents continued to appear, such as Azuma Takeko in Tokyo, and Tsubouchi Naoko, but of course in a different style from that disliked by male readers.

Thus the correspondence column of *Chūō bijutsu* was very attractive in its early phase, but soon two correspondents in the March 1918 issue blamed the editorship outright for the recent decline of the column, and pointed out that regular correspondents were disappearing from it.[30] In 1919 the column was discontinued.

I should also like to discuss the decline of the correspondence column in *Mizue* magazine, especially after the great earthquake in 1923. The decline reflected, it seems, partly the fall in popularity of water-colors, and partly the growth in readership. A correspondent in the December 1922 issue deplored the recent trend where beginners, instead of starting their Western-style painting education in water-colors, were going straight into oil painting.[31] He was afraid of the neglect of water-colors, even among amateurs. But seen from the diffusion of the medium, this situation was the unavoidable result of popularization, or was the fruit of the spread of art education, a result which the magazine itself had sought for many years.

Another reason is somehow related. In the March 1918 issue the editor suggested that the magazine's circulation had doubled.[32] This growth had not failed to affect the relationship between the editor and readers. In my view, the editorship was losing direct contact with its early reader–student and was thus forced to change its policy in order to reach the general public. Moreover, in the mid-1920s the publishing world faced a critical, even revolutionary, situation brought about by a series of cheap books called *enbon* which were priced at only one yen each. The popular magazine *Kingu* would boast a circulation of one million copies, while several other series attracted several hundred thousand subscribers. This situation was actually reflected in the pages of art journals. For example, *Chūō bijutsu* changed its cover to one designed by Tōgō Seiji from the January 1928 issue, emphasizing the three new directions or genres by which it sought to gain popularity: art, movies, and literature.

In the mid-1910s, the issue of people's art had been hotly debated, but now the masses had actually appeared on stage. This new situation in the later 1920s silently and steadily broke the old art establishment as the masses found their own form of art. It reached its zenith around 1930 when there should have been no need for a correspondence column of the earlier type. Amateur painters thus literally lost the respectable position they had had in the past. In art journals they were forced into silence by the advent of the masses. This symbolic pantomime surely anticipated the fate of people of Japan in other fields in the 1930s and 1940s.

Notes

1   The first national modern museum after the Western model was established in 1872 by the Ministry of Education, but it was not a so-called art museum. After moving from one ministry to another, in 1889 the museum was reorganized as an imperial museum under the jurisdiction of the Imperial Household Ministry, putting more emphasis on the collection of art objects than before. In February the same year Tōkyō Bijutsu Gakkō (Tokyo School of Fine Art) was opened with the three departments of painting, sculpture, and design. For details, see *Tōkyō Kokuritsu Hakubutsukan hyakunenshi*, Tokyo, Tōkyō Kokuritsu Hakubutsukan, 1973; Tōkyō Geijutsu Daigaku Hyakunenshi and Henshū Iinkai (ed.), *Tōkyō Geijutsu Daigaku hyakunenshi*, Tokyo, Ongaku no Tomosha, 1987.

2   For the Hakubakai, see the recent exhibition catalog with detailed documentation for the centenary of its establishment, *Starting Anew in the Meiji Period: A Retrospective Exhibition of Paintings from the Hakubakai Group 1896–1911*, Tokyo, Bridgestone Museum of Art, and other museums, 1996–7.

3   The figures are quoted from Nittenshi Hensan Iinkai (ed.), *Nittenshi*, vol. 5, 1981, Tokyo, Nitten, p. 570, for the twelve Bunten showings, and from vol. 11, 1983, p. 672, for the fifteen Teiten ones.

4   Kon Wajirō and Yoshida Kenkichi (eds), *Kōgengaku: Modernologio*, Tokyo, Shunyōdō, 1930, pp. 258–63.

5   See, for example, ibid., p. 77.

6   For this, see my article " 'Ginzara' jidai no Tōgō Seiji," in ex. cat. *Tōgō Seiji ten*, Kagoshima City Museum of Art, 1994, unpaginated.

7   During World War II the magazine changed its name to *Shin bijutsu* (New Art) between the September 1941 issue and the November 1943 issue. Thereafter it was called *Bijutsu* (Art) from the January 1944 issue to the July/August 1946 issue.

8   For details, see the ex. cat. *Taishō gajin netwâku: Taguchi Kikutei ga hiraita Chūō bijutsu*, Akita, Akita Museum of Modern Art, 1996.

9   During World War II the magazine changed its name to *Seikatsu bijutsu* (Life Art) from September 1941 to November 1943.

10   "Kaikoku," *Mizue*, no. 1, July 1905, p. 18.
11   Gotō Kogai, untitled correspondence, *Mizue*, no. 7, January 1905, p. 20.
12   For Ruskin's deep influence in Japan, see the detailed essays in the catalog *Ruskin in Japan*, Kamakura, Museum of Modern Art, 1997.
13   B.K., "Sekisan Bekken," *Mizue*, no. 46, January 1909, pp. 25–6.
14   See my contribution, "The Non-Continuity of the Avant-Garde," trans. by Chiaki Ajioka, in the ex. cat. *Modern Boy, Modern Girl*, Sydney, Art Gallery of New South Wales, 1998, p. 138.
15   Ryokuyō, "Akitaken no fūkei," *Mizue*, no. 57, December 1909, p. 19.
16   Henja (the editor), untitled statement, *Mizue*, no. 57, December 1909, p. 20.
17   Shiroya sei, "Ane no moto e," *Mizue*, no. 73, March 1911, p. 34.
18   Sankyaku dōjin, "Yo wa naniyue ni e wo egakitsutsu ariya," *Mizue*, no. 105, November 1913, p. 29.
19   Mizu no awa, "Nōgyō ka geijutsu ka," *Mizue*, no. 150, August 1917, pp. 35–8.
20   Ōshita Tōjirō, "Mizue go shūnen shokan," *Mizue*, no. 64, July 1910, p. 39.
21   Kisha (a staff writer), "Dokusha no pēji ni tsuite," *Atorie*, vol. 3, no. 10, October 1926, p. 107.
22   Miki Sadao, "Gadan kyūshō-roku," *Atorie*, vol. 2, no. 1, January 1925, p. 147.
23   Sugita Hideo (Ei Kyū), "Gaji zakkō," *Atorie*, vol. 4, no. 1, January 1927; Sugita, "Shin," *Atorie*, vol. 4, no. 2, February 1927. For this artist, see my article "Hihan sareru ishi — Ei Kyū no geijutsu to shōgai," in Honma Masayoshi (ed.), *Ei Kyū sakuhinshū*, Tokyo, Nihon Keizai Shinbunsha, 1997, pp. 10–33.
24   Iwamatsu Jun, "Tomicha no e," *Atorie*, vol. 4, no. 7, August 1927; Iwamatsu, "Nihon no manga," *Atorie*, vol. 4, no. 9, September 1927; Jun [Iwamatsu Jun], "4 jōhan danpen go," *Atorie*, vol. 5, no. 5, May 1928.
25   Banjii, untitled statement, *Chūō bijutsu*, vol. 2, no. 1, January 1915, p. 118.
26   See the illustration in *Mizue*, no. 31, December 1907, p. 13.
27   Tsubouchi Naoko, untitled statement, *Chūō bijutsu*, vol. 2, no. 2, February 1916, p. 115.
28   Tsubouchi, untitled statement, *Chūō bijutsu*, vol. 2, no. 3, March 1916, p. 119.
29   Fujishima Shūka, untitled statement, *Chūō bijutsu*, vol. 2, no. 2, March 1916, p. 114.
30   Matsui Senoo, "12 gatsugō o mite," *Chūō bijutsu*, vol. 4, no. 3, March 1918; Takada Keichū, "Dokusharan no shinkō o nozomu," *Chūō bijutsu*, vol. 4, no. 3, March 1918.
31   Nakai Shōji, "Mizue no kachi," *Mizue*, no. 214, December 1922, p. 34.
32   Anonymous answer to a question posed by Shitsumon sei, *Mizue*, no. 157, March 1918, p. 41.

CHAPTER FOUR

On Rationalization and the National Lifestyle
Japanese Design of the 1920s and 1930s

Kashiwagi Hiroshi

The 1920s and 1930s in Japan were marked by a proliferation of social reform movements and tremendous changes in the national lifestyle. Modernization, industrial rationalization, and Westernization were in vogue; somewhat paradoxically, nationalist sentiment was also on the rise. Put broadly, developments in modern industry, science and technology, and economic systems caused many great and rapid changes in lifestyles, social conditions, and structures of community networks. As these changes unfurled, Japan had to create a new, modern idea of society to replace the old traditional society. Ideas and images for this new environment appeared as discourse on the creation of a better society, and were often portrayed as the Utopian dream of a perfect society in the near future.

Such Utopian visions gave rise to conflicting social ideologies such as socialism, capitalism, and fascism, each of which argued for its particular version of Utopia, and can also be seen as a factor contributing to the outbreak of World War II. Meanwhile, market forces and methods of mechanical production were shaping a particularly twentieth-century consumer society. Mass-consumer society accelerated the destruction of vestiges of the traditional, class- and occupation-related social institutions that had until then been implicitly accepted, and reorganized economic and social life according to capitalist market theory.

Japanese society and culture around the 1920s were characterized by their shift toward modernization; however, the definition of "modernization" was never clearly distinguished from those of "Westernization" and "industrial rationalization." Later on, from the 1930s on into World War II, modernization became entwined with the twin concepts of nationalism and "Japanese particularity," further complicating the situation. Given this confusion of terms, the debates that arose in the period about managing the conflicting notions of "modern and traditional" and "Western and Japanese," and about overcoming these contradictions, seem quite natural. Japanese modern design and the modernizing process were not only causes of these dilemmas, but had to engage directly with these dilemmas themselves.

A social product, design changes according to the conditions of the time. The appearance of modern design as a phenomenon of early twentieth-century Japan is thus a response to the changes in social conditions and living environments occurring at the time. As such, a look at Japanese modern design, and its characteristics in the 1920s and 1930s, should shed light on some aspects of modern Japan. This chapter considers Japanese modernization with respect to design movements of the 1920s and 1930s.

New lifestyle images and the emergence of designers

Modern design was first consciously created in Japan in the late 1910s and 1920s. When migration to metropolitan centers like Tokyo and Osaka boomed dramatically, cities were transformed into nexuses of consumer society, and consumer goods like automobiles and home electrical appliances found their way, sometimes unfamiliarly, into daily life.

Never referred to as *kakumei* (revolution), these changes were referred to most often with terms like *kaizen*, *kairyō*, and *kaizō* (improvement, reform, transformation), language which expressed quiet, anxious anticipation for the creation and completion of a new society. The words *kaizō* and *kairyō* were in vogue as expressions, and succinctly encapsulated popular opinion of the era. The very ideas of reform and improvement were themselves seen as expressions of the new and modern, and overlapped with the idea of "modernity" then in fashion. Thus a magazine entitled *Kaizō* (Reform) began publication in 1919, and the word also became popular as a boy's name.[1]

The popularity of "reform" and "improvement" can be attributed to the influence of two events in particular: the great success of the Russian Revolution, and Ford's industrial rationalization and mass production of the Model T Ford. The Russian Revolution helped nurture dreams of transforming old social systems into new societies and living environments, while Fordism's newly created system, concepts, and effects on industrial reform were discussed widely in manufacturing nations around the world and strongly influenced reform in thought and practice in Japan. As words in vogue, "reform" and "improvement" represented the desire to transform an old society into something new; this transformation was the aim of Japan's process of modernization.

The Japanese experience of modernization is unique in that concepts such as improvement, reform, and transformation were first proposed and carried out concretely as the adoption of Western-style housing and living styles. In 1916, Hashiguchi Shinsuke established the Jūtaku Kairyō Kai (Association for Improved Housing). Hashiguchi had already founded Japan's first construction company specifically for housing, Amerikaya (American Home Shop) in 1909, in an attempt to popularize American-style housing in Japan.

Misumi Suzuko, a main proponent of the Taylorization of housework, was also active in the Association for Improved Housing. Taylorism's application to housework was not a singularly Japanese innovation. In the United States, Christine Frederick (1883–1970) had set up a model kitchen for research in effective housekeeping in the Applecraft Home Experiment Station at her home in Greenlawn, Long Island, New York, after graduating from Northwestern University in 1906.[2] Her fame spread nationwide, and in 1912 she became an editor for *The Ladies' Home Journal and Practical Housekeeper.* An article she wrote for the journal that year was published as a book in 1913, and was read throughout the United States and abroad, particularly by architects in Germany, where it indirectly influenced the Bauhaus movement.[3]

Bunka Seikatsu Kenkyūkai (Cultured Life Research Group), another example of the life improvement movement, was founded in 1920. Its founder, Morimoto Kokichi, called for the improvement of living conditions suited for new cultural lives in the new era, and established Bunka Fukyūkai (Society for Cultural Diffusion) for the same purpose in 1922. These and other groups were similar in their efforts to transform old, traditional ways of living and to diffuse the resulting new lifestyles throughout Japanese culture.

As reform movements sprang up in the private sector, Japanese public administrators began promoting lifestyle improvement as well. The Monbushō (Ministry of Education, Science and Culture) presented the Seikatsu Kaizen Ten (Lifestyle Improvement Exhibition) in 1919, and established the Seikatsu Kaizen Dōmeikai (Alliance for Lifestyle Improvement) as a related organization the following year. The Alliance targeted for improvement almost all areas of daily life — from clothing, housing, and food, to social interaction — and represents a state attempt at reform. The activities of these and other groups present one aspect of the development of movements for the reform of daily life from the late 1910s through the 1930s and into World War II.

Lifestyle design according to Western furniture

At the same time as reformers were proposing lifestyle reform, designers intent on creating new environments for living were emerging and establishing organizations to carry out their ideas.[4] New design groups such as Moriya Nobuo's Kinomesha and Kurata Chikatada's Keiji Kōbō (Ideal Form Atelier) were not simply concerned with having their ability at design recognized, but aimed at ordering new lifestyles through design.

Moriya Nobuo, a professor at Tokyo Kōtō Kōgei Gakkō (Tokyo High School of Industrial Arts, now the Engineering Department of the University of Chiba), a pioneer furniture and interior designer, had organized the design group Kinomesha in 1927 with Katō Shinjirō, Moriya Isaburō, Suzuki Tarō, and others. One of Kinomesha's main purposes was the spread of Western-style furniture and the

Fig. 1 *Design by Keiji Kôbô,*
Chair with tatamizuni, *leg guard,*
for use on tatami *mats, 1930s*

"Western lifestyle" this entailed. More precisely, Kinomesha's presentation of "Western lifestyle through furniture" meant the use of chairs.

Moriya was also concerned with the aesthetic values of Western-style furniture design, writing in one catalog that "articles of furniture that are most related to our lives ... should link aesthetic value to living."[5] This relation of living design to the aesthetic was common among designers of the time, including Kajita Megumi and Saitô Kazô, and for Kajita it meant furniture designed as though appearing in theatrical stage sets.

In 1928, Kurata Chikatada, also a professor at the Tokyo High School of Industrial Arts, organized the design group Keiji Kôbô (Ideal Form Atelier), with furniture designers such as Kobayashi Noboru, Matsumoto Masao, and Toyoguchi Katsuhei (Fig. 1). As with Hashiguchi of the American Home Shop and Morimoto of the Research Group on Culture and Living, the organizers of the Ideal Form Atelier held that the Westernization of living meant its rationalization as well. For its designers, this Westernization, brought about mainly by sitting on chairs instead of on the floor, was rational and thus signified a new cultured or cultural life; thus, Ideal Form Atelier designers tried to make Western-style living the standard for living in modern Japan, an attitude reflected even more intensely in the principles of the Alliance for Lifestyle Improvement, as will be discussed later in this chapter. With design targeting the rationalization of production through standardization, the Ideal Form Atelier set out to create a model of a "standardized" life. As one Atelier manifesto from 1935 stated:

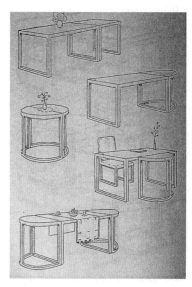

Fig. 2 *Seikatsu Kaizen Dômei,*
Exhibition of improvements to everyday
domestic products, 1930

We would like to set a standard for every article of furniture in a room ... Our aim is to

Fig. 3 *Seikatsu Kaizen Dōmei,
Exhibition of improvements to
everyday domestic products, 1930*

simplify form, and to make an integrated and unified standard for construction materials … Purchasing chairs will be as easy and acceptable as buying ready-made clothes.[6]

Influenced by the Bauhaus idea of organizing the environment entirely from the industrial system, Kurata's conceptions of design formed the nucleus of Ideal Form Atelier activities. Kurata's writings often comment on Bauhaus design, and also introduce design by Le Corbusier, and chairs by the Bauhaus's Marcel Breuer as well as by Le Corbusier and Charlotte Perriand.

While the Ideal Form Atelier was unsuccessful at shifting its design into the actual arena of industrial production, the group's designs for products for everyday life are based entirely on the condition of mass industrial production. By the mid-1930s, this idea had grown stronger in Japanese social thought, and ultimately became absorbed into political activity as a "standardized lifestyle for the national citizenry."

Seikatsu Kaizen Dōmeikai (Alliance for Lifestyle Improvement)

Developed, led, and run under government guidance, the Alliance for Lifestyle Improvement also encompassed the activities of many civil organizers, activists, and designers working toward the remodeling and improvement of daily life, and reflected national sentiment favoring the need for a better, improved lifestyle.

In the first issue of its magazine *Seikatsu Kaizen* (Lifestyle Improvement), the Alliance appealed to readers to rationalize their *ishokujû no seikatsu* (housing/clothing/diet system), and to simplify complicated social rituals and relationships, in an article called simply "Seikatsu Kaizen Dōmeikai no honryô" (The Function of the Alliance for Lifestyle Improvement).[7] Strengthening the national polity through national rationalization, one of the Alliance's main objectives, was thus carried out on a personal level, through the intervention into citizens' daily lives, rather than on a national level through manufacturing and industrial policy[8] (Figs 2 and 3).

As part of its mandate, the Alliance organized a number of committees pertaining to specific reforms in housing, diet, and clothing. Sano Toshikata, a professor at the University of Tokyo, presided over Jûtaku Kaizen Chôsa Iinkai (Research Committee for Improved Housing) with Tanabe Junkichi, an advisor for the Shimizu-gumi construction company, as vice-president. Other members of the committee included: architect Ôkuma Yoshikuni; Kogure Joichi, furniture designer and professor at the Tokyo High School of Industrial Arts; Kon Wajirô, Waseda University professor and founder of the "Kôgengaku" (Modernology) school of research on popular culture and life; Tanahashi Gentarô, director of the Education Museum at Ochanomizu (the Alliance's office was also located in the Education Museum); silviculturist Tamura Tsuyoshi; Taga Kazutami, Governor of Mie Prefecture; Inoue Toshiko, professor at Japan Christian Women's University; and Ôe Sumi, domestic scientist and president of Kaseigaku Kenkyûjo (Tokyo Academy of Domestic Science), renamed the Tôkyô Kasei Gakuin in 1926.

The Committee's 1924 research report, *Jûtaku kagu no kaizen* (The Reform of Domestic Furniture), addressed six main themes, all of which have long been considered as typically representing the direction of reform movements in 1920s Japan:

1. Homes should incorporate chairs, rather than sitting on the floor.
2. Domestic floor plans and facilities should be based on the family, rather than around visitors, as is currently the case.
3. Domestic structural facilities should shun decoration and place weight on hygiene and the prevention of accidents.
4. Gardens should not be for mere entertainment, as is currently the case, but should place weight on having practical use in preventing accidents.
5. Furniture should be simple but strong, in keeping with the reform of the house.
6. Public housing (apartment houses) and garden city facilities should be constructed in accordance with the circumstances of the megalopolis.

Of the six, points one, two, and six are particularly important, as they lay out the era's underlying policies of Westernizing daily life, creating a lifestyle centered around the family, emphasizing functionality and effectiveness, and following a "garden city" plan.

In particular, the use of chairs over sitting on the floor was explained as follows: sitting on the floor "does not fit with a free and active life," "wastes time and diminishes work efficiency," and is "disadvantageous from a sanitary perspective." Furthermore, sitting on the floor binds Japan to a "double lifestyle," namely both Japanese and Western habits of living. Finally, the use of chairs is the international standard:

> *The chair-style is the international style — not only Westerners but also our neighbours the Chinese follow this style, which proves that it has many advantages. Of course, it will be distressing for us to abandon our conventional style of life, but we must move quickly*

to disallow continuing to sit on the floor alone in the face of progress in all other areas of the improvement of daily life.[9]

This transition to chair-style also entailed such necessities as improving and remodeling kitchen layouts, not simply the use of tables and chairs.

After the Meiji period, the public and private spheres in Japan were most commonly distinguished by two different design styles, the "Western" and the "Japanese." Customs penetrated into clothing as well as architecture and interior design, with men wearing Western-style suits in public places and Japanese clothing at home. The creation of a distinction between public and private is a phenomenon seen with processes of modernization around the world, but in the case of Japan, this distinction overlapped with the distinction between Japan and the West. Such a "double life" started in the elite upper class, but gradually diffused to the middle class as it became a state which people admired and aimed to achieve. The Alliance for Lifestyle Improvement's propositions, then, were a denial of such a "double life" in the name of simplicity, rationalization, and functionality in the middle-class lifestyle.

If the "rejection of a double life," "family-centered life," and "Westernization of the domestic environment" were the themes for creating a standardized style of domestic life, "garden city planning" was the keyword for the standardization of the urban lifestyle. The Committee's report offered further explanation for its sixth point as well in an indictment of the poor conditions in some urban areas (in Tokyo): "In large urban areas, rapid city development and soaring land prices [have] meant that houses were built over-crowded; conditions in these areas have poor lighting and ventilation and are not suitable as healthy living environments."[10] The Committee called for the construction of "suitable cooperative housing" and pointed out that "unified planning for the construction of housing and roads has yet to be carried out," recommending the development of garden cities and suburban housing.

Slums were a common consequence of nineteenth-century capitalism worldwide. Tokyo too had its fair share of poor housing conditions from the late Meiji period on, prompting reports like Yokoyama Gennosuke's examination of Tokyo shanty towns, *Nihon no kasō shakai* (Lower Strata Society in Japan), and the Ministry of Agriculture and Commerce's *Shokkō jijō* (Situation of Workers and Craftsmen). Japan's rapid influx of people into the cities following World War I caused conditions to worsen severely, making "urban problems" and "housing problems" near-synonymous by the 1920s. The image of the garden city, first proposed by Ebenezer Howard, was a solution grasped by architects and designers around the world, including the Alliance for Lifestyle Improvement.

Thus the problems of urban slums and absolute poverty became one starting point for modern urban planning. Like the interior designers of the American Home Shop and Morimoto's Cultured Life Research Group (Seikatsu Kairyōkai), the Alliance for Lifestyle Improvement's actual proposal for the improvement of living conditions began with the adoption of Western, rational ways, seen as a totally new cultural life.

From total cultural life toward total warfare — Kogure Joichi

While a Westernized and thus more rational, family-centered, and cultured *bunka seikatsu* (cultural life) was the ideal proposed by reformers in the early 1920s, by the early 1930s this ideal had shifted toward a lifestyle supporting the national defense system. Furniture designer Kogure Joichi's comments on furniture design show this transition clearly.

A pioneer of Japanese modern design, Kogure assisted in the creation of the interior and furniture design curriculum for the Tokyo High School of Industrial Arts at the time of the school's founding in 1922, and served on the housing committee of the Alliance for Lifestyle Improvement. Kogure promoted the use of chairs and the Western living style throughout his life, and practiced his vision of lifestyle improvement in his own house as well. In 1930, he described his experience reforming his home in *Wagaya wo kairyō shite* (Having Reformed My House), in which he explains how to renovate Japanese-structured spaces to fit Western taste and provides experimental furniture designs (Fig. 4).

Kogure's fundamental attitude toward design was to achieve the rationalization and modernization of both household and society, a notion shared in the abstract by contemporaries like Kurata and Moriya as well. Kogure, however, recommended unique practical methods by which to carry out these changes. A man in a patriarchal society, he nonetheless saw men as constituent members of the family rather than as

Fig. 4 *Kogure Joichi, Experimental unit furniture design, from his book* Wagaya wo kairyō shite, *1930*

automatic heads of the household, and believed that housework should not be wives' sole responsibility. Rather, the household environment was to be designed so that all members of the family could perform their duties in a rational manner:

> In the kitchen, then, when the equipment in the kitchen is divided into categories, it falls basically into four groups according to purpose: facilities for washing dishes and food, facilities for food preparation, facilities for boiling and grilling, and facilities for the storage of food and dishes. The foods prepared are placed finally on plates, and the process is complete when there are facilities for placing these plates.[11]

By distinguishing kitchen work as four functions — namely, work employing water, food preparation, heat, and storage — Kogure perceived kitchen work as a flow of activity in a space. Understanding the family as a cooperative unit, he broke down individual activities and assigned them to spaces according to function. A designer working from a functionalist perspective, Kogure attempted to achieve improvements in domestic life through rationalization, and also recommended the rationalization of industrial production, suggesting the implementation of standardization and mass production.

Kogure saw the domestic environment as organized by function rather than by conventional systems of social institutions, and saw such organization as carried out in the design of domestic space and furnishings. This stance was soon expanded into discourse on national productivity — as with the Alliance for Lifestyle Improvement, Kogure's ideas were coopted on a national level as the Japanese nation demanded productivity through the rationalization of family and society for national defense.

In 1941, the year war broke out on the Japanese–American front, Kogure published a collection of essays entitled *Watashi no kōgei seikatsu shōshi* (On My Way of Designing). "Jūgo kokumin seikatsu no gōrika" (Rationalization of the Way of Life on the Home Front), included in the collection, argued for the rationalization of daily life for the defense of the nation. Kogure's perceived purpose of domestic rationalization thus shifted from that of bringing happiness to the family to that of securing the nation, and Kogure's focus moved from the family unit to a more exterior one, the Japanese nation itself.

Distinctions between private and public, and between family life and the outside world, grew with the development of the capitalist system, and evolved gradually into a conception of the home as a shelter from the economic world. At the same time, however, the home was considered to function as a site of both reproductive work like child-raising and of refreshment and recovery from the day at work. Thus reorganized, the family unit served as a support unit for the capitalist system in the modern era. With modern society's inseparable linkage between nation and economic system, such a relationship between family and society also implies a direct relation between the family and the nation.

In the early days of the Alliance for Lifestyle Improvement, Kogure did not intend to make the family a unit to support the national defense structure; however, given the historical context, the Alliance's intentions to make the household the basic unit of the nation began to correspond with that idea, differences in original aim notwithstanding.[12] This shift was not unique to Kogure — the entire movement to reform society through design, including its declarations on rationalization, renovation, and standardization, was to be assembled and reorganized into an integral part of the system to control the family.

Systematization and Japanism

While the Alliance for Lifestyle Improvement strove for rationalization at the household level, the Shōkōshō (Ministry of Commerce and Industry, the present Ministry of International Trade and Industry) proposed to rationalize production through design. These two corresponded to each other as representatives of living and production.

In 1928 the Ministry of Commerce and Industry established the Kōgei Shidōsho (Design Educational Research Center, first president Kunii Yoshitarô) as part of an attempt to use design to revitalize industry in an economy badly damaged by the Great Depression. The Design Educational Research Center tried to rationalize design and to make it applicable to volume production. Like Kogure and Kurata, the Center worked toward design that would rationalize both industry and daily life; not surprisingly, many of the organization's members, including Toyoguchi Katsuhei and Kenmochi Isamu, both part of Keiji Kōbō, and other graduates of the Tokyo High School of Industrial Arts, were influenced by Kogure and Kurata.

In 1933 the Center invited German architect Bruno Taut to Japan to lecture at the Center, hoping to grasp the rise of modern design through contact with him. Later, in 1940, the Center invited Charlotte Perriand, a French furniture and interior designer known for the chaise-longue she designed with Le Corbusier. During her stay in Japan, Perriand designed a similar chair made out of bamboo. With these and other invitations, the Center sought to encourage the development of international, rational design in Japan.

Ministry official Kishi Nobusuke (who was charged with war crimes after World War II but later became Japanese Prime Minister) and Yoshino Shinji were responsible for creating the Design Educational Research Center. In the 1930s their project explicitly concerned industrial rationalization, but this project almost inevitably included lifestyle rationalization as one of its goals. The rationalization sentiment recreated itself in Yoshino and Kishi's program of industrial rationalization as a national political agenda in the 1930s, and the new generation of designers such as Toyoguchi went along with the flow of this project. Rationalization and reform, once cultural movements, thus became political ones, just as industrial rationalization aimed at rescuing the nation from economic crisis was transformed into a rationalization campaign

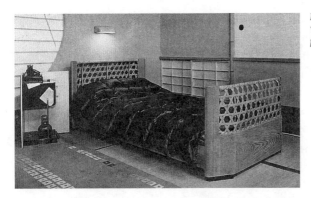

Fig. 5 *Sugiyama Sekishino, Western-style furniture with Japanese bamboo, 1937*

aimed at building and controlling the nation for the war regime. These movements can be seen in the enactment of the National Mobilization Law in 1938.[13]

The 1930s also saw the rise of the ideology of Japanism. While rationalization and modernization were linked with Westernization, Japanism was connected to images of traditional Japanese culture. If the coexistence of rationalization and Japanism was itself a paradox, it was also an inevitable and logical consequence of the Japanese rationalization process, given rationalization's connection to Westernization in Japan. Japan could only notice its own cultural identity through encounters with a different culture, that of "the West;" thus a sense of Japanese national identity — Japanism — came about with modernization.

As the activities of the Design Educational Research Center and the Ideal Form Atelier attest, Japanese modern design in the 1930s adopted some of the modern, rational design attributes of Le Corbusier, Perriand, and the Bauhaus. Such designs were recognized as an image or metaphor for the twin poles of industrial and domestic rationalization. At the same time, the question of how to express Japanism in design became frequently discussed among Japanese designers. The *teikan yôshiki* (Japanese gable-roof style), together with architectural style and furniture design which incorporated Japanese materials such as bamboo and Nishijin-ori textiles, were two new design trends born out of this discussion (Figs 5 and 6).

Nishikawa Tomotake, a designer active in the Design Educational Research Center, wrote in his 1935 *Kôgei gairon* (Outline of Crafts and Design) that:

> *table lamps made of bamboo or concrete architecture with Japanese-style pediments appeared as Japanese style. However, we must not see them as possessing "youthfulness", "hopefulness," "a sense of the national citizenry" or "real Japanism." It is a misunderstanding to say that this is truly design with Japanese characteristics; it can come only from the confusion of anachronism.*[14]

Nishikawa's criticism is for architecture incorporating the *teikan yôshiki* gable-roof style, and for Western design made with Japanese materials. As he further explained,

"Western modern designers have been saying that they learn much from Japanese rationalization and standardization ... Le Corbusier said he gained much useful information from Japanese traditional architecture."[15]

The use of horizontal and vertical lines in Bauhaus architecture can be seen as resembling Japanese traditional architecture and interior design; the argument that Western modern design has elements in common with Japanese traditional design became so persuasive as a result of such similarities. Such an interpretation evades, rather than resolves, the contradiction between Japanese traditional design and machinery and functional modern design.

In 1941 the Ministry of Commerce and Industry held the Kokumin Seikatsu Yôhin Ten (Exhibition of Products for the People's Everyday Life), and explained the logic behind the exhibition as follows: "Nations advanced in national defense demand the people to standardize and rationalize in housing, clothing and diet, the fields of basic living environment ... Our new nation too, given the times, demands even further standardization in everyday life and in products."[16] Accordingly, products, furniture, tableware, and the like were exhibited as models for a national standard.

Total warfare, whether for capitalism, socialism, or fascism, integrates all people into its war or struggle. Such modern rationalism affects even the arena of design, making World War II a driving force for the further advancement of Japanese modern design. Phrases like "difficult situation," "serious situation," and "war preparation" —

Fig. 6 Sugiyama Sekishino, Western-style furniture with Japanese Nishijin-ori textiles, designed in 1937

the language of total warfare — expresses a sense of emergency, circumstances in which the divisions between the personal and private fade. State reinforcement of a national consciousness worked to make all equal under its system, leading later to the principles of the Greater East Asia Co-prosperity Sphere.

Wartime design can thus be seen as being used to orient citizens toward the interests and needs of the nation. This happened as well during the Meiji era, when Japan was strongly influenced by Western culture first through products which were then later understood through language. Standardized design for a national lifestyle explicitly showed the population that they were treated equally under a system moving toward total warfare.

As such, World War II had already constructed the route to Japanese postwar society. Claims of an equal society did not begin with postwar Japan; the Japanese population was formed into a common society, one linked to the strengthening of the nation, under the prior system of total warfare. Japan's postwar democracy is thus associated with the national sentiment created by total warfare and carried out in design for wartime everyday life.

Notes

1   In Japanese, different characters with different meanings can have the same sound, so the name *Kaizō* could be written with a variety of characters.

2   Glenna Matthews, *Just a Housewife*, Oxford, Oxford University Press, 1987, p. 168.

3   Dolores Hayden, *The Grand Domestic Revolution: History of Feminist Design for American Homes, Neighborhoods and Cities*, Cambridge, Mass., MIT Press, 1981, p. 265.

4   In the 1920s, many designers proposed improvements and reforms while also promoting design as an industrial business in Japanese society. In 1926, Teikoku Kōgeikai (Imperial Society of Industrial Arts), an association of design professionals, was established with over 100 members, making it an unprecedentedly large organization. Members included Yasuda Rokuzō, Rokkaku Shisui, Hata Masakichi, Kunii Yoshitarō, Kogure Joichi, and Miyashita Takao. The group's goals were to revitalize the industry with new designs and to promote exports. In contrast to the Japanese traditional arts and crafts previously exported, however, the Imperial Society of Industrial Arts strove to create a new trend of exporting new designs. In addition, the Society was highly conscious of the role of designers, modeling itself after the Deutsche Werkbund (DWB). Their monthly magazine influenced design at the time, much like the Ministry of Commerce and Industry's Design Educational Research Center publication, *Kōgei nyuusu*.

5   In the catalog for the Kinomesha Exhibition of 1927.

6   Keiji Kōbō (ed.), *Seisan kōgyōteki kagu*, Tokyo, Kōyōsha, 1935, p. 2.

7   The Alliance for Lifestyle Improvement (ed.), *Seikatsu Kaizen Dōmeikai no honryō, Seikatsu kaizen*, vol.1, 1921, publisher's imprint page. The Meiji Restoration beginning in 1868 saw a drastic change in Japanese manners and interpersonal relationships. These new manners, based initially on those of the ruling class from the preceding Edo period, were integrated and transformed into a new lifestyle for the middle class from the Meiji era onwards. Many publications described the new manners and rituals, modeled after the mix of traditional Edo and European industrial bourgeois manners considered appropriate for the new Meiji ruling class, the minor and lower samurai class. If power always rests ultimately in patterns of corporeal, daily life, the new Meiji ruling class thus visualized the base of their political power in the establishment of a new order of manners and rituals. Given this relation between power, social ritual, and daily life, the Alliance for Lifestyle Improvement aimed at changing lifestyles by creating a new, simplified set of manners and gestures.

8   As the third article of the Alliance for Lifestyle Improvement's charter stated,
"Members of this association must make an effort to achieve our aims of improving the residential, dietary

and sartorial lifestyle and social manners by the following:
- We should keep our promises on time.
- We should take care not to be a nuisance when visiting, introducing and making requests.
- We should reject the custom of seeing one's family off at the station.
- We should reject the customs of exchanging presents at the New Year, midsummer, the year end and Christmas."

Alliance for Lifestyle Improvement (ed.), *Seikatsu kaizen*, vol. 1, 1921, publisher's imprint page.

9   Research Committee for Improved Housing (ed.), *Jūtaku kagu no kaizen*, Tokyo, Seikatsu Kaizen Dōmei, 1924, pp. 5–8.

10   Seikatsu Kaizen Dōmeikai (ed.), *Jūtaku kagu no kaizen*, 1928, p. 8, explains that, "planning with a garden city style has many advantages. Garden city plans include building of houses, stores, retailers, schools, hospitals, parks, roads and squares, which has many advantages for the aesthetic values of the place, effective use of public space, and revivifying of the environment. Statistics show a remarkable decline in death rate in the garden cities. Therefore we recommend constructing a garden city and space for suburban life and facilities."

11   Kogure Joichi, *Wagaya wo kairyō shite*, Tokyo, Hakubunkan, 1930, p. 240.

12   Kogure Joichi, "Jugo kokumin seikatsu no gōrika," in his collection of essays *Watashi no kōgei seikatsu shōshi* which was published on the occasion of his sixtieth birthday. He states: "In the early days of the outbreak of the Chinese War, our way of life was perceived as an important issue on the home front as a basis for the construction of national defense. The reinforcement movement developed from that time. Through radio and newspapers, I appealed to the public to understand the importance of improving the home. In December 1939, Kokumin Seishin Sōdōin Honbu (Headquarters for the General Mobilization of Popular Morale) asked me to go to the town of Kanaki in a rural part of Aomori Prefecture, to lecture the youth of the town on 'sanitation and the reform of household economic facilities.' It is an unforgettable memory" (p. 304).

13   Looking back at the history of industrial rationalization, the Ministry of Industry and Commerce established a Temporary Council for Industrial Improvement in 1930 which acted as the core for the promotion of industrial improvement. In 1934, Yahata Iron Manufacturing, a state-owned company, merged with private iron manufacturers, making iron the most important base industry to come under government control and administration. In 1936 the Law for Automobile Manufacturers legalized the use of automobiles and engines as weapons during the war.

14   Nishikawa Tomotake, *Kōgei gairon*, Tokyo, Kōseikai, 1935, p. 146.

15   ibid., p. 212.

16   Kōgyō Chōsakai (ed.), *Kōgei nyuusu*, 1944, p. 6.

Chapter Five

Japanese Modernism and Consumerism
Forging the New Artistic Field of "Shōgyō Bijutsu" (Commercial Art)

Gennifer Weisenfeld

"Things cannot be presented 'naked.' They must be packaged."

Hamada Masuji[1]

Imagine strolling down one of the main boulevards in the Ginza. It is the early Shōwa period, the late 1920s. The streets are lined with bustling commercial establishments. You are engaged in *"ginbura"* (an abbreviation of the expression *"Ginza de burabura suru"*), referring to the activity of casually strolling and window-shopping in this high-profile commercial area. On all sides there are department stores and various shops with decorative show windows displaying textiles, clothing, household goods, books, and the like (Fig. 1). Lined with advertising signboards, billboards, and banners, the street has been transformed into an exposition-like environment through design. Then day turns to night and a flood of electric light transforms the street scene into an even more dramatic theatrical stage illuminated from above.

This transformation of the urban environment — what was referred to by many critics at the time as the "artification" of the streets — was sustained by a vibrant modern Japanese design movement, increasingly stimulated by worldwide trends in the visual arts.[2] Traditionally an artisanal field in Japan, design was established as a major area of "artistic" endeavor in the first few decades of the twentieth century. This gradual recognition of design's aesthetic as well as functional value has shaped its evolution and defined its central importance in the sphere of Japanese visual arts ever since. The construction of a new social status for design was not a coincidental development. It was consciously and aggressively forged by designers and design theorists who sought aesthetic and social legitimacy for the profession. Hamada Masuji (1892–1938), one of the most vocal design theorists of this period, had a major impact on the development of the modern Japanese design movement during its critical formative stage in the late 1920s and early 1930s. By publicly endorsing art as a means of persuasion and systematizing the specialized requisite knowledge, Hamada helped launch a new

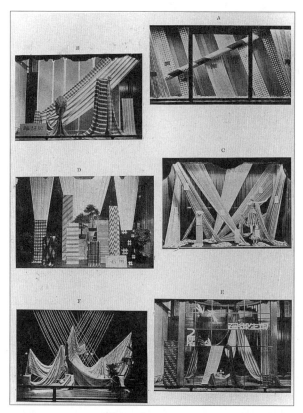

Fig. 1 *"Six varieties of expressive beauty created with the sentiment and display of commodities: Show window displays of various textiles." In Kitazawa Yoshio (ed.),* Gendai shōgyō bijutsu zenshū, *vols 1–24, Tokyo, Ars, 1928–30 (hereafter abbreviated as GSBZ), vol. 4, ill. 3.*

professional field of artistic practice that explicitly and unapologetically put aesthetics in the service of commerce. For Hamada, products could not merely be placed in the market to speak for themselves, "naked" so to speak. They required skillful packaging, and who better to design this packaging than artists who understood the affectivity of visual stimuli.

Principal among Hamada's works was a twenty-four-volume illustrated compendium of commercial design with annotation and theoretical analysis published by Ars from 1928 until 1930. The series, published in both hard- and softcover editions, was titled *Gendai shōgyō bijutsu zenshū* in Japanese and *The Complete Commercial Artist* in English.[3] Hamada edited and co-wrote the publication together with over sixty well-known professional journalists, educators, and practitioners active in the design field. For the first fifteen volumes, he was one of six editorial committee members including: Watanabe Soshū (chief editor of *Zuan to kōgei* (Design and Crafts) magazine, Tatsuke Yoichirō (director of the Japanese Advertising Study Association (Nihon Kōkoku Gakkai)), Nakada Sadanosuke (managing committee member of the Association of Commercial Artists (Shōgyō Bijutsuka Kyōkai)), Miyashita Takao (professor at the Tōkyō Kōtō Kōgei Gakkō (Tokyo Higher School of Arts and Technology)), and Sugiura Hisui (advisor to the design division of Mitsukoshi department store). For the final nine volumes, Hamada was elevated to chief editor.

The series was distributed through direct subscription sales, selling between 1500 and 2000 copies to small commercial retailers and major Japanese companies such as Lion Dentrifice, Kao Soap, Maruzen, Hoshi Pharmaceutical, and Shiseido cosmetics, who were pioneering sponsors of innovative design work that was produced either in their newly established internal design divisions or solicited through public design competitions. Similarly, newspaper companies, which relied on commercial advertising for financial support, and emerging advertising firms such as Mannensha, Hakuhodō, and Nihon Denpō Tsūshinsha (now known as Dentsū), acquired copies of the set as reference materials. This bountiful sourcebook of commercial artforms and techniques served as both a record of original design work being produced during the period and an invaluable tool for disseminating the most up-to-date design practices to small retail shops that could not afford to employ full-time designers but still sought to invest their advertising and displays with creative aesthetics. The Ars series was one of several important design compendia and textbooks published at this time, indicating the expanding market for explanatory design texts and the expansion of the commercial design field in general.[4]

This chapter will focus on the important contribution of Hamada Masuji to the discourse on design during the peak of his activities from 1926 until 1932. Hamada's design theory combined modernist fine-art aesthetics with the "progressive" values of industrialism: rationalism, efficiency, effectiveness, applicability, and pragmatism. To this was added a touch of popular psychology and visual perception theory, and a strong dose of Marxian social utopianism to produce Hamada's own distinct brand of "commercial art," dubbed *shōgyō bijutsu*, a recently coined neologism of the period (c. 1926).[5] In Hamada's lexicon, *shōgyō bijutsu* was the "general term for all practical art (*jissai geijutsu*)." It was, in other words, a form of "artistic industry" (*bijutsuteki sangyō*).[6] But Hamada further clarified: *shōgyō bijutsu* was not merely any art used in advertising, what was commonly called "*kōkoku bijutsu*" or "*senden bijutsu*." Rather, it was art that formally embodied its commercial function. It required the skillful manipulation of aesthetics to "attract the consumer's eye" and "make the product stand out," effects that would further commercial interests.[7] With this attitude, Hamada paved the way for both a commercialization of aesthetics and an aestheticization of commerce.[8]

Modernism was Hamada's tool of choice for undertaking this process of aestheticization. He redirected the visually evocative aesthetic strategies of autonomous abstract art that undergirded modernism to serve a more clearly functional purpose, beginning with the general assertion that "form itself resonated with people in distinct ways."[9] It was the designer's job to maximize and direct this resonance in the mind of the consumer. Hamada and his colleagues closely followed international developments in modernism and the avant-garde through publications, exhibitions, and by traveling abroad. Adapting Le Corbusier's famous dictum that architecture was "a machine for living," Hamada produced his own mechanical metaphor, declaring "art as a machine with a purpose." The implication was that art could function pragmatically through applied design, which was manipulable in a manner akin to the precise calibrations of a machine.[10] Industrial development as a whole became the inspiration for Hamada's commercial art, as its vigor supplied the designer's "energy."[11]

While *shōgyō bijutsu* now principally refers to two-dimensional graphic design, in the late 1920s and in Hamada's writings, it was a more inclusive term, comprising three-dimensional forms such as show windows, and architectural structures used for advertising, such as kiosks and storefronts. It also overlapped with elements of industrial design, known as "*sangyō bijutsu*" or "*sangyō kōgei*," which included product design. Japanese design historians have identified a gradual conceptual shift around the turn of the century from the long-standing artisanal notion of design (*ishō*) to one which implied more personal intentionality and professional standing on the part of the designer, expressed in the increasingly common terms *zuan* (design), *dezain* (design), and *shōgyō bijutsu*.[12]

Commercial art came to the fore in Japan during the period between the end of the Russo-Japanese War in 1905 and the beginning of the war in China in around 1931, when many forms of culture were being "massified" and commodified. The importation of new technologies from Europe and the Untied States beginning in the late nineteenth century brought a momentous change in the relationship between culture and industry in Japan. Innovations such as the rotary press, the wireless, photography, movies, recording technology, and railroads enabled the production of a cheap and easily reproducible culture that could be efficiently disseminated throughout the nation. What has been termed by scholars as a modern "culture industry" (*bunka sangyō*), consisting of mass publishing, mass media, and mass entertainment, relied on these new technologies.[13] The so-called massification (*taishūka*) of Japanese culture was also predicated on the cultivation of a literate consumer public that extended beyond the elite classes of society. The implementation of a nationwide education system in 1872 had significantly increased literacy and facilitated this trend.

While there were still great disparities in wealth among the Japanese populace, the standard of living was generally rising for most sectors during the interwar period.[14] This was particularly true for the expanding middle class, as well as a segment of this population who became *nouveau riche* (*narikin*) due to the boom economy during World War I. Increased prosperity provided many middle-class Japanese people with extra money and time to spend on recreation. It stimulated and transformed an urban leisure economy that had been developing since Tokugawa times. This period saw a rapid expansion of consumerism, especially among women, for goods and entertainment. The "modern girl" (or "*moga*" as she was commonly known) was just one particularly visible member of this expanded consumer public.

The rapid boom in consumerism produced valuable work opportunities for artists in the commercial sector. Many commercial establishments, from department stores to major manufacturers, were establishing internal design divisions in order to develop effective visual and verbal strategies to advertise and market their products. These divisions were often manned by artist–designers, many of whom, after studying at prestigious art schools and private ateliers around the country, became specialists in commercial design.[15] At the same time, a host of new design and craft schools were being established around Japan, most notably the Tōkyō Kōtō Kōgei Gakkō (Tokyo High School of Industrial Arts) opened in 1922, to meet the demands of increased industrial production and commercial activity.[16] Individual groups and companies all over Japan began sponsoring academic study sessions on advertising and design, which concentrated on analyzing major modern trends. This was so widespread that Kawahata Naomichi has gone so far as to dub the 1930s "the era of design study groups," identifying over sixty associations known to have formed during this time.[17]

The study of design from a historical perspective, however, has several obstacles. Principal among them is the difficulty of identifying designers and attributing their works, as commercial art was often not signed and the designers themselves were often not named in company histories, even though they were clearly instrumental in establishing brand images in the public imagination. As Louisa Rubinfien's work on the companies Kao Soap and Ajinomoto has definitively shown, there was an important shift to product brand name recognition from the turn of the century, beginning with the establishment of a trademark registration law in 1884. And brand image definition played a crucial role in the success of these companies.[18] This included everything from logos to innovative and colorful package design. In this respect, the Ars series presentation of thousands of executed designs and design plans, many of which were labeled with the artists' names, made a strong statement about the important role of designers. Hamada argued, principally to the art community, that designers needed to be pulled out from behind the scenes and given the social recognition they deserved. He was, however, faced with deeply ingrained biases. Despite the lack of a clear distinction between arts and crafts in premodern Japanese artistic practice, a new term distinguishing the fine arts, "bijutsu," had come into use well over fifty years prior to Hamada's activities, around the time of the Vienna World's Fair in 1873. Having seen the social status enjoyed by artists in Western countries, many Japanese artists returning from abroad fought to establish fine art as an autonomous sphere of cultivated intellectual endeavor worthy of social recognition. In the process, however, they rigidified the previously fluid boundaries among the fine arts, decorative arts, and crafts, thus creating a self-conscious artistic hierarchy on the model of the West. This categorization was then reinforced by the establishment of an official salon in 1907 sponsored by the Ministry of Education, called the Monbushō Bijutsu Tenrankai (abbreviated as "Bunten"), which was dedicated to exhibiting fine art.[19]

By the 1920s, this hierarchical mentality was well inculcated through the art establish-ment and art education, although in actual practice the areas still blended. Most artist–designers themselves did not consider design activity their principal artistic contribution and emphasized their "pure art" (*junsei* or *junsui geijutsu*) work as being of greater aesthetic importance.[20] Art historian Michelle Bogart has noted a similar enduring prejudice against commercial art in the American context during the same period. She attributes this partially to power politics within the field of fine art as "efforts to claim jurisdiction over art [was a] means of acquiring authority."[21] Informed by Marxist theories of culture, Hamada was blunter in assigning blame. "Pure art," he claimed, was "controlled by bourgeois ideology," serving only the needs of the ruling class. It was his foremost goal to redress this artistic hierarchy, elevating commercial art to the level of so-called pure art. Due to its intrinsically compelling nature, commercial art, Hamada felt, would eventually eclipse all forms of art for art's sake.[22] In the meantime, just naming the field was a significant act in the then climate of the Japanese art world, as it identified a vast realm of artistic production that went entirely unacknowledged. Hamada lamented that "in some respects, it can be said that *shôgyô bijutsu* has not yet been born in Japan."[23]

Indeed, out of all the full-time designers working during the prewar period, only a handful had public recognition. For high-visibility projects, it was common for artists already well established in the world of fine arts to be commissioned to paint a work that would then be used for advertising purposes. This work was generally not pictorially intended to represent a particular product or industry. Rather, businesses sought to invest their trades with the refined image of fine art, thereby distancing themselves from direct association with commerce. This reflected a persistent Edo-period social bias against those directly involved with commercial activity, partially rooted in neo-Confucian morality. Thus, posters of "beautiful women" (*bijinga*), which had been used for hundreds of years to represent style, sophistication, and elegance, were still the most appealing for promotional purposes. *Portrait of a Woman*, by the renowned academic oil painter Okada Saburosuke, from 1907, for example, was quickly adapted into the now famous Mitsukoshi department store poster with the simple addition of the store's name.[24] Like many of his academic colleagues, including his illustrious teacher Kuroda Seiki, Okada produced paintings for commercial use throughout his career. Magazine covers, such as a year-long series for *Shufu no tomo* (The Housewife's Companion) magazine in 1923, and a commemorative calendar for the same publication in 1927, were just a few examples. Still, the professional identity of these artists was always solidly situated within the lofty precinct of fine arts.

One artist–designer who was able to establish a public reputation in the graphic arts, paving the way for activist–designers like Hamada, was undoubtedly Sugiura Hisui. In fact, Hisui was one of the editorial committee members of the Ars design series. From 1910 until 1934, Hisui was the chief designer at Mitsukoshi department

store. The popularity of his *art nouveau* and *art deco*-inspired designs catapulted him
into national recognition in the Japanese art world. Most of Hisui's designs still relied
on elements of the *bijinga* tradition, but they displayed a new concern for graphically
accentuating the identity of the sponsor. This included, for instance, the direct incorporation of the modern architectural structures of the department store buildings. The
store was also represented synecdochically in posters through the display of its promotional magazine *Mitsukoshi*, well known for publicizing new consumer trends. In
one widely circulated image, the magazine was conspicuously presented on the lap of
a seated female figure, quickly recognizable as an example of the "new woman"
(*atarashii onna*) by her hairstyle, apparel, and modern domestic surroundings. A direct
connection was implied between the store and the woman's stylish new lifestyle.

Hisui's solid training in the fine arts under the tutelage of Kuroda Seiki, and his
strong personal ties to the fine arts community, gave his design endeavors social status
to which others of equal ability could only have aspired. He used his position to promote the graphic arts in the public eye and within art education. Hisui formed a design
study association called the "Group of Seven" (Shichininsha). The Group published a
magazine titled *Affiches* (Posters 1927–29, 1930), holding annual poster shows of
domestic and international work during the same period. Perhaps one of Hisui's greatest contributions as a design proponent was the introduction of the concept of "total
design." Taking his lead from European *art nouveau* designers, he supported the
notion of designing the entire lived environment. His legacy to design pedagogy is pre-
served at the prestigious Tama Art University (Tama Bijutsu Daigaku, formerly Tama
Teikoku Bijutsu Gakkō), which he helped found in 1935 and where he served as
school president for many years.[25]

Like Hisui, Hamada Masuji was also trained in fine art, first in Western-style
painting at the White Horse Society Western-style painting studio run by Kuroda and
his students, and then at the academic Pacific Painting Society studio. After this he
entered the Tokyo School of Fine Arts sculpture division. And like so many of his contemporaries, he began freelancing as a commercial designer while still in school. In
1926, he and a group of young colleagues formed the Association of Commercial
Artists (Shōgyō Bijutsuka Kyōkai) (Fig. 2) which published the periodical *Shōgyō
bijutsu* (Commercial Art) from 1930.[26] The Association mounted yearly exhibitions,
mostly in fine art venues that were reviewed with great interest in both the art and popular press. The group were referred to as "artists of the streets" because of their impact
on the look of the urban environment.[27] Association chapters were established
throughout the country — in Osaka in October 1927, followed by Nagasaki, Sendai,
Iwate, and Hiroshima.[28] They opened a study center from 1929. Three years later
Hamada established his own design school, the Shōgyō Bijutsu Kōsei Juku, in
Totsuka. This was a three-year program for certification as a commercial artist. All the
while he continued to participate in many published roundtable discussions.

In addition to producing the Ars compendium, Hamada wrote a two-volume set of textbooks, *Shōgyō bijutsu kyōhon* (Textbooks for Commercial Art), for would-be designers and published numerous texts explaining the conceptual elements of design in the early 1930s.[29] Still, the most comprehensive expression of his theory of *shōgyō bijutsu* was published in the final volume of the Ars series, a 100-page essay explicating the theoretical underpinnings of commercial design and the social implications of the field. Hamada called commercial art "art with a purpose" (*mokuteki no bijutsu*), as distinct from pure art or art for art's sake which was produced entirely for aesthetic appreciation and individual expression.[30] His theory centered around the notion of purpose. Thus, how efficiently, effectively, pragmatically, and appropriately a work served its purpose were the main criteria for evaluating its worth, while pure art was measured by the gauges of beauty and aesthetic pleasure. In *shōgyō bijutsu* the new scientific credo of the age that came hand in hand with industrialism was expressed in buzzwords such as rationalism (*gōri*), exactitude (*seikaku*), clarity (*meiryō*), suitability to purpose (*gōmokuteki*), and a host of others. Hamada argued that this form of art addressed the real-life conditions of a modern industrial society under capitalism. It was less elitist, appealing to the mass consumer. Hamada believed that in the end the practical or applied arts would actually enable the artist to break through the limiting bonds of subjectivity in pure art.[31]

Heralding a new consciousness for design, Hamada advocated the independence of the designer vis-a-vis the client. And, design should have a conceptual — and even social — underpinning that would function beyond purely monetary objectives. This signaled a new combination of the spiritual and the materialist. Design would transform a product into a commodity by mediating between the producer and the market,

Fig. 2 *Association of Commercial Artists (Shōgyō Bijutsuka Kyōkai), c. 1926. Hamada Masuji is seated second from the left in the first row.*

generating image and desire. Commercial art was "that which went beyond pure purpose; it [was] what inspired love, attachment (aichaku)," enabling the "spiritual elevation of commerce."[32]

Hamada's "commercial art" tended to emphasize production, downplaying consumption as the "bourgeois" component of modern commerce. He claimed that the "main purpose of commerce was to enhance the prosperity and livelihood of the masses" and that "mass production would solve problems by producing only practical, necessary items rather than consumer demand items."[33] Yet despite his claims to the contrary, consumption was still the essential flip side to Hamada's commercial art strategies. It was the implied, and hoped for, consequence of these techniques. Moreover, it was developments in the consumer market that fueled the expansion of the commercial design field as much as, if not more than, increases in production. This fundamental contradiction remained unreconciled in Hamada's writings.

Hamada also gave little serious attention to the issue of a product's merit or the designer's possible complicity in creating "false need." Instead, he somewhat naively asserted the importance of "sincerity" when promoting a store and its products, warning simply that "deception will be discovered." Additional slogans, such as "move away from profiteering and towards social meaning," are repeated throughout Hamada's text, showing a heavy reliance on the integrity of the producer and the designer to safeguard the interests of the consumer.[34] Yet it is undeniable that the same effective strategies Hamada was championing were often effective precisely because they persuaded consumers to purchase superfluous items.

Color, composition, and materials were just a few of the elements Hamada advocated employing to make a product stand out, to accentuate its special features, and to attract the eye of the consumer. He drew upon the abstract formalist strategies of modernist and avant-garde art to produce visual "agitation" (sendô).[35] Many of these techniques were pioneered by progressive artist–designers abroad, such as the Russian and international constructivists, the Dutch artists of De Stijl, and the diverse group at the Bauhaus in Germany, who were attempting to integrate fine art with social praxis through design. Their work was predicated on the notion that a designed environment could alter the perception and action of its inhabitants. Artists associated with the Bauhaus figured prominently in Hamada's examples, owing to the fact that one of his close colleagues and a member of the publication editorial committee was the avid Bauhaus proponent Nakada Sadanosuke (1888–1970). Nakada had visited the Bauhaus in the early 1920s and was among the first to introduce the school's work to a Japanese audience beginning in 1925.[36]

Tatsuke Yoichirô, one of the other Ars editorial committee members, compared the work of Japanese commercial artists to that of the Wiener Werkstätte and other joint craft–industry initiatives.[37] Tatsuke was director of the Japanese Advertising Study Association and published on international trends in design practice. His 1926

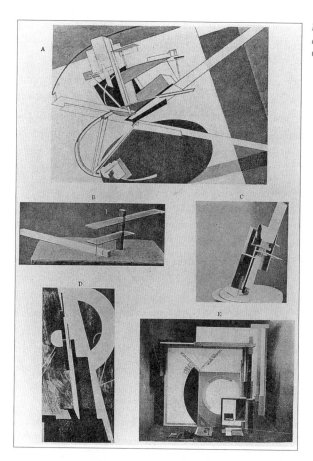

Fig. 3 *"Constructivist works and commercial art constructions." In GSBZ, vol. 24, ill. 9.*

survey *Oubei shôgyô posutâ* (European and American Commercial Posters) presented a systematic analysis of the conceptual underpinnings of the poster as a form of mass communication and then went on to feature a broad array of historical and contemporary examples from around the world.[38] In the light of this strong internationalist orientation, it is not surprising that Hamada's articulation of *shôgyô bijutsu* corresponded with developments in Euro-American design that the historian Paul Greenhalgh has designated the international "Modern Movement," particularly the period within this movement which he has called the "Pioneer Phase" — from World War I until the early 1930s. This refers to a group of avant-garde artist–designers who, like their Japanese counterparts, put forth a vision of how the designed world could transform human consciousness and improve material conditions. These designers tended to have a holistic and absolutist world-view, and their foremost concern was to break down barriers between aesthetics, technology, and society to produce for the mass of the population.[39]

Hamada's final essay in the compendium best illustrates the relationship between commercial art and international art developments. It begins with a series of illustrations showing various modernist and avant-garde works of art. Among each grouping is at least one piece labeled "*shōgyō bijutsu*," demonstrating the easy conversion of modernist "isms" into styles for the commercial realm. Figure 3 shows a group of constructivist works. The images labeled A and D are by the Russian constructivists El Lissitzky and Natan Altman. Images B and C are two Bauhaus material studies, fundamental exercises in the school's primary course, which served as a transitional stage between art and design. The piece on the lower right, E, is identified as a show window display for a German stationery store. The surrounding works employ lively abstract compositions, dynamic asymmetry, bold projecting diagonals, strong contrast and effective manipulation of materials, and, unlike the black-and-white reproductions here, bold color contrasts in the original images, particularly red, black, and white. The show window displays similar techniques. Even the German text that reads: "Why, why, why drive yourself crazy, please use our instruments" visually accentuates the composition by its off-kilter, perpendicular positioning in relation to the geometric forms.[40] The layering of square components that diminish in scale draws the eye down toward the right corner and to the goods displayed below. The books and writing implements lie on the platform and are inserted into the display.

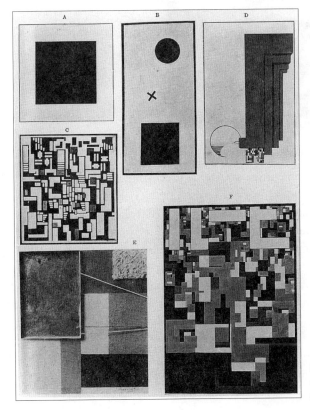

Fig. 4 *right "Suprematism and directions for its practical application." In GSBZ, vol. 24, ill. 6.*

Fig. 5 *"Background display props that harmonize the best with the presentation of letters." In GSBZ, vol. 4, ill. 57.*

In Figure 4, Hamada presents an array of abstract paintings. Images A and B are suprematist works by the Russian artist Kasimir Malevich. Image C is by the De Stijl principal, Theo Van Doesberg. Image E is a collage-construction created as a homage to Van Doesburg by the Japanese artist Murayama Tomoyoshi.[41] And Images D and F are by Hamada himself. Image D is identified as an experimental "rational composition" for use in a poster, with no product explicitly mentioned. Image F, in the right corner, is identified as a design for a beer poster. Mirroring Van Doesburg's work to the left, Hamada produces a lively decorative backdrop that simultaneously camouflages and reveals the *katakana* letters for "beer" looming above. Immediately below, one can make out the shape of a bottle, its label, and perhaps even roughly discern figures seated at tables in a café. The abstract composition subtly discloses its figurative content to the viewer. A leap of imagination is invited.

In the numerous other similar comparisons, all styles are shown to have practical design applications in terms of the structure of display, the exploitation of material qualities, or as lively background images to draw attention to products and advertising text. Another volume in the series illustrates actual examples of Japanese show windows, several experimenting with modernist design techniques. One display (Fig. 5 top) presents "new cinnamon felt hats" on sale at Maruzen. In the Maruzen window, the emphatic curve of the display echoes the rounded shape of the hat brim connecting the display with the displayed. The use of only two hats and their geometric, architectonic shapes accords with the minimalist, structured form of the display. The tipped hat playfully acknowledges the presence of the viewer. The window reproduced below (Fig. 5 bottom) advertises international newspapers and magazines, announcing a display of samples on the top floor of the store. Here the bold black grid of the display props structures the visual field of the window, creating easily legible compartments for text and commodities. This is accentuated through color contrasts of black, white, and presumably primary colors.

Some of the most intriguing examples of show windows in the Ars series were those for the display of fabrics, one of the most common commodities advertised at the time. The composite of photographs in Figure 1 attests to the tremendous creativity of these projects. The material malleability of the fabric enabled a range of visually striking display compositions. A visual texture was created through overlapping and juxtaposition. Bold diagonal sweeps of material were used to catch the viewer's eye,

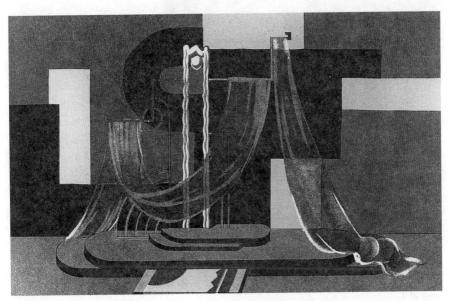

Fig. 6 *Nakazato Kenzō, "Display prop for various dyed goods for the modern woman who demands a lyrical mood."* In GSBZ, vol. 4, ill. 13.

Fig. 7 *"The road to commercial art in 3-dimensional plastic arts form."* In GSBZ, vol. 24, ill. 12.

carrying it from one side to the other. In certain cases, the fabric almost appears like shafts of light illuminating a stage or projecting into the sky. In others, mannequins (referred to as *chinretsu ningyô*, display dolls, or *chôkoku ningyô*, sculpture dolls) are shown draped in cloth, inviting the consumer to imagine herself enveloped by the sensual material and eliciting a bodily response. The extant black-and-white photographs cannot do justice to the actual kaleidoscopic color of the displays. Just an inkling of their resplendence, however, can be garnered from a vibrant sketch provided by Nakazato Kenzô for a prospective fabric display in the Ars series (Fig. 6). He similarly takes advantage of the sinuous and diaphanous quality of the material. Here the organic draping of the fabric is contrasted with the more geometric and rectilinear composition of the backdrop behind.

Hamada drew inspiration from modernist art for even the most basic elements of display platform design and props. In Figure 7, he set his own plastic arts window display (labeled C below), among sculptural works by the De Stijl designer Georges Vantongerloo (labeled A above), and a sculptural motif for a Bauhaus stage design by

Kurt Schmidt and Georg Teltscher (under the letter B). The massing of volumetric forms on the show-window stage and the effective use of props for structuring window space was a central concern. In fact, it was likened to theatrical stage design. This experimentation is documented in many systematic studies and charts of various stepped stage platform options and backdrop organization systems such as seen in Figure 8. The systematization of this information in diagrams and sketches was invaluable for pedagogic purposes. Moreover, it lent the subjective artistic endeavor of design an air of scientific credibility, as if to imply that through methodical study absolute results could be guaranteed.

The compendium served as a kind of pattern book of design ideas, all at one's finger-tips for easy reproduction or modification. Not only were new, modern styles employed to imbue commodities with a stylish aura, but new technologies and materials associated with modern industry were proffered as a means to create an exciting spectacle for the consumer. Display functioned both inside the show window and out-side the store itself. The "sales street decoration" (*uridashi gaitō sōshoku*) was used as a temporary prosthetic for the front of the building. According to Hamada, these struc-tures were designed to elicit a psychological response based on "group mentality." That is to say, they were expected to pique the curiosity of pedestrians, relying on the assumption that if one person stopped, soon a crowd would congregate.[42] As a gateway to the commodity exposition within, the decorative entrance, whether an arch or a pillar, was intended to produce an atmosphere of excitement. Slick modern materials like glass, metal, and electric lighting went a long way in facilitating this effect. The rendering in Figure 9 shows just one of the many outlandish and elaborate plans proposed for this

purpose in the Ars series. In this design by Ishimoto Kikuji, a founding member of the Secessionist Architecture Association (Bunriha Kenchikukai), structural members were used to broadcast advertising information. The medallions here exclaimed the "large sale." The vertical column would display the date. The ABC lettering on the cornice would presumably be customized to the particular location. On a slightly smaller scale, advertising pillars could similarly be used to coax the consumer into the building.

Hamada saw unlimited potential for advertising in outdoor public spaces. The compendium illustrates a range of outdoor advertising strategies such as kiosks, sand-wich-boards, decorated automobiles and

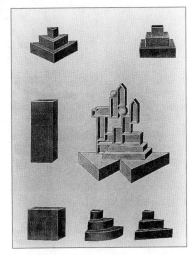

Fig. 8 *"Standard box-shaped display stands and their expressive appearances."* In GSBZ, vol. 4, ill. 42.

Fig. 9 *Ishimoto Kikuji, "Sales street decoration for the storefront." In GSBZ, vol. 10, ill. 5.*

trucks, and large-scale painted and electric or neon signboards. Of course, many of these modes of advertisement already existed in some form or another dating back sometimes as far as the seventeenth century. Street kiosks, known as "advertising towers" (*kōkokutō* or *sendentō*), were pillars or small buildings that functioned primarily as architectural signboards, such as those used for promoting Maruzen ink and Kirin beer erected at the Japan Peace Memorial Exhibition in Tokyo in 1922. A number of scholars have discussed the related spectacular environments of the exposition fairground and the department store.[43] This, of course, included both the indoor environment of the store and the transformed theater of the street outside. Many designers and display companies were involved in both areas.

Along with trains and ships, automobiles and trucks were the representative new transportation technologies of the modern age. For advertising purposes they were effective because they enabled mobile promotion, circulating through the urban population. Furthermore, it was argued that a moving device was infinitely more visually stimulating than a stationary one. This was not lost on avant-garde designers in Russia who had been using painted trains as a principal agitprop technique for several years since the revolution. Hamada's suggested design for an advertising truck (Fig. 10) — the generic text reading "advertising" — allowed for easy substitution of individualized copy.

The innovative and expressive use of new kinds of typography (*zuan moji*) in commercial advertising was a major strategy for producing an eye-catching and modern look. The shape, size, and hue of printed text, its position and composition, all

Fig. 10 *Hamada Masuji, "Decorated vehicle for the advertisement of sales." In GSBZ, vol. 10, ill. 4.*

Fig. 11 *Fujii Kiyoshi, "Three varieties of signboard design for standing in fields." In GSBZ, vol. 7, ill. 38.*

became important design components. Visual and textual elements were highlighted through combination and conscious juxtaposition to accent both two- and three-dimensional forms. Designers labored to evoke the pictorial and expressive qualities of letter forms. This, of course, was not new in Japan and other Asian countries that possessed strong calligraphic traditions. Modern Japanese designers found the two syllabaries, *hiragana* and *katakana*, Chinese characters, and now romanized letters as well, fertile ground for experimentation. One of the first comprehensive explications of typography, titled *Zuan moji taikan* (Typographic Handbook), was published by the poster designer Yajima Shūichi several years before the Ars series. In the introduction to Yajima's book, architect and Tokyo Imperial University professor Takeda Goichi argued that there was a need for new letter forms to fit modern commodities. And he concluded that "beautiful typography [was] the most effective way of promoting the worth of a commodity."[44] Takeda echoed the contemporary widespread recognition of the import-ance of typography in visual communication and for the encouragement of consumption.

Experiments in the so-called rational or new typography of European and Russian artists also skillfully integrated text and image to produce a powerful tool for commercial and political ends. It was in 1928 that the German typographer Jan Tschichold published his ground-breaking handbook, *Die neue Typographie* (The New Typography), considered by scholars to be "unsurpassed as the best single document" displaying the developments in modernist typography.[45] Japanese designers quickly became aware of such new developments in Western modernist typography, mostly through published sources and a few exhibitions of poster design. In his book-length study of developments in avant-garde art abroad, Murayama Tomoyoshi quoted the Bauhaus instructor Laszlo Moholy-Nagy on the importance of typography in the visual arts:

> *Printing technology is the most powerful form. It must be a clear means. It must be specially emphasized . . . First, all printed works must have the clarity of a singular meaning. They must be easy to read. No a priori aesthetic knowledge must be necessary . . . letters must not be forced into a square form. Corresponding with the essence and purpose of the printed matter, we must allow an unrestricted use of typefaces, letter arrangements (i.e., not always organizing the letters in straight or parallel lines), and geometrical forms and colours.*[46]

As recommended by Moholy-Nagy, the Ars design compendium offered a host of typographic and compositional strategies for maximizing visual effect, once again readily appropriated or adapted by any designer for use in any circumstance. In the three beer advertisement signboards by Fujii Kiyoshi (Fig. 11), the designer draws attention to the images by using stark primary colors, dynamic diagonal compositions, and bold typography. He also accentuates the nominal identity of the beer through motif. From left to right the beers are named: "Star beer," "Moon beer," and "Sun beer," and corresponding representations are seen in the images.

An equally significant new instrument for the development of commercial art was photography, a topic which has been well studied and will not be greatly elaborated upon here.[47] Photography, or more specifically photogravure, was incorporated into advertising around 1910. The vast majority of represented images, as in graphic works, were pictures of beautiful women. Photographs lent advertisements an aura of reality because they purported to record the truth. According to Hamada, people trusted photographs more than any other medium. They were reliable and clear, two key components for promoting confidence in the consumer. A photograph was the next best thing to being able to present the commodity itself. In fact, it was better, because photographs could be cleverly manipulated to produce certain visual and emotional responses while maintaining the semblance of unmediated representation.[48] Designers in the 1920s seized on the techniques of modernist or "new photography" (known in Japanese as "*shinkō shashin*") for commercial (and political) purposes, particularly the creative fusing of disparate images and texts in photomontage. 'By combining two or more images, by joining drawing and graphic shapes to the photograph, by adding a significant spot of color, or by adding a written text," observes Christopher Phillips, the designer could "divert the photograph from what it 'naturally' seems to say," and "underscore the need for the viewer's active 'reading' of the image." [49] In the commercial arena, this was employed to create a non-linear promotional narrative that metonymically linked the paired correlates of text and

Fig. 12 Arai Sen, *"Original
advertising photograph (soap)."*
In GSBZ, vol. 4, ill. 5.

image — the product and its concept. It provided a multiple, but still controlled, perspective that sought to sway the viewer/consumer through the accumulation of layers of meaning that always returned to product and company identity.

In the compendium, Arai Sen presents a humorous combination of women's faces and large typography to promote the fictitious *"bigan"* (beautiful face) soap (Fig. 12). Arai's eye-catching composition is animated by the dynamic zig-zagging layout of seemingly disparate photographic and textual fragments; dramatically cropped images of glamorous, exotic Western women from Hollywood movies are interspersed with the product brand name and the repeated English word "soap." The eye is drawn from the upper left-hand corner across the page to the right where it ricochets off the head of an attractive woman, whose enticing stare establishes direct eye contact with the viewer. The composition then reverses the course of the viewer's gaze back to the left, from where it is jerked in reverse once again to the right and down to the bottom of the page. The composite as a whole is somewhat tenuously anchored at the bottom by the incongruous image of the Little Rascals all clustered together staring intensely at a superimposed object labeled "soap" held in the grasp of the central figure. Part of the appeal of this image, and photomontage in general, is precisely its incongruity — the reframing of unrelated images through self-conscious coordination that forces the viewer to reconsider the "natural" meaning of the image. Since this design mock-up was merely a proposal and not an actual advertisement, its effectiveness in the market-place unfortunately cannot be gauged. But the increasing use of photomontage in Japanese commercial design throughout the 1930s attests to the popularity and, one can surmise, efficacy of this form.

In arguing for the systematic application of visual art techniques in commercial design, Hamada successfully helped forge the new category of artistic production labeled "shōgyō bijutsu," which imbued art with a purpose and aestheticized com-merce. Seeking to influence consumers by visually manipulating their perception of goods, daily life, and even the urban environment, he attributed to commercial art the potential for promoting social change through innovative forms and new functions. The Ars compendium and Hamada's other voluminous writings served as invaluable tools for disseminating these new conceptions of design. They also publicized the names of individual designers generally engaged behind the scenes in this process.

Together with a broad range of activist–designers, Hamada and his circle of col-leagues in the Association of Commercial Artists spearheaded a movement to con-struct a new social status for design, legitimating commercial art as a significant area of artistic practice. This in fact marked a convergence of concerns between modern designers and fine artists around the world. Artists active in the "new art movement" (shinkō bijutsu undō) in Japan and various avant-garde groups abroad were increasingly seeking to incorporate a more productivist perspective into the realm of fine arts in an effort to make their work more applicable to the conditions of daily life, while those in the commercial art sphere sought to aestheticize their production by applying mod-ernist visual techniques to everyday design. The abundance of publications on various areas of design practice, the explosion of design study groups, and the establishment of educational programs in design as independent institutions or within fine art acad-emies by the early 1930s greatly reinforced the importance of this area of artistic pro-duction in the Japanese art world. Moreover, the incorporation of a crafts section into the official annual salon sponsored by the Ministry of Education in 1927 was an important step in elevating craft, and by extension design, in the academy and the public eye. Finally, the active participation of designers in state initiatives from cloth-ing reform to propaganda production promoted them to an advisory level equivalent to other members of the intelligentsia such as university academics.

This, of course, did not mean that there was not still plenty of resistance to Hamada's project. There were prominent artists, such as the celebrated nihonga (Japanese-style) painter Yokoyama Taikan, who were adamantly opposed to the incor-poration of design under the rubric of fine arts because of its aesthetic unworthiness. The social recognition of design and the designer in Japan in the public, official, and fine arts arenas was a gradual process that only culminated in the postwar period.

"The real beauty of art is found in our surroundings, in our daily life — in produced objects and practical goods," wrote Hamada.[50] This adulation of the utilitarian nature of industrialism was mixed with a Utopian vision that aimed to reach a mass audience. It questioned the recondite premises of art for art's sake, searching for a new form of applicability, because, in Hamada's words, if "beauty in art is to be esteemed, it must speak to everyone. It is assumed that to appreciate art one must be educated and cultivate knowledge. But does beauty need to be difficult to understand?"[51] While Issey Miyake and Yokoo Tadanori may not be what Hamada had in mind when he put forth his populist vision of "*shōgyō bijutsu*," they are certainly the living legacy of his project.

Acknowledgments

I would like to take this opportunity to thank several people who provided helpful comments on earlier drafts of this chapter: Christine Guth, Jordan Sand, John Clark, and Laura Coyle. I would also like to express my great appreciation to Kawahata Naomichi for allowing me to study the extensive design-related materials in his collection and for sharing his insights into Japanese commercial design.

Notes

1   Hamada Masuji, "Shōgyō bijutsu sōron," in Kitazawa Yoshio (ed.), *Gendai shōgyō bijutsu zenshū*, vol. 24, Tokyo, Ars, 1930, p. 13.

2   In his essay, Hamada quotes various responses to the Association of Commercial Artists' work and exhibitions that appeared contemporaneously in Japanese newspapers such as *Kokumin shinbun, Yamato shinbun, Yorozu chōhō, Nihon shinbun, Maiyū shinbun,* and *Minato shinbun*. All refer to the group's art as an "art of the streets" (*gaitō bijutsu*), and one reporter writing for the *Yorozu chōhō* noted that the group was calling for a comprehensive "artification of the daily life of the masses" (*taishū seikatsu no geijutsuka*). Ibid., pp. 10–11.

3   Kitazawa Yoshio (ed.), *Gendai shōgyō bijutsu zenshū*, vols 1–24, Tokyo, Ars, 1928–30. Hereafter abbreviated as *GSBZ*.

4   According to extensive research conducted by Kawahata Naomichi, some of the important commercial publications on design theory and practice during this time were: Dr. Anna Berliner, *Japanische Reklame in der Tageszeitung* (Japanese Newspaper Advertisements), Stuttgart, C.E. Poeschel Verlag, 1925; Sugiura Hisui and Watanabe Sōshu, *Zuan no bigaku* (The Aesthetics of Design), Tokyo, Atelier-sha, 1931; Sugiura Hisui and Watanabe Sōshu, *Zuan no kenkyū* (Study of Design), Tōyō Seikōkan Shuppan, 1934; and *Zuan shin gihō kōza* (Course on New Methods of Design), vols. 1–7, Tokyo, Atelier-sha, 1932–33.

5   The term "*shōgyō bijutsu*" was coined around 1926, but only came into regular parlance in the early 1930s.

6   Hamada, "Shōgyō bijutsu sōron," *GSBZ*, vol. 24, p. 15.

7   ibid., pp. 11–13.

8   ibid., p. 62.

9   ibid., p. 14.

10 ibid., p. 85.

11 ibid., p. 16.

12 According to design historian Kayano Yatsuka, the term "*dezain*" and its newly coined Japanese translation "*zuan*" were both introduced into the Japanese lexicon at the time of the Vienna World's Fair in 1873. Kayano Yatsuka, *Kindai Nihon no dezain bunkashi 1868–1926*, Tokyo, Fuirumu Ātosha, 1992, pp. 56–58. The term "*ishō*" continued to be used interchangeably or in combination with "*zuan*" throughout the prewar period. Anne Gossot, "L'affiche publicitaire et le *gurafikku dezain* au Japon (1854–1960)," *Histoire de l'art*, no. 24, December 1993, p. 82. Kashiwagi Hiroshi, "Nihon no kindai dezain," in *Kenchiku to dezain, Nihon bijutsu zenshū, kindai no bijutsu IV*, no. 24, Tokyo, Kōdansha, 1993, p. 169. For the influence of Asai Chū in the transformation of the conception of design in Japan, see Christophe Marquet, "Asai Chū to 'zuan'," in *Kenchiku to dezain*, pp. 178–9, 182.

13   Minami Hiroshi and Shakai Shinri Kenkyūjo, *Taishō bunka*, Tokyo, Keisō Shobō, 1965, pp. 118–19; Ishikawa Hiroyoshi and Ozaki Hatsuki, *Shuppan kōkoku no rekishi*, Tokyo, Shuppan Nyūsusha, 1989, pp. 12–14. It was around this time that the term "marketing" was first coined.

14   Sydney Crawcour, "Industrialization and Technological Change, 1885–1920," in Peter Duus (ed.), *The Cambridge History of Japan: The Twentieth Century*, Cambridge, Cambridge University Press, 1988, p. 387.

15   The Tokyo School of Fine Arts (Tōkyō Bijutsu Gakkō, present-day Tōkyō Geijutsu Daigaku) was, in 1896, one of the first art schools to establish a design section. Later, in May 1923, the section was subdivided into a division for design (*zuan*) and a division for architecture (*kenchiku*). Independent design schools, however, had been established prior to this in the mid-Meiji period as part of a larger governmental initiative to promote product design and national industry for the benefit of the Japanese economy. Tokyo Higher Industrial School (Tōkyō Kōtō Kōgyō Gakkō) was originally founded in 1881 as Tokyo Worker's School (Tōkyō Shokkō Gakkō), renamed Tokyo Industrial School (Tōkyō Kōgyō Gakkō) in 1890, and then renamed as a higher school of crafts in 1901 with the addition of an industrial design department (*kōgyō zuanka*). A parallel institution, the Kyoto School for Industrial Arts (Kyōto Kōtō Kōgei Gakkō), was established in the Kansai area in 1902.

16   According to Mori Hitoshi, these schools were established in the period after the government had taken an active role in developing design education as a means of promoting production and industry during the Meiji period. For a detailed discussion of the school curriculum, see Mori Hitoshi, "The 1930s of [sic] Tokyo Kōtō Kōgei Gakkō," in Matsudō Kyoiku Iinkai (ed.), *Shikaku no Shōwa 1930–1940*, Matsudō, Matsudō Kyoiku Iinkai, 1998, p. 23.

17   Kawahata Naomichi, "Kokusaku senden ni okeru datsu shōgyō bijutsu no nagare," in *Shikaku no Shōwa 1930–1940*, p. 143.

18   Louisa Rubinfien, "Commodity to National Brand: Manufacturers, Merchants, and the Development of the Consumer Market in Interwar Japan," Harvard University, PhD Dissertation, 1995.

19   For a discussion of the construction of the term "*bijutsu*," see Kitazawa Noriaki, *Me no shinden*, Tokyo, Bijutsu Shuppansha, 1989, pp. 105–55. It was not until 1927 that the Bunten (renamed the Teikoku Bijutsuin Tenrankai (Exhibition of the Imperial Academy of Fine Arts) in 1918 and abbreviated as Teiten) inaugurated a crafts (*kōgei*) section in which industrial arts were also exhibited.

20   Hamada, "Shōgyō bijutsu sōron," *GSBZ*, vol. 24, p. 15.

21   Michelle Bogart, *Artists, Advertising, and the Borders of Art*, Chicago, University of Chicago Press, 1995, p. 7.

22   Hamada, "Shōgyō bijutsu sōron," *GSBZ*, vol. 24, pp. 9, 32, 34.

23   ibid., pp. 3, 15.

24   Takashina Shūji, "Taishū geijutsu no seiritsu to modanizumu," in *Geijutsu to kōkoku*, Tokyo, Sezon Bijutsukan, 1991, pp. 183–4.

25   At Tama, Hisui placed special emphasis on design pedagogy in the school curriculum. For more information on Hisui's career, see *Sugiura Hisui, Nihon modan dezain no kishu*, Tokyo, Tabako to Shio no Hakubutsukan, 1994.

26   The Association also published the *Shōgyō bijutsu shinbun* in 1931. Several other Association members also went on to write actively on design, one of the most prominent among them being Murota Kurazō, who published the long-running, more mainstream periodical, *Advertising World* (Kōkokukai), which ran for 194 issues from March 1926 until the end of 1941. James Fraser, Steven Heller, and Seymour Chwast, *Japanese Modern: Graphic Design Between the Wars*, San Francisco, Chronicle Books, 1996, pp. 88, 97. Murota also published several books, including *Shin kōkoku kōsakuron*, Tokyo, Seibundō, 1935.

27   See note 2.

28   Hamada, "Shōgyō bijutsu sōron," *GSBZ*, vol. 24, p. 12.

29   In addition to his series of textbooks, Hamada's publications include: *Shōgyō bijutsu kōsei genri*, Tokyo, Kōyō Shoin, 1935; and *Shōgyō bijutsu kōza*, 5 vols, Tokyo, Ateliersha, 1937–38. Hamada also wrote regularly for the journal *Kōgei jidai*, which ran from December 1926 until October 1927.

30   Hamada, "Shōgyō bijutsu sōron," *GSBZ*, vol. 24, pp. 27–9, 32, 50.

31   ibid., pp. 57–8.

32   ibid., pp. 70–1.

33   ibid., p. 66.

34   ibid., p. 74.

35   ibid., p. 13.

36   Nakada Sadanosuke, "Kokuritsu Bauhasu (I)," *Mizue*, no. 244, June 1925, pp. 2–7; Nakada Sadanosuke, "Kokuritsu Bauhausu (II)," *Mizue*, no. 245, July 1925, pp. 8–12; Nakada Sadanosuke, "Bauhausu Goki," *Mizue*, no. 248, October 1925, pp. 37–8; Nakada Sadanosuke, "Warutā Guropiusu Suisan," *Kenchiku shinchō*, vol. 6, no. 10, October 1925, pp. 1–5; Nakada Sadanosuke, "Bauhausu o kataru," *Kōgei jidai*, vol. 2, no. 1, January 1927, pp. 113–22. The avant-garde artist Murayama Tomoyoshi, leader of the group Mavo, was also instrumental in introducing the design theories of artists associated with the Bauhaus, particularly Laszlo Moholy-Nagy. See Murayama Tomoyoshi, *Kōseiha kenkyū*, Tokyo, Chūō Bijutsusha, 1926.

37   Quoted in Hamada, "Shōgyō bijutsu sōron," *GSBZ*, vol. 24, p. 22.

38   Tatsuke Yoichirō, *Oubei shōgyō posutā*, Tokyo, Nihon Kōkoku Gakkai Shuppan, 1926.

39   Paul Greenhalgh (ed.), *Modernism in Design*, London, Reaktion Books, 1990, pp. 5–22.

40   The original text in German read, "Warum, warum, warum Kopfzerbrechen, verwenden sie bitte unsere Hilfsmittel."

41   See Mizusawa Tsutomu, chapter one in this volume, for other references to Murayama.

42   Hamada Masuji, "Uridashi gaitō sōshoku no gainen to shōgyō bijutsu," in *Uridashi gaitō sōshokushū*, vol. 10, Kitahara Yoshio (ed.), *Gendai shōgyō bijutsu zenshū*, Tokyo, Ars, 1928, pp. 4–5.

43   See Hatsuda Tōru, *Hyakkaten no tanjō*, Sanseidō Sensho, no. 178, Tokyo, Sanseidō, 1993.

44   Quoted in James Fraser et al., *Japanese Modern*, p. 123.

45   Robin Kinross, "Introduction to the English-Language Edition," in Jan Tschichold, *The New Typography*, trans. by Ruari McLean, Berkeley, University of California Press, 1995, p. xv.

46   Murayama Tomoyoshi, *Kōseiha kenkyū*, p. 69. Hamada discusses similar statements by Moholy-Nagy in Hamada, "Shōgyō bijutsu sōron," *GSBZ*, vol. 24, p. 87.

47   See Nakai Kōichi, *Komasharu foto*, vol. 11, *Nihon shashin zenshū*, Tokyo, Shogakukan, 1986. Particularly noteworthy in this area is the work of Iizawa Kohtaro concerning the development of "new photography" (*shinkō shashin*) in Japan, its relationship to the Bauhaus in Germany, and its later impact on Japanese advertising. See, for example, Iizawa Kohtaro, "The Bauhaus and Shinkō Shashin," in *Bauhausu no shashin corokiumu*, Kawasaki, Kawasaki-shi Shimin Myūjiamu, 1997, pp. 134–9.

48   Half of volume 14 in Hamada's design compendium was dedicated to explicating the vast range of effective uses of photography in commercial art. See Hamada's essay "Shashin oyobi manga ouyō kōkoku no gainen," in Kitazawa Yoshio (ed.), *Shashin oyobi manga ouyō kōkokushū*, vol. 13, *Gendai shōgyō bijutsu zenshū*, Tokyo, Ars, 1928, pp. 3–8. Other contributions to the same volume included an essay by Nakada Sadanosuke, "Shashin no shinkeikō to sono ouyō kōkoku," pp. 9–14, which further explicated the development of avant-garde photography techniques that were being applied in German advertising design, including photomontage, photograms, and x-ray photographs. Nakada's piece was followed by a series of more practical "how to" sections beginning with a contribution by the *shinkō shashin* photographer Kanamaru Shigene, a leading figure in photography education in Japan and the founder of a commercial photography studio involved in publicity and advertising called Kinreisha in 1926, in which the author explained the range of photographic technologies and devices currently available. Kanamaru Shigene, "Kōkokuyō shashin no seisakuhō," pp. 14–21. Other essays explained the relationship between various printing technologies and photography, the use of airbrushing, the effectiveness of different models and locations, and the use of films in advertising.

49   Christopher Phillips, "Introduction," *Montage and Modern Life, 1919–1942*, Cambridge, Mass., MIT Press, 1992, p. 28.

50   Hamada, "Shōgyō bijutsu sōron," *GSBZ*, vol. 24, p. 77.

51   ibid., pp. 75–6.

CHAPTER SIX

The Cultured Life as Contested Space
Dwelling and Discourse in the 1920s

Jordan Sand

Taishō "culture"

The coupling of "Taishō" with "culture" has become so common in descriptions of the era as to have acquired a retrospective sense of inevitability. We speak of Taishō culture not only because certain political and social configurations of the 1910s and 1920s — party governments, prosperity derived from World War I era production, the beginnings of social welfare, and so on — sustained what appears retrospectively as a recognizable culture, but because the idea of "culture" itself saw a boom (to use a later Japanese loanword) at a particular moment in the 1920s. Yet few Japanese were speaking of "culture" before 1920, the ninth year of Emperor Taishō's fifteen-year reign. Further, the connotations of *bunka* in this first period of widespread use differ markedly from what is implied by *bunka* today. We need, therefore, to distinguish our retrospective Taishō culture, a historiographic construct, from the "culture" which occupied a peculiar position in elite and popular discourse during the 1920s.[1]

A familiar set of polarities typically serve to distinguish Meiji "civilization" (*bunmei*) from Taishō "culture" as two moments in the development of the national character: public Meiji/private Taishō, nationalist Meiji/cosmopolitan Taishō, self-sacrificing Meiji/self-cultivating Taishō, productionist Meiji/consumerist Taishō. In particular, Taishō has been characterized as individualistic, in a reaction to the public and nationalistic character of Meiji. Viewed as discourses rather than manifestations of *Zeitgeist*, *bunmei* and *bunka* appear in a somewhat different light. "Civilization" in Meiji was a unitary discourse. Intellectuals might debate the means of achieving it, but they had no dispute over the nature of "civilization" itself. Taishō "culture" (and here we should emphasize the quotation marks to stress that this is the *rhetoric* of the era), by contrast, provided the terms for an emergent competition over cultural goods. The retrospective picture of Taishō intellectuals turning to "culture" in a reaction against the state-centered ideology of Meiji derives from a highly selective intellectual history. The discourse of "culture" in the 1920s signifies more the fragmentation of public discourse than intellectual rejection of dominant ideology. This is because, unlike "civilization," the material definition of "culture" fluctuated in the market, following the logic of fashion.[2]

We can be fairly precise about the beginnings of the "culture" boom, which is to say the popularization of the term, and the emergence of a popular culture of "culture houses," "culture pots," "culture knives," and "culture diapers." Two points of departure suggest themselves: 1920 and 1922. Nineteen-twenty saw the establishment by economist Morimoto Kōkichi of the Bunka Seikatsu Kenyūkai (Cultured Life Research Group). The Group published two periodicals containing lectures for women's higher school graduates, *Bunka seikatsu* and *Bunka seikatsu kenkyū*. There is little to suggest that these were themselves market successes on a very large scale, but after their appearance the phrase "cultured life" appeared frequently elsewhere in popular publications, which were quick to adopt themes and catchphrases from official, academic, and high-cultural sources if they showed mass-market potential.[3]

Nineteen-twenty-two provided Taishō "culture" with an iconic site: a cluster of fourteen model houses, labeled "Culture Village," built at the Peace Exposition held that summer in Ueno Park. These houses were the winning entries in a competition, judged by members of the Society of Japanese Architects as new models for living. Ōkuma Yoshikuni, Professor of Architecture at Tokyo Imperial University, was official village "headman." Newspapers and magazines referred to the small, eclectic-looking houses on display as "culture houses" (*bunka jūtaku*). As Japan's first model house exhibition, the village initiated a style of event that would be repeated under commercial auspices countless times afterward. The name "Culture Village" was also borrowed by private developers building new residential districts in the suburbs of Tokyo and elsewhere after 1922.

The sponsors of Culture Village promoted such Westernizing modifications as the use of chairs over the traditional practice of floor-sitting, and removal of the long surrounding corridors (*engawa*) and sliding doors characteristic of detached houses in Japan at the time, in favor of fixed walls and windows. Although competition guidelines focused on specific aspects of planning and construction, popular discourse treated any house with new features not found in the common run of vernacular housing as a "culture house." The most commonly noted characteristics were colored roof tiles, glass windows, walls of narrow, painted clapboards or mortar on the exterior, and white lace curtains and rattan furniture inside.[4]

Promoting a blend of bourgeois family ideology and scientific management ideas for the home, Morimoto's "Research Group" differed little in its message from the government-sponsored Seikatsu Kaizen Dōmeikai (Alliance for Lifestyle Improvement), which had been established one year earlier, also with the intention of enlightening middle-class housewives. Culture Village in Ueno was inspired by similar concerns. In some cases, membership overlapped — village "headman" Ōkuma, for example, also sat on the Housing Committee of the Daily Life Reform League. In this sense, "culture" ideologues merely carried on the tradition of top-down reform campaigns instituted since Meiji in the pursuit of "civilization."[5] "Culture," however, possessed a capacity for positive appeal that prescriptions for reform lacked. So did the promise of new goods. Culture Village, after all, was addressing the fair-going public not through verbal exhortation, but directly, through attractive new houses. And as canny advertisers began promoting a plethora of new "cultured" commodities, discourse of the "cultured life" too highlighted the allure of modernity's tangible products.

The Taishō cultural intermediary

The historiography of Taishō culture has evoked for us images of a new generation of consumers on the scene in the city of post-World War I Japan, members of the "new middle classes" (shin chūkansō). The press of the time seems seldom to have used this term, but awareness of the changing landscape of class is evident in such terms of the day as "the educated unpropertied class" (yūshiki musan kaikyū), and the ironic "paupers in Western clothes" (yōfuku saimin).[6] Today's understanding of the Taishō new middle class is mediated through the words of journalists and other intellectuals in the popular press of the time. As we try to glimpse Japan's first modern consumers in these popular sources, it is easy to overlook the presence of another new player in the development of urban mass culture, namely the popularizing intellectual himself, whose fortunes were ineluctably tied to those of the new middle class. Adopting an idea from Pierre Bourdieu, I will refer to such popularizers (and we may include a very small number of women among them) as cultural intermediaries. Bourdieu's cultural intermediary is an intellectual located at the unstable edge of the intelligentsia, selling his (or her) own lifestyle to the rising petit bourgeoisie.[7] The cultural intermediaries of Taishō were purveyors of new, largely Western, tastes — writers, designers, and entrepreneurs who made a living teaching readers of mass-market books and women's magazines the ingredients of cosmopolitan modernity. We might describe the "cultured life" as the contemporary label for the product such people purveyed.

Yet, as the ironic characterization of middle-class "paupers" suggests, the actual buying capacity of the new middle classes was extremely limited, particularly with regard to houses and the other "consumer durables," such as refrigerators and automobiles. The culture house phenomenon thus marks the beginning of fashion in housing, more than a transformation of living standards for most Japanese (or even most Tokyoites). Actual houses were being built in new styles and materials that seemed outlandish, but only a fraction of the urban population could afford to buy them. Most so-called culture houses were small and built for rental, and, for practical as well as financial reasons, even these remained mere fantasies for many readers of Shufu no tomo (The Housewife's Companion). As is often the case, but perhaps to an even greater extent than elsewhere, the consumption of dream images ran far ahead of

Fig. 1 Visitors to the Peace Exposition at Ueno in spring 1922 view the model houses at Culture Village (from Takanashi Yūtarō (ed.), Bunka mura no kan'i jūtaku, Tokyo, Kōyōsha, 1922).

the consumption of goods. Not until the "my-home" boom of the 1960s would a majority of Japanese attain the incomes necessary to realize these dreams.

The Taishō cultural intermediary entered a field of production already occupied by reform-minded members of the bourgeois elite who had dominated higher education and publishing since the late nineteenth century. A comparatively small group of ideologues had controlled the magazines and other print media through which images of modernity were promoted, as well as dominating the new cultural professions, from journalism to architecture. Not until the World War I years did major magazines represent other voices.[8] The distinction between the older generation of bourgeois proselytizers and the upstart cultural intermediaries was one not only of generation, but also of motives. Meiji bourgeois proselytizers exhorted their audience in the faith that they acted for the good of the nation, but not expecting that the class boundaries that guaranteed their own privileged position within it were open to all traffic. Since their interests often aligned with those of the state, they commonly formed organizations in alliance with particular ministries for didactic campaigns directed at the masses. The Daily Life Reform League was one such organization. Where these people saw a nation in need of guidance, Taishō cultural intermediaries saw a diverse and competitive market.[9]

The massification of print and the exponential growth of reading publics permitted the intervention of these less privileged cultural producers into the schema of state agencies, possessors of legitimate culture and national citizenry. The older group of bourgeois proselytizers, rich in both social capital (comprising primarily ties to the Meiji state) and cultural capital (primarily Western knowledge), now shared the field with both a vanguard of Taishō intellectuals, rich in cultural capital but lacking the kind of access to political power possessed by their Meiji predecessors, and the more marginal cultural intermediaries, who sought to assert their own legitimacy by making the dominant culture more accessible. In an expanded market of ideas and goods after World War I, challenges thus arose against both traditional practices associated with the "feudal" pre-Meiji past and the progressive ideas of the Meiji and post-Meiji intel-lectual elite. This is attested by press reactions to the government-sponsored cam-paign for daily life reform. The *Asahi* newspaper, for example, ridiculed members of the Daily Life Reform League as pompous aristocrats who claimed to speak for the middle classes but had little understanding of how the true middle class lived.[10] But criticizing the proselytizers did not de-legitimize their product. The rhetoric of cul-tural reform itself could still be appropriated. In many criticisms, others' "daily life reform" or "cultured life" was judged mistaken, and the "true cultured life" said to lie elsewhere. Writers on both "daily life reform" and "the cultured life" thus wrote polemically, posing their models consciously against one another. In short, contest developed among the various progressive-minded players sharing the space of these vaguely defined reform projects.

Picturing the culture house

At Culture Village, elite architects had met the mass market for the first time. The ur-event of the exhibition also aptly expressed another aspect of the culture house phenomenon, one affecting the physical as well as the discursive landscape of the city — what I will call a specularization, or rendering-visible of the dwelling. This happened in four ways.

First, in the most obvious sense, the houses at Culture Village were for looking at. Ironically, they were not for going into, since visitors were allowed to enter the houses only by special invitation (Fig. 1). This made them more purely visual objects (or objects for voyeurism), since it limited the typical fair-goer's experience of them to peering into door-ways and through windows. Here, for the first time, were detached houses, a quintessentially private architectural form, built expressly for public display.

Second, in magazine advertisements and elsewhere in the mass media after the exposi-tion, depictions of houses became popular symbols, used to evoke both progress and domesticity. The Ajinomoto Company, makers of monosodium glutamate, advertised their product in the newspapers of late 1922 with a sketch of a steep-roofed half-timber style

Fig. 2 *"Appropriate to the Name of Culture."*
Advertisement for Ajinomoto flavoring.
Reprinted from Shinbun shūroku Taishōshi
dai 10 kan, *Tokyo, Taishō Shuppan Kabushiki*
Gaisha, 1978, p. 518.

Fig. 3 *(three photographs) Culture houses stood out from their surroundings, in contrast to traditional urban detached houses, which were hidden behind walls and hedges. Gables facing the street and second-story windows further distinguished them. (a) Street in Hirosaki City (from Miyazawa Satoshi (ed.),* Nihon no bijutsu: Machiya to machinami, *Tokyo, Shibundō, 1980). (b) New houses built along the Odakyū private rail line in Tokyo (*Nihon chiri taikei, Dai Tōkyō hen, *Tokyo, Kaizōsha, 1929). opposite (c) House of Baron Tokuse Hideo (*Kenchiku shashin ruiju dai 4 ki dai 7 kai: Bunka jūtaku 1, *Tokyo, Kōyōsha, 1923).*

house and the words, "appropriate to the name of Culture" (Fig. 2).[11] Soap companies and other makers of products for home use employed similar images. These were the first advertisements in Japan to exploit the now-common shorthand of representing consumer satisfaction in the form of a cosy home.

Third, in the architectural pattern books that proliferated in the 1920s, a new mode of depicting dwellings appeared. Authors included perspective sketches and stylized freehand elevations where formerly only floor plans and an occasional hard-line elevation had been made to suffice. Houses were consciously rendered as aesthetic objects, using single-point perspective, especially, which gave primacy to vision, creating allure and embodying the eye of possessive individualism.

Fourth and finally, culture houses were dwellings rendered visible literally, for the new houses appearing in suburban neighborhoods of the time were more available to view from nearby streets. Surrounded by low fences rather than the high walls and hedges that had been usual for detached houses, often two stories where most of their neighbors were one, with gables facing the street side, and dormers or attic windows cut into the gables rather than the traditional heavy, unbroken mass of roof tile (as if the eyes of the culture house were set higher on the head than native eyes), culture houses were conspicuous additions to the landscape (Figs 3a, 3b, 3c).

The opening scene of Goshō Heinosuke's film *Madamu to nyōbo* (The Neighbor's Wife and Mine, 1930) plays upon the character of the culture house as specular object. Strolling among the open lots of a sparsely populated suburb where new development is just beginning, Shibano, the film's protagonist, approaches a painter at his easel. The painter is studying two houses visible in the distance — one a typical rental house of the day, the other a white-stuccoed "Western-style" cottage, an icon of "culture." His canvas depicts only the Western house. The role the two houses play in the ensuing story neatly evokes the contradictory relationship between the new middle-class consumer and the culture house. Shibano's family moves into the plainer house, where we see scenes of typical domesticity. A vampish jazz singer occupies the Western house next door. Her daring lifestyle makes the white-stuccoed cottage a place of threatening seductions for Shibano.

From the 1870s, high-ranking officials in the Meiji government had built independent Western pavilions (yōkan) for the purpose of reception on their estates. The equivalent for men of lesser means was a Western room or suite of rooms affixed to one side of the house, appointed with chairs, tables, curtains, and the other necessaries of a Victorian parlor, to be used as a reception room and study. Houses built in this manner were known as wayō setchū, or "Japanese-Western eclectic." The opposition of Japanese and Western in wayō setchū was functional as well as stylistic. Two complete material and cultural systems were embodied in the contrast of kimono and Western clothes, chair-sitting and floor-sitting, sliding paper shōji and glass windows. The early eclectic house posed a monolithic Westernness against the indigenous, dictating not only distinct materials and construction for each, but a distinct planning system and orthography.

During the World War I economic boom, the clear stylistic dichotomy between West and East became more complexly nuanced. Pattern books, the collections of house plans, photos, and specifications written originally for builders, began to develop a popular market at this time and exploded in number in the early 1920s. Their contents reveal the monolithic West being replaced by a catalog of national types from which to borrow. As the stylistic palette became richer, facades came to manifest clear distinctions of taste. "Culture" signifying both the illusion of a universal measure of value and the desire for what was newest, was making houses part of the endless differentiating process of fashion. It would be a mistake to imagine, however, that the new fashions connoted by "culture" were universally embraced. On the contrary, satires and criticisms are easier to find in writing on the culture house and other "cultured" goods than earnest propaganda. "Culture" started depreciating in the rhetorical market even before the original Culture Village had closed its gates. Each particular feature of the culture house quickly suffered ridicule from some quarter.

"People think a Western-style house has to have red tiles to be new," wrote the architect and educator Nishimura Isaku in 1922. "The red tiles called 'French tile' are too red, and uninteresting in shape. The ones I find the most repulsive, and also the ones I see most often, are the cement tiles with some ochre-like pigment applied to the surface." Nishimura went on to criticize steep roofs, broad gable boards, and the fashion for painted half-timbers. In a capping condemnation, he remarked, "what Japanese do thinking it's new is always out of date in the West." Blaming recent German design trends for the current fad, he urged readers to throw away their German pattern books.[12]

During and after the Ueno Exposition, writers in the architectural and popular press offered similar assessments, some focusing on aesthetic features, others on questions of practicality.[13] This range of criticisms should not be read as evidence that "the public" rejected new house designs. What was taking place, rather, was a multiplication of publics, public purveyors, and public spokesmen, and a fragmentation in the field of taste. Underlying this was the larger breakdown of a unitary progressive discourse resulting from the participation of a vastly expanded educated class. Nishimura's criticism of culture houses may be seen in this context as the position of a vanguard intellectual finding his monopoly of Western knowledge challenged in the market by the superficial knowledge of parvenus without comparable cultural capital. Pattern-book and magazine writers were quick to adopt features of dominant-class aesthetics and to promote them with an enthusiastic tone of consumer liberalism. Responding to the incursion of these new players in the game, the "taste-makers" — both established and avant-garde — sought to shift the ground. Thus, in the late 1920s, elite architects and writers were finding that the culture house idea had "gone too far" or been "poorly executed" by ignorant builders. This became a standard trope in the introductions to books by elite architects, including the architect who had presided over the original "Culture Village" in 1922.[14]

Cultural contest in two texts

Comparison of two examples from the welter of popular books on house design published in the 1920s may serve to luminate the contrast between establishment architect and cultural intermediary. Yamada Jun's *Ie o tateru hito no tame ni* (For the Person Building a House, 1928) (Fig. 4) and Nose Kyūichirō's *Sanjū tsubo de dekiru kairyō*

Fig. 4 *"A Japanese Style Culture House" (from Yamada Jun,* Ie o tateru hito no tame ni, *1928). Use of windows instead of sliding doors and surrounding corridors, in addition to the absence of garden walls, mark this as a "culture house."*

jûtaku (Reformed Houses Under Thirty Tsubo, 1924) are two books written for general audiences. They both follow a common formula, combining critical pronouncements on the present state of Japanese middle-class housing with the authors' own house designs and simple descriptions, including a minimum of technical information. Both authors promote their designs as culture houses, using the common rhetoric of the era; the houses are described as scientific, efficient, and hygienic. But other aspects of their descriptions, and of the designs themselves, differ significantly. While I have only limited information about the background of the authors, the writing and architectural designs in these two works delineate two strategies in the field of "culture house" production, each suggesting the characteristics of a distinct social position.

The difference of social position is suggested first in what the two books tell of their authors' biographies. Yamada Jun, we learn from his introduction, was a graduate of Tokyo Imperial University who had completed the proverbial "grand tour" of Europe and the United States in 1922. *For the Person Building a House* also contains two prefaces praising Yamada's work, the first by Satō Kōichi, Professor of Architecture at Waseda University. In contrast, little can be gleaned about Nose Kyūichirō. While Yamada is a well-documented figure in the history of the Society of Japanese Architects, Nose is unrecorded in the institutional history, and is today little more than the author of a paperback found in a used-book shop. His name is preceded by no title, and his text bears no preface by a senior member of the profession.

The two texts take different positions in relation to their readership and to the building trade. Yamada defends the boundaries of the architectural profession, beginning with a condemnation of the general run of culture houses (which by 1928 was formulaic), and including long diatribes against ignorant builders (even describing violent confrontations he had had on construction sites), and against clients who do not give complete authority over the design to their architects. By contrast, Nose is a populist. The cultured life, he tells us, does not require "money or dance lessons." His criticism is saved for people who do not understand that the cultured life is the "simple life." While Yamada emphasizes the sanctity of the specialist's role, Nose teaches readers to draw house plans.

Two distinct culture-house aesthetics emerge from the two texts' illustrations and language, and from the house designs themselves. Nose's book contains only sketches, in a stylized, uneven freehand, while Yamada includes photographs and hard-line plans, with center lines drawn through fixtures and furniture. We recognize Nose's inclusion of his own sketches as distinctly modern, because they communicate a sense of artistic spontaneity through the medium of mechanical reproduction. It also intimates to the reader the simplicity of the houses, and the ease of designing one's own (Fig. 5). Yamada's use of illustrations, and particularly photographs, is also unequivocally modern, but this is the modernity of scientific rationalism, in which the image claims to represent objective information.

The preferred modifiers in Nose's and Yamada's writing further imply the difference of positioning in the social field. Nose's aesthetic gives primacy to immediate
effects, described with adjectives such as "simple" and "cheerful" (kan'i, tanoshii).
Yamada's aesthetic implies lineage and codification, through adjectives such as
"authentic" and "harmonious" (jun, chôwa shita). Categories of architectural style are
vague for Nose, whose designs are generally in an unspecified eclectic style. Yamada's
designs are stylistically eclectic too, but the elements of the mix are carefully distinguished. His examples include houses from various parts of Europe, the United States,
and Japan, classified by national origin of both the designer and the style employed.
Yamada thus demonstrates his expertise as an aesthetic arbiter in the classification of
national styles and periods. He finds his own aesthetic resolution in a fusion of English
Gothic revival and "authentic" Japanese style. Yamada's architectural strategies thus
reveal the position taken by established intellectuals faced with the challenge of popular
imitators. While making proprietary claims on Western knowledge, the source of all
that could be vanguard, he speaks at the same time from the comfort of an elite native
style already canonized as "authentic," the source of all that could be traditional.

Nose's designs call for color, promoting red roof tiles and painted wood, in contrast to the traditional grays and browns of unfinished wood and earth which Yamada's
designs maintain. Flower boxes are the final accent to Nose's culture houses. Bright,
unconcealed, quick to grow, and immediately gratifying, they are the antithesis of the

Fig. 5 *"A New Style of House" (from Nose Kyūichirō, Sanjū tsubo de dekiru kairyō jūtaku, 1924). Nose's aesthetic
gives primacy to immediate effects, and the style of rendering suggests spontaneity and do-it-yourself simplicity.*

traditionally status-marking Japanese garden adopted by Yamada, which is subtle, hidden from outside view, and gradually cultivated, presupposing commensurate investment in personal cultivation.[15]

Nose's embrace of "Western style" in its most visible forms — that is, in the exterior appearance of the house and its garden — recalls Bourdieu's portrait of the petit bourgeois who invests "in the minor forms of legitimate cultural goods," seeking to "[make] his home and himself look bigger than they are."[16] Nose may be seen, in effect, to be taking what was most readily available, the superficial and easily reproduced elements of a European house style. Put in less Veblenesque manner, the visual charm of the new, the progressive, and the imported, worked most upon those who were not invested with the old, the conservative, and the indigenous, and most immediately upon those who lacked, or did not care for, the intellectuals' more subtle criteria for distinguishing the genuinely avant-garde. Popular-market culture houses as a whole were often accused by intellectuals of being "Western" only on the outside, with little Western furniture in their conventional *tatami*-mat interiors. An elite architect like Yamada was in a position simultaneously to defend indigenous tradition (as he chose to define it) and to claim authority over which non-indigenous elements were significant and worthy of adoption.

Practical settings

The houses in these two books contrast equally as settings for social practices, suggesting the differences in the circumstances of their intended audiences. Yamada's plans have a discrete guest reception room, usually set next to the *genkan*, with Western furniture. Nose creates open plans without guest rooms or dining rooms, asserting in his text, "people who say they need a guest room and dining room don't understand anything about the cultured life. These are the same people who think that the cultured life is just dancing and playing the piano." Such criticisms of conservative standards and the outmoded up-to-dateness reflected in the classic "high-collar" accomplishments, whose acquisition took an investment of time, evoke the denial of class cultural markers that Bourdieu describes as part of the petit bourgeois "dream of social flying, a desperate effort to defy the gravity of the social field." In a subtle move against social hierarchy, Nose furnishes one corner of the living room with an L-shaped bench and chairs. Note that there is no seat of honor (*kamiza*) in this arrangement (Fig. 6).[17]

Yamada's reception rooms are studied adaptations of European interiors, but the author points out that the furniture has been arranged "with consideration of Japanese customs." This appears to refer to the placement of two armchairs directly facing one another across a small table in front of a mantelpiece, replicating in furniture the positions of host and guest in traditional elite practices of reception, with the mantle as *tokonoma* (Fig. 7). Western guest rooms of this kind, set next to the *genkan*, were the products of Meiji-period architectural reform. At the same time, elsewhere in the plan,

Fig. 6 *"A Small Single-story House" (interior) (from Nose Kyūichirō, Sanjū tsubo de dekiru kairyō jūtaku, 1924). Thwarting the spatial demands of formal reception, Nose designs a living room with L-shaped fixed seating.*

Yamada situates two linked *tatami* rooms across a corridor from the kitchen and maid's room. This reflects the so-called central corridor plan, also a product of late Meiji architectural reform, but carrying over the functions of similar large *tatami* spaces (*zashiki*) present in the houses of propertied families from earlier. Large *zashiki* were necessary for occasions such as weddings and funerals in propertied houses. Nose's houses have no large contiguous *tatami* spaces, as his presumed client does not carry the obligations of inheritance. In addition, few have maid's rooms.[18]

Finally, the houses in these two books differ strikingly in size. House designs in pattern books had been getting steadily smaller as architects came in contact with a broader market in the 1910s, but some of the houses represented in Nose's book are tiny indeed (for example, 320 square feet or 30 square metres). While Yamada's work reflects the trend toward smaller house design, the houses depicted are still well outside of the "middle" range of the housing stock of the time. *For the Person Building a House* includes houses with floor areas over 2000 square feet (186 square metres) among drawings labeled "small houses."[19]

These are only two texts, and their authors cannot stand in proxy for economic classes. The contrast, however, suggests that the proliferation of different "culture house" models represented a diffusion of the social field, and a competition of values among cultural producers. The consumers are more elusive. Were market-survey data of the kind Bourdieu used for France of the 1970s available for Taishō Japan, it might be possible to map each house type onto a particular "class fraction" in a similarly sociometric way. Here we can at least suggest what the logic of such a mapping might be. As small culture houses became common, those who already held property and houses (members of the haute bourgeoisie, we could call them) were positioned to become defenders of native tradition — just as elite architects and other representatives of the upper class in the field of cultural production often were. Those with the most cultural capital of Western knowledge could criticize the "false" or superficial

West of the new Japan (as did Nishimura Isaku and literati like Nagai Kafû, who built his own eccentric, but "truly Western," house, with no *tatami* on the floor, in 1920), while those struggling to join the field by acquiring their first house partook of the features of the dominant-class forms they could afford. Within this "petit bourgeoisie" one might further discern two tendencies: those whose middle-class status derived from jobs in modern industries and commerce and rested on secondary education would have been the primary consumers of the more overtly Western-oriented style and relatively unhierarchical plan of the stereotypical small culture house, while small entrepreneurial capitalists would tend to build or acquire the more hierarchically planned and conservative (though still modern) "eclectic-style" houses with one Western reception room. Hence it is not surprising to find evidence suggesting that the radically new culture houses tended to be built in the commuter suburbs, while houses built in the more conservative "eclectic style" with the interior corridor plan predominated in older neighborhoods.[20]

Beyond distinction

Yet, different meanings might be found in both cultured life discourse and in the culture consumer's moves in social space. As suggested by the instance of the inheriting son who occupies the permanent homestead while second and third sons go off to urban jobs and smaller houses, even siblings may differ markedly in their housing situations. Since the category of class is only meaningful if class traits are visible at the level of the family (which reproduces them), distinctions of house form do not correlate with class in any simple, mechanical sense.

It is possible, however, to interpret the work of cultural producers within the class-based categories provided by Bourdieu, yet still allow other factors to complicate the consumer profile. We could call Nose Kyûichirô's promotion of "simple living" making a virtue of necessity, and his criticism of dominant cultural practices the petit

Fig. 7 *Reception room designed in consideration of Japanese reception customs "without losing the traits of pure Western style architecture" (from Yamada Jun,* Ie o tateru hito no tame ni, *1928). Two armchairs face one another perpendicular to the fireplace, like host and guest in front of a* tokonoma *alcove.*

Fig. 8 "What is the Cultured Life?" postcards, by cartoonist Iizawa Tenyō (early 1920s). Wife: "Goodbye. You mustn't leave the house while I'm out. If I have visitors, please be sure to receive them politely." Husband: "Come home early." Wife: "Social duties won't allow it. I'll come home when I please." Reprinted from Shimizu Isao, Manga ni egakareta Meiji Taishō Shōwa, Tokyo, Kyōikusha, 1988, p. 94.

bourgeois "dream of social flying," yet still allow that many actual occupants of the small culture houses Nose designed possessed the same class background and education (or even came from the same families) as Yamada's wealthier clients. To accommodate such contingencies requires a very fluid model of social class with the potential for innumerable gradations.[21] The more politically significant issue, however, is whether class was really the main arena in which "cultured living" was being contested. The negative image purveyed by dominant intellectuals reveals that the occupants of these little houses on the margins of the city were themselves situated on the margins of legitimate culture. But must we regard the "petit bourgeois" consumer as Bourdieu insists, "in every respect a bourgeois writ small" or could he (or *she*) have been a less totally subjugable subject?

There are suggestions that the vanguard of cultured living was doing more than merely struggling to emulate the lifestyle of the elite without the fancy trappings. If we shift our focus from class to gender, social transgression rather than conformism appears to emerge at the core of the cultured life. Criticism of the cultured life as seen, for example, in *"Bunka seikatsu to wa"* (What is the Cultured Life?), a set of cartoon postcards printed in the early 1920s, equates "culture" with the threat of an inversion of gender roles (Fig. 8). This perceived threat bore direct relation to culture *houses*, because one of the features of many of the new houses was that, with fewer doors to the outside, they were easier to lock up and leave empty. Writers in the women's magazines stressed the freedom this afforded housewives, who no longer had to stay at home all day to watch the house.[22]

The culture house also represented isolation of the conjugal couple from the extended family, with dangerous social and erotic implications. Here, the very diminutiveness of Nose's smallest house designs offered a challenge to traditional authority, because these were spaces conceived for two or at most three. Journalist Yumeno Kyūsaku wrote caustically that the "cultured life" had no room for old folks or children.[23] In the scandalous and enormously popular novel *Chijin no ai* (A Fool's Love, 1924, translated into English as *Naomi*), Tanizaki Jun'ichiro rendered explicit the unspoken supplement to this traditionalist male critique by turning the intimate space of the culture house into the setting for a masochistic fantasy of female erotic domination.

This is not to say that the cultured life was all about sexual liberation, or perversion, or male fears of female sexuality. Male intellectual critics saw the cultured life tied to indulgence of private desires in many forms. It bears noting that the fantasy initially concocted by Tanizaki's Jōji, which forms the basis of the whole novel, is one of "playing house," and that the first thing Jōji and Naomi do is to find a culture house and decorate it together. Tanizaki refers to the stage for their pas de deux in quotation marks as a "fairy-tale house." This is a quotation in a quite literal sense, since similar phrases were common in the home design features of magazines such as *The Housewife's Companion*. Like Nose's pattern book of culture houses, women's magazines described the new models they proffered as "cosy" (*kojinmari shita*), "comfortable" (*igokochi yoi*), bright (*akarui*), and cheerful (*tanoshii*). Written for and sometimes by women, articles objectified "home" not merely as the site of childrearing and domestic labor, but as a personal artistic project.

In a more subtle way than the unbridled promiscuity of Tanizaki's Naomi, the feminine tastes represented in *The Housewife's Companion* challenged gender categories formulated in the course of Meiji modernization. Articles on house style and interiors positioned the female consumer–reader beyond the bounds of her established duties as "good wife, wise mother," and beyond her traditional aesthetic purview, which had been limited to the decoration of her own body for male consumption. Here, through the cultural mediation of *The Housewife's Companion* and other publications, she could look and choose in the male sphere of architecture. The regime of domesticity — domestic hygiene, domestic economy, and all the other rationalizations the Daily Life Reform League advocated — was assigning women new authority as modern homemakers. Specularization of the house as mass image now licensed extending that authority to the aesthetics of the domestic environment.

Articles about house design in *The Housewife's Companion*, at least those whose author was identified, were almost all by men. The magazine did have female reporters, however, and commonly ran descriptive pieces based on visits to new houses by members of the magazine staff, some of whom were women.[24] One early piece of this kind, written in 1920 (before the birth of the neologism "culture house") under the byline "Tsuruko," describes a "small Western house" the writer had spied from the train near Ôfuna station, south of Tokyo.[25] The writer tells of her encounter with the house almost as if recounting a romantic intrigue, from her first glimpse of it through the train window to the moment she strikes up the courage and gains admittance. Painting the scene in words, her description evokes mystery and visual allure:

> at dusk, with the setting sun glowing red on the white walls and on the glass of the bay window containing flowers, a fine wisp of smoke rising from the green chimney, one is impressed with a certain storybook-like poignancy. In the morning ... the red tiles of the roof are bathed in the brilliant light of the sun, and with the curtains in the window open, the sight of a day about to begin appears beautiful and vivid, as if one were looking at it through a magnifying glass.[26]

Announcing her physical mobility through the story of discovery, then sketching a verbal tableau of unusual intimacy, she adopts a role seldom available to women at the time: pursuing and visually possessing the object of her desire. The exotic shapes and bright colors of the Western house make it a peculiarly specular object. At the same time, what enables the reporter's fantasy is the fact that her object is also something safe, an icon of domestic bliss.

Even the sanctioned, thoroughly feminine pursuit of *shugei* — small handcrafts such as needlepoint, lace, and knitting — was breaking gender boundaries in the culture house. The decoration of formal rooms in the bourgeois house, which consisted mainly of selecting objects for the decorative alcove, had previously been considered a male prerogative. As writers on *shugei* sought new applications for the expertise they purveyed, they urged female readers to decorate otherwise spartan interiors with small items of their own manufacture. The use of fabric to wrap, cover, and drape, combined with the choice of rounder, softer forms of furniture, such as the ubiquitous rattan chair, contributed to a tactile feminization of the home.[27] In *The Housewife's Companion* of June 1926, an anonymous article on interior decorating for summer encouraged readers to sew light printed-cotton curtains to hang in front of the cabinets and *shoin* window, spread pieces of linen crossing one another over a table, hang a cover over the electric light, and if the *tatami* mats were not new, spread something called "Taiwan Panama" over them. The author of the article may have been a man, but he represented little of the older canon of male taste (which limited decorative objects to the *tokonoma* alcove), treating the room rather as a creative opportunity for female readers. The accompanying illustration depicted a room occupied by two women in kimono, with a small boy sitting on a rattan chair in the background.[28] In late 1925, the indomitable architect–ethnographer Kon Wajirō cataloged all of the belongings in the three-room house of a young Waseda University colleague and his wife. In addition to such items redolent of the "cultured life" as the Mitsukoshi-bought rattan furniture, the piano, and the gramophone with Western record collection, the inventory is characterized by the prominence of decorative odds and ends made by the mistress of the household, including cushions, two lampshades, and curtains.[29]

The liberal ethics of cultural intermediaries permitted a blurring of boundaries between masculine architecture — a modern, Westernizing, and public pursuit — and feminine personal ornament, considered traditional, native, and private. This kind of transgression did not threaten the social order in the way that the freedom to leave the home did, but it formed part of a general destabilization of the established, homologous categories that had defined domestic interiors as well as public space. For an elite architect like Yamada, the women's magazine reader, with little legitimate cultural capital of her own, embodied the undiscriminating middle-brow consumer whose emergence threatened the hegemony of rational bourgeois men.[30] Beyond the regimes of hygiene and efficiency, or enveloped in the same house with them, here was a domesticity that was playful, indulgent, and, in the eyes of some, transgressive. The culture house was both a place the modern woman could leave and a site for her to remake.

Concluding thoughts: Everyday life in question

One way around the question of whether to read the "cultured life" as conforming to predictable class categories or as something more radical is to zoom out from the intimacy of the home and take in the whole landscape of everyday practices. Satō Kōichi's preface to Yamada Jun's book speaks of a recent "awakening to daily life (*seikatsu*)." Morimoto and others wrote in a similar vein of making the transition from "existence" (*seizon*) to "living" (*seikatsu*). This *seikatsu* can only be understood as the material life generated by modern capitalism, a world of new commodities to be negotiated. Houses are typically the largest, most durable of commodities, the last in which permanent investments are made. This is part of the economic logic behind Bourdieu's notion of *habitus*, the congeries of dispositions that structure an individual's perceptions and tastes, which is ultimately rooted in the domestic environment. What happens when the form of the dwelling, as an objectification of daily life, is brought to the surface of consciousness, made negotiable?

The dominant class of Meiji embraced reform, sacrificing a considerable measure of the stability of a dominant-class *habitus*. The new middle classes of Taishō could go a step further because they had less tradition to part with, so that a certain anti-conventionalism could appear to be the proper convention to follow. The 1920s in Japan, then, were a period when houses, household goods, and domestic space were coming to be manipulated politically, not only in the state politics of "housing," but (indeed, far more extensively) in the social politics of the mass market. In a fragmented social space, cultured life discourse could not be contained entirely within the normative, as it generated images that implied alternately the exposure of everyday practice to the even light of rationality and the pursuit of secret fantasies in a hidden space of play.

Notes

1   The source for much scholarly understanding of Taishō culture is the still-authoritative study by Minami Hiroshi, *Taishō bunka*, Tokyo, Keisō Shobō, 1965.

2   A classic analysis of the meaning of "culture" for Taishō intellectuals is offered in Harry Harootunian, "Introduction: A Sense of an Ending and the Problem of Taishō," in Harootunian and Bernard Silberman (eds), *Japan in Crisis: Essays in Taishō Democracy*, Princeton, Princeton University Press, 1974, pp. 3–28. Like Kamishima Jirō and the other Japanese scholars he critiques, Harootunian restricts his focus to "culture" (and "culturalism" — *bunkashugi*) in the field of thought (*shisō*).

3   On Morimoto, see Terade Kōji, *Seikatsu bunkaron e no shōtai*, Tokyo, Kōbundō, 1995, pp. 92–104.

4   These are the characteristics cited by Nishiyama Uzō, *Nihon no sumai*, 2, Tokyo, Keisō Shobō, 1976, p. 66.

5   On the Daily Life Reform League and other similar campaigns directed at women, see Sheldon Garon, *Molding Japanese Minds: The State in Everyday Life*, Princeton, NJ, Princeton University Press, 1997, pp. 115–45, and Chino Yōichi, *Kindai Nihon fujin kyōiku shi: taisei nai fujin dantai no keisei katei o chūshin ni*, Tokyo, Domesu Shuppan, 1979.

6   "Yūshiki musan kaikyū" from a newspaper article reprinted in Fujiya Yōetsu, "Mejiro bunka mura," in Yamaguchi Hiroshi (ed.), *Kōgai jūtakuchi no keifu: Tōkyō no den'en yūtopia*, Tokyo, Kajima Shuppankai, 1988, p. 153. "Yōfuku saimin" from Ishizuka Hiromichi and Narita Ryūichi, *Tōkyōto no hyakunen*, Tokyo, Yamakawa Shuppan, 1986, p. 128.

7   Pierre Bourdieu, *Distinction: A Social Critique of the Judgement of Taste*, trans. by Richard Nice, Cambridge, Mass., Harvard University Press, 1984, pp. 360–6. In Bourdieu's model of society, players in a given cultural field deploy goods, discourses, and everyday practices in a competition of taste. Individual position is determined by the volume of economic and cultural capital each player possesses. The relative amounts of different forms of capital distinguish "class fractions." Formal education, Bourdieu stresses, has a particularly powerful role in reinforcing class dispositions. In Japan's case, since higher education involved a lot of Western texts, knowledge of the West became an important marker of educational and cultural capital.

8   *Shufu no tomo* (published from 1917) and *Kingu* (1925) are usually considered to be the first vehicles of a more genuinely "mass" print culture. Maeda Ai describes the generational transition among writers of the popular fiction which these magazines serialized. See Maeda, "Taishō kōki tsūzoku shōsetsu no tenkai, fujin zasshi no dokusha sō," in *Kindai dokusha no seiritsu*, Tokyo, Iwanami Dōjidai Raiburarii, 1993, pp. 211–83.

9   On the relationship between bourgeois reformers and the state, see Sheldon Garon, *Molding Japanese Minds: The State in Everyday Life*, Princeton, NJ, Princeton University Press, 1997. On the increasingly competitive market for positions in the bourgeois professions, see Earl Kinmonth, *The Selfmade Man in Meiji Japanese Thought: From Samurai to Salaryman*, Berkeley, Calif., University of California Press, 1981.

10   *Tōkyō Asahi shinbun*, December 21, 1921, p. 5.

11   Reprinted in *Shinbun shūroku Taishōshi dai 10 kan*, Tokyo, Taishō Shuppan Kabushiki Kaisha, 1978, p. 518.

12   Nishimura Isaku, *Sōshoku no enryō*, Tokyo, Bunka Seikatsu Kenkyūkai, 1922, p. 69.

13   Fujiya Yōetsu, "Heiwahaku bunka mura shuppin jūtaku no sehyō ni tsuite," *Nihon kenchiku gakkai taikai gakujutsu kōen kōgaishū*, October 1982, pp. 2363–4.

14   Ōkuma Yoshikuni, "Sōsetsu," in Jiji Shinpō Kateibu (eds), *Ie o sumiyoku suru hō*, Tokyo, Bunka Seikatsu Kenkyūkai, 1927, p. 6.

15   Ironically, Yamada does not illustrate "tasteful" Japanese gardens, instead accompanying photographs of his houses with critical remarks about the gardeners hired by his clients spoiling the visual effect of the

architecture. The implication is that the house and garden ought to be a self-contained *Gesamtkunstwerk*, composed under the direction of the architect.

16   Bourdieu, *Distinction*, p. 321.

17   Social reformers at the turn of nineteenth the century had used seating arrangement and the shape of the table to embody horizontal social relations. A group called the "Band of Idealists" gathered in 1902 at a T-shaped table "set without any formal seating order or ranking." In Nose's designs we see this anti-hierarchical vision being marketed for the first time. See David Ambaras, "Social Knowledge, Cultural Capital, and the New Middle Class in Japan, 1895–1912," *Journal of Japanese Studies*, vol. 2, no. 1, 1998, pp. 1–33.

18   It should be noted that the absence of these spaces is not necessarily a direct gauge of economic class, as non-inheriting second sons from property-owning families could maintain small households.

19   Two thousand square feet is substantially larger than the average house size for any occupational category listed in a survey of "middle-class" housing conducted by the Tokyo Prefecture Social Bureau in 1921. The survey included bank professionals making over 300 yen per month. Tōkyōfu Shakaika, *Tōkyōshi oyobi kinsetsu chōson chūtō kaikyū jūtaku chōsa*, Tokyo, Tōkyōfu Shakaika, 1923, p. 45 (chart).

20   For houses on the interior corridor plan in an older residential development, see Inaba Keiko, "Abe-sama no tsukutta gakusha machi Nishikatachō," in Yamaguchi (ed.), *Kōgai jūtakuchi no keifu*, pp. 48–60. Since few small culture houses have survived, it is difficult to ascertain where they were most concentrated. In a 1925 survey near Asagaya station in the western suburbs of Tokyo, Kon Wajirō judged 20 percent of the 588 houses he counted to be "culture style" (*bunka shiki*), while only 5 percent were "eclectic." Kon Wajirō, "Kōgai fūzoku zakkei," reprinted in Kon Wajirō and Yoshida Kenkichi, *Moderunorojio "Kōgengaku,"* 1930 (facsimile edition, Gakuyō Shobō, 1986), p. 115.

21   This is in fact the kind of model Bourdieu appears ultimately to adopt in *Distinction*, although he seeks to demonstrate that every class fraction can be defined on the basis of empirical criteria.

22   This is mentioned, for example, in "Anka de tateta benrina ie," *Shufu no tomo*, vol. 1, no. 1, March 1917, p. 36.

23   Yumeno Kyūsaku, "Gaitō kara mita Tōkyō no rimen" (1924), reprinted in *Yumeno Kyūsaku zenshū*, vol. 2, Tokyo, Chikuma Bunko, 1992, p. 141.

24   Shufu no Tomosha (ed.), *Shufu no Tomosha no gojūnen*, Tokyo, Shufu no Tomosha, 1969, p. 174.

25   Tsuruko, "Shumi to jitsuyō o kaneru chiisana yōkan," *Shufu no tomo*, December 1920, pp. 126–7. The author is almost certainly Matsuda Tsuruko (Tsuruji), the magazine's first female reporter. *Shufu no Tomo no gojūnen*, pp. 65, 88.

26   Tsuruko, "Shumi to jitsuyō," p. 126.

27   The association of textile production and women is found in almost all cultures since neolithic times. I do not mean to claim that pliability, softness, and roundness are intrinsically female characteristics, however. The point is rather that *shugei*'s feminization of the domestic interior functioned through terms provided by a Western discourse of femininity which construed them as such. This aesthetic development cannot be subsumed solely to either gender or national–cultural polarities — the different cultural variables constantly articulate with one another.

28   "Ippen shita natsu no shitsunai sōshoku," *Shufu no tomo*, vol. 10, no. 6, June 1926, p. 33. When the magazine sponsored a *shugei* competition in 1923, entries were judged by a panel of men. *Shufu no Tomosha no gojūnen*, pp. 110–11.

29   Kon Wajirō, "Shin katei no shinamono chōsa" (1926), reprinted in Kon and Yoshida, *Moderunorojio "Kōgengaku,"* pp. 164–5.

30   I borrow this interpretation from scholars in other contexts. Janice Radway's analysis of critics' attitudes toward middle-brow cultural institutions like the Book-of-the-Month Club makes an analogous point for the literary field. See Radway, "On the Gender of the Middlebrow Consumer and the Threat of the Culturally Fraudulent Female," *South Atlantic Quarterly*, vol. 93, no. 4, Fall 1994, pp. 871–93. See also Andreas Huyssen, *After the Great Divide: Modernism, Mass Culture, Postmodernism*, Bloomington, Ind., Indiana University Press, 1986. Nishikawa Yūko notes the same point with regard to male Japanese architects in the postwar period. Nishikawa, "Otoko no ie, onna no ie, seibetsu no nai heya: zoku sumai no hensen to 'katei' no seiritsu," in Wakita Haruko and Susan Hanley (eds), *Jendaa no Nihonshi 2: shutai to hyōgen, shigoto to seikatsu*, Tokyo, Tōkyō Daigaku Shuppankai, 1995, p. 623.

CHAPTER SEVEN

The Café
Contested Space of Modernity in Interwar Japan

Elise K. Tipton

Why study cafés? In 1978 Steve Bradshaw wrote a book on café society which, so far as he knew, was "the first attempt to evoke the atmosphere of those nights" in cafés which fostered major cultural and political movements such as Impressionism, Surrealism, and the French Revolution,[1] but he wrote nothing about cafés in Japan, nor anywhere outside Europe or the United States. His EuroAmericanism is probably not surprising to scholars of non-Western societies, but also notable is his claim for the originality of his subject. This points to the recent direction of historians' attention to social sites and institutions like the café which provided the context for popular culture.

Although the "new social history" has become a respectable field since Bradshaw wrote, its relative newness in the historical profession raises the question of why café society merits scholarly consideration. In particular, in the case of Japanese history of the 1920s and 1930s, why should we redirect attention away from the important political developments which are bound up with explaining World War II? The answer lies in the writings of Japanese contemporaries themselves, who saw the café as a central symbol of modernity. In these writings we can see that, like modernity as a whole, the café provoked reactions running the gamut from glowing praise and enthusiasm to severe moral condemnation and rejection.

In one contemporary writer's eye, the café was not simply *one* symbol of modernity, but in fact *the* symbol of modernity. According to Murobushi Kôshin (Takanobu), the modern city meant liberation, not only liberation of the townspeople (*chônin*) from their low status in the feudal hierarchy of classes or liberation of the intellect from the Neo-Confucian orthodoxy, but also liberation for women, for relations between men and women, and for drinking. The café symbolized this modern liberated spirit and, as a symbol of the process of modernization, ranked in significance with establishment of the Diet. In fact, Murobushi went further, claiming that the café was even more signifi-cant than the Diet! Why? Because whereas constitutional government represented the aspirations of the ruling elites, the café expressed the ideology of the petit bourgeiosie. According to Murobushi, the Diet represented the "dying enlightenment" of the older generation, while the café represented youth and the future. In other words, if in historical periods the Diet represented the early bourgeois era, the café represented the late bourgeois period.[2]

The café, to Murobushi, was unique to the modern city. Earlier civilizations had enjoyed alcoholic beverages and coffee — the former a narcotic, the latter a stimulant — but none united the two "dialectically" like the café. Socrates drank alcohol in the house of a prostitute, but he never knew a café. Neither did the Romans. What Murobushi meant is that none of these earlier figures had ever known a *Japanese* café. In his claims he was in effect defining the café as symbolic of both a universal and a distinctively Japanese modernity. While eschewing his hyperbole and glorification of the café, I would like to focus on certain elements in Murobushi's and other contemporary depictions of the café and to highlight those aspects of universality and particularity.

The pre-earthquake café

The Japanese café of the 1920s and 1930s was not only unlike cafés that Westerners would most likely envisage, but also unlike the Japanese café of earlier times. The first one appeared in Tokyo in 1911, or, more precisely, the first to be called a "café" was established then, for Western-style eating places had existed in Japan since the 1870s. Its name, "Kafê Purantan" (Café Printemps), revealed its European, and especially French, inspiration (see Fig. 1). At this time Western food was still in the process of

Fig. 1 Café Printemps, after 1911

gaining popularity, so it was "ultra-modern boys" and especially writers, intellectuals, and artists, such as the novelist Ozaki Kôyô's disciples, who gathered at Café Printemps and the other cafés established at this time.[3] In fact, the owner of Café Printemps was the Western-style painter Matsuyama Shôzô. These people wanted a gathering place in the city where they could talk freely and drink, a place like the salons for artists and intellectuals in Europe. During its first six months, Café Printemps even operated as an intellectuals' salon with a club membership of about thirty-five painters, novelists, musicians, politicians, and critics.[4] Although the requirement of membership was soon dropped, artists and intellectuals continued to dominate the clientele, which inhibited others from participating in café life. Sitting around on wooden chairs at tables with white

Fig. 2 *Waitresses and patrons at Café Lion, after 1911*

tablecloths, they ate Western food and enjoyed the wide variety of Western cocktails proffered by the café waitresses. Ishikado Harunosuke observed in 1934 that the service provided by the waitresses differed totally from that of the present. The Café Printemps's waitresses were elegant and beautiful, and what he described as "noble virgin-types" were respected. Cafés at this early stage were places where one ate Western food, and where the service was of secondary importance.[5]

This applied as well to large cafés such as Kafê Raion (Café Lion), which was established in Ginza four months after Café Printemps's success. Three stories tall, it presented a fashionable and imposing sight whose trend-setting modernity attracted people seeking something new in Western restaurants. Café Lion became famous for its thick and tender beef steaks which cost about 50 sen. In contrast to the predominantly artist–intellectual patrons of Café Printemps, the patrons of Café Lion came from other walks of life as well. Situated at the main intersection in the center of Ginza, the café invited in many more ordinary people visiting the busy district, although the café for "the masses" was still to come. Patrons entering Café Lion could first stop at the bar or salon, and then proceed to the second-floor dining and entertainment rooms where they might listen to the singing of a Shinbashi geisha. Alternatively, they might go up to the Renaissance-style third floor where, if required, they had the novel choice of relieving themselves in either Western or Japanese toilets.[6] The young waitresses, dressed demurely in kimonos and white aprons, simply served food (see Fig. 2).[7] According to Ishikado, the waitresses gradually began to change from around

1915–16, in his eyes deteriorating as they began to offer erotic services and in some cases develop a paramour relationship with certain customers. Until the Great Kantō Earthquake of 1923, however, Café Lion remained a well-known and popular place primarily for food rather than the service itself, and cafés mainly attracted an intellectual, cultural clientele.

The "café era"

According to Ishikado and many other pre-World War II commentators, this changed after the earthquake, which became a major dividing point in the history of cafés and of Tokyo as a city. The earthquake created the conditions for a new phase in the history of Japanese modernity as well, which we can see reflected in the changing nature of the café. It is no exaggeration to describe the decade after the earthquake as "the café era." The number of cafés and café waitresses shot up sharply and rapidly — contemporaries referred to "massification" (taishūka). In 1922 there were twenty cafés on Ginza's main street; in 1929 there were fifty.[8] In 1925 a Central Employment Agency survey counted 7319 café waitresses in Tokyo and 4230 in Osaka.[9] According to a police survey just four years later, the number of waitresses in Tokyo had jumped to 15,559, working in 6187 cafés and 1345 bars.[10] A later national survey in 1940 found that there had been 27,532 cafés and bars throughout the country and 66,840 waitresses in 1930. The number of cafés and bars climbed to a peak of 37,065 in 1934 and thereafter declined to 29,064 in 1940. The number of waitresses continued to increase beyond 1934, reaching a peak of 111,700 in 1936 before it decreased to 91,946 in 1940.[11]

In Tokyo after the earthquake, cafés had sprouted up "like bamboo shoots after a rain" all over the city,[12] but were concentrated in entertainment districts known as "sakariba'" (literally, bustling places) such as Ginza, Asakusa, Kanda, Shinjuku, and Shibuya. In terms of defining modernity, we need to focus our attention on Ginza. Ginza had represented the modern since its reconstruction in the Meiji period. During the previous Tokugawa period it had not been a bustling commercial center compared to the Nihonbashi area to the north, but after a fire in 1872 the governor of the city decided that Ginza should be rebuilt in brick to act as a model of fireproofing for the rest of the city. This suited the desire of influential political leaders, such as Inoue Kaoru and Mishima Michitsune, to give Tokyo a modern, meaning European, appearance in order to help achieve elimination of the unequal treaties.[13] The new Ginza — or Bricktown, as it was known — was built in the Georgian style to the designs of the English architect Thomas Waters. It failed to inspire further fireproof construction, but did attract what we might call tourists to look at it as a model of "civilization and enlightenment."[14] Thereafter began the custom of "ginbura," or strolling in Ginza, which was to have its heyday in the 1920s and 1930s.

Although associated with the modern from the 1870s, it was not until after the earthquake that Ginza became a symbol of modernity for all Japanese. According to

Andô Kôsei, people in the countryside used to think of Asakusa or perhaps Ueno or Nijûbashi when you said "Tokyo," but by 1930 what they immediately thought of was Ginza.[15] Modern department stores catering to the new office employees and salaried classes emerged from the ashes of the earthquake to draw the crowds during the day. Instead of selling only expensive specialty or imported items as in the past, temporary department stores had offered all sorts of goods for everyday living in response to the needs of urban dwellers in the wake of the earthquake. Department store owners had in this way discovered what was to become in the post-World War II period a vast new market.

However, during the interwar years the crowds were not always able to buy, nor did they have to because of a revolution in modes of retailing. Mitsukoshi had already introduced glass display cases after the Russo-Japanese War in its Nihonbashi store, so that customers could readily see the goods for sale and browse instead of requiring a salesperson to bring them out from a storage area.[16] An innovation after the earthquake, however, brought in the masses — customers did not have to take off their shoes.[17] Ginza department store dining rooms also eliminated the necessity of sitting on *tatami* floors to eat. It now became respectable to keep on one's coat as well as shoes when sitting on a chair at a Western-style table. Women, notably a growing number of middle-class working women, for the first time felt comfortable eating out in public.[18] "Window-shopping" (*ginbura*) became the typical way to pass the time in Ginza during the day, as we see in numerous photographs of "modern girls" (*modan gâru* or *moga*) and "modern boys" (*modan bôi* or *mobo*) breezing along the streets or gazing into shop window displays as described by Gennifer Weisenfeld's in chapter 5. It is what the social commentator Gonda Yasunosuke had in mind when he located "modern life" (*modan seikatsu*) in the streets of the city, rather than in middle-class homes or working-class areas.[19]

According to Gonda, cafés, along with bars, restaurants, dance halls, and cinemas, acted as extensions of the streets.[20] The post-earthquake cafés and bars turned Ginza into an entertainment as well as commercial center, a gathering place by night as well as by day. Like the post-earthquake department stores, these invited in the masses, but especially young people among the new middle class of office workers, salespeople, and minor government officials. As many commentators put it, the cafés and bars made Ginza a "theater" or "stage" upon which modern life was performed.[21] And it was a "first-class stage." Ginza continued to exude class and elegance as well as the new and the beautiful.[22] Shops in the suburbs carrying anything new attached "Ginza" to their names — Ginzadô, Ginzatei, Kafê Ginza.[23]

Cafés flourished in other districts, especially Asakusa and increasingly Shinjuku, but they did not possess the top-class image of Ginza cafés. Before the earthquake, Asakusa, in particular Rokku, the Sixth District, had been the most popular *sakariba* for modern entertainments. After the earthquake it remained the most bustling of *sakariba* and the place to go for the latest movies and musical reviews, but although Asakusa cafés attracted masses of people from all over the city and of all classes and all ages, they were "cheap and easy" and lacked the high tone of Ginza cafés.[24] The lower education level of café waitresses in Asakusa compared to Ginza reflected these differences.[25] The smaller proportion of young people there compared to patrons in Ginza also foreshadowed Asakusa's gradual decline in the 1930s. Kawabata Yasunari, Nagai Kafū, and other famous Japanese writers maintained a soft spot for Asakusa, but even Kawabata said that Asakusa never produced anything of high quality. By the end of the 1930s it had truly given way to Ginza, as chronicled in Takami Jun's novel *Ikanaru hoshi no shita ni* (Under What Stars).[26]

Shinjuku also thrived in the late 1920s as extensions of the railway network stimulated growth of the western suburbs. Between 1920 and 1930 the population of Tokyo City declined from 2.2 to 2.1 million, whereas the population of the five surrounding counties (*gun*) increased from 1.2 to 2.9 million.[27] The westward and southward expansion of the population had begun in the early 1920s, but the earthquake accelerated the trend. Most of the new suburban dwellers came from the white-collar salaryman class, often referred to as "*yōfuku saimin*" (poor people in Western-style clothes), who were seeking cheaper housing. The extension of private as well as public railways enabled them to commute to the city to work.[28] The private railway companies also built or encouraged residential development, many of which were "culture houses" that Jordan Sand writes about in Chapter 6, and offered free or discounted rail fares for a certain time period to attract potential residents.[29] Shinjuku thrived as a transfer point for these commuters from the western suburbs, with a new station completed in 1925.[30] Mitsukoshi opened a branch store in 1924, and the forerunner of Isetan department store opened in 1926. One of the new private railway companies also opened up a retail business named Keiō Paradise in its terminal building.[31]

Entertainment flourished along with retailing. Shinjuku's licensed brothel quarter benefited from the earthquake destruction of the old Yoshiwara pleasure quarter. Modern cafés also mushroomed, and in the evening Shinjuku was more crowded than Ginza.[32] Some Shinjuku cafés had their waitresses dress in Western clothes, but the area appeared "more vulgar," even if more lively than Ginza.[33] According to Edward Seidensticker, "the modern boy and modern girl went to extremes thought unseemly and in bad taste by high Ginza."[34] Despite the common observations of vulgarity, some Shinjuku café waitresses reflected the new intelligentsia who also lived in larger numbers in the suburbs after the earthquake — "Marx boys" were conspicuous in Shinjuku cafés. According to one survey, Shinjuku café waitresses possessed a somewhat higher educational background than that of Ginza café waitresses, and considerably higher than that of Asakusa café waitresses.[35] Probably they were wives or daughters of the "*yōfuku saimin*" middle-class salarymen who lived in the western suburbs beyond

Shinjuku. Nevertheless, as a contemporary concluded, "although it is called the Great Shinjuku, there still lingers the mood of the outskirts."[36]

After the earthquake, many large cafés appeared on the main street of Ginza and also dozens of small cafés in the back streets, but it was not just greater numbers and the larger scale of the establishments that created "the café era" and new characteristics of the modern. As in pre-earthquake times, modern still meant Western, which is reflected in the names of the new cafés and bars being derived from English — Gondora (Gondola), Ginza Paresu (Ginza Palace), and Gurando Ginza (Grand Ginza). Their architecture and interior decor also continued to be foreign–inspired. In some cases this was attraction to the foreign as the exotic. Kafê Taigâ (Café Tiger), with its Chinese paintings on the walls and Chinoiserie decorative motifs, provides a striking example of this.[37] More common, however, was a shift in foreign influences from European to American ones, which was also evident in other aspects of urban culture. Modern now was increasingly associated with American things — speed, movies, and jazz. All three were directly or indirectly manifested in the cafés of the late 1920s and early 1930s.

The big new cafés of Ginza transformed the visual images of the modern city in both their interiors and exteriors. From the outside their blazing red and blue neon signs lit up the main street, a vision captured by a popular song of 1932, "Hana no Tôkyô" (Flowering Tokyo):

> Yoru no Ginza wa hotaru kagu
> Ren no kokoro o chirachira to
> Maneku hikari ni manekarete
> Kite miru tsuki no hosoi koto

> Ginza at night is a "firefly cage,"
> The flickering feeling of love.
> Drawn by the inviting lights
> I came and saw the moon. How thin it was.[38]

Moonlight could not compete with the dazzling "red lights, blue lights" of the Ginza cafés and bars (see Fig. 3).[39] Inside, the red and blue of the neon lights reappeared in stained-glass windows, and the use of silvery, light-reflective building materials, such as stainless steel, aluminum, glass, mirrors, and spotlights, reinforced the overall impression of brilliant light and contributed to a sense of modernity and richness. Café Maru and Ginza Palace led the way in these design innovations. On its first floor, Café Maru used silvery yen-shaped motifs on the partitions between tables, elsewhere light-reflective panels on the walls and shimmering decorative circles (see Fig. 4). Ginza Palace similarly made lavish use of glass mosaic tiles, milky white glass, metallic plates, and aluminum-plated pillars, and illuminated its ceilings with a ring of blue-colored neon lights.[40]

Fig. 3 *Ginza Palace, 1932*

Fig. 4 *Café Maru, fourth floor, 1932*

With these new cafés the distinction between cafés and bars on the one hand and *kissaten* (coffeeshops) on the other became clear. *Kissaten* were places where one went for a meal, not to enjoy alcoholic beverages. Cafés, like bars, offered Western alcoholic drinks, but could provide more food than bars and were usually more Western in their menus, décor, and ambience.[41]   Jazz music, big band not blues, contributed to the Western ambience and satisfied patrons' desire for a fast "tempo." Not all cafés played music, however.

The rise and fall of "ero" service

What came to distinguish the cafés of the late 1920s and 1930s from both their Japanese predecessors and their ostensible Western models was the changed role of the café waitresses (*jokyū*). In Murobushi Kōshin's depiction of the Japanese café, the café waitress was both the flower and spirit of the café. He observed that, unlike a European café, a Japanese café did not require music to be a café. One could even imagine a café in Japan without alcohol, he declared, but one could not imagine a café without waitresses.[42] From this we can see that the café in Japan after the earthquake had become a different place from its Meiji and even Taishō antecedents. It was no longer a place where Western food and drinks were of primary importance. Rather, service, and increasingly erotic service, became its chief attraction. However, while

Murobushi acknowledged the sexual attraction of the waitresses, he denied the café's primary function and appeal as a place for arranging sexual assignations. In his view the young generation was interested in "platonic" and "romantic" love, not sex, so it was an atmosphere of love (ren'ai) that brought young people to the café.[43]

Other commentators, though not as enamored of the café, also noted that the café provided one of the few places where young men and women could meet and mingle socially. In fact, there was no other place where young women and men could interact as easily, cheaply, or directly as in a café.[44] Geishas were expensive, too expensive for the young salarymen who comprised the majority of café patrons, and too complicated to arrange. One had to go through prescribed procedures at an introductory meeting (machiai) and follow certain etiquette to be entertained by a geisha. "Modern men want a flaming moment of pleasure," noted Murashima Yoriyuki.[45] In this "time of speed" the café enabled men to enjoy an erotic atmosphere openly and easily.[46] Moreover, modern young people wanted romance and an object for their sexual life which the café waitress as a "modern girl" provided.[47] Again, according to Murashima, it was less carnal desire than a "love feeling" (ren'ai kibun) that drew young men to the café.[48]

For women, the café in some views played an important role in their liberation. It offered an opportunity for work to young women without particular education or training, as well as opportunities for free love.[49] The 1920s saw the opening up of new occupations for women, especially middle-class women.[50] Besides farming and textile or other factory work, women could engage in work outside the home as typists, nurses, teachers, department store clerks, bus conductors, and switchboard operators. Young women from poor rural or urban families, however, did not possess the education or skills for many of these new jobs, nor for the traditional entertainment job of a geisha, and compared to farm or factory work, work in a café was less arduous even though the hours were long. It was also commonly thought that café waitressing paid more money than other jobs, and the celebrity status of some café waitresses attracted even well-known actresses to open cafés in Ginza.[51] According to a 1930 survey, café waitresses pointed to, first, a good income and, second, freedom as good aspects of their job.[52]

It is true that the waitresses were not employed as prostitutes and that men could have gone directly to either a licensed or unlicensed prostitute if sex was what they wanted. Prostitution was to remain a legal institution until 1956 despite the efforts of some Christian moral reformers to abolish it.[53] Nevertheless, several factors worked to push many café waitresses into prostitution after hours, and this became the basis for moral condemnation by a wide variety of social commentators and for the association of cafés with a social climate of "ero-guro-nansensu" (erotic-grotesque-nonsense). The café waitresses' provision of erotic or "ero" service also became a reason for their falling victim to police repression and control during the late 1920s and 1930s.

A number of explanations may be offered for the eroticization of the café waitress. Miriam Silverberg links it to a Japan-specific history of the sale of women's eroticized services in the medieval (c. 1150–1600) and early modern (c. 1600–1850s) periods, but at the same time emphasizes its modern context by pointing out a certain degree of agency played by the waitress in the commodification of eroticism.[54] Unlike the geisha, the café waitress was not bound like a slave by a contract to the café owner, nor did she have to accept just any patron into a sexual relationship like a licensed prostitute.[55] Hayashi Fumiko's best-selling novel *Hōrōki*, about a café waitress, on the one hand suggests the difficulty in reality of leaving an undesirable café. The heroine at one point wanted to quit a café patronized mostly by students and others who did not bring in much money for her, but she lacked the courage to leave because the café was very busy and short-staffed. She and another waitress finally slipped out through a window early one morning before anyone else was awake.[56]

On the other hand, surveys on café waitresses revealed high turnover rates, which indicate that waitresses moved from café to café quite easily. Ōbayashi Munetsugu's study of Osaka waitresses in 1930 found that almost one-third had worked at their present job five months or less and the majority between six and twelve months.[57] With the rapidly increasing number of cafés in the mid- and late 1920s, the demand for waitresses escalated too. People opening new cafés tried to hire waitresses from other cafés rather than advertising for new and inexperienced women. Then, when the Depression reduced patronage, café owners tried to lure more customers by hiring more waitresses. Large cafés in Tokyo and Osaka had 100 or more waitresses.

Hiring is not quite the right word here, for the café owner did not pay any wages to the waitresses, which is the reason that Depression-period café owners could increase the number of waitresses without increasing their expenses. In fact, it was the waitress who had to pay the owner for her meals and the employment of the cooks at the café. She was also responsible for the cost of any drinks, food, matches, or other items consumed by her patrons. Hayashi's heroine in *Hōrōki* at one point has to go to the police station to try to recover money from a man who left without paying for the meals and drinks he bought for himself and the waitresses. She succeeds, but if she had not, she would have had to pay the café owner herself.[58] Until 1929, café owners also collected fines (called *kisoku* in Osaka and *desen* in Tokyo) to penalize waitresses for being late for work (between 50 sen and 1 yen) or absent (between 1 and 2 yen, more for a weekend), and in addition charged them for any damage to furnishings caused by patrons.[59]

A waitress's remuneration came from tips, which in 1929 averaged about 2 yen a day in a big city *sakariba*, but about 50 sen on the outskirts of a city or in a country town. Contrary to popular belief, most waitresses did not earn a lot of money. At the end of the 1920s only a little over 2 percent earned more than 100 yen per month. Average incomes ranged between 30 and 50 yen per month, compared to the starting salary of 70–75 yen per month for a male clerk working for the Tokyo Metropolitan Government.[60] The money did not come in evenly over the course of a month, but peaked at the end of the month when salarymen were paid and dwindled with the thickness of their wallets around the middle of the month.[61] Out of this income the waitress also had expenses related to her work — kimonos (a new one each season), cosmetics, hairdresser, and laundry costs. A significant proportion of waitresses nevertheless saved some money each month, and many gave it to their families. This reflects the fact that the reason most commonly stated for becoming a waitress was financial, in particular to help with the family budget.[62] In Ôbayashi's survey of almost 2000 café waitresses in Osaka, although the largest proportion of waitresses lived with both parents (35.56 percent), a large number were supporting their divorced or widowed mothers (17.75 percent).[63] Another surprisingly large percentage (22.32 percent) were married.[64]

Both Marxist and non-Marxist social critics and government social agency officials blamed the tipping system and café owners' exploitation for the eroticization of café waitresses and the increasing incidence of prostitution after hours. Relying on tips encouraged waitresses to develop their skills at coquetry and seductive manipulation to obtain a larger tip, even though this sometimes meant they had to endure a man's disgusting behavior, as one respondent put it.[65] One government official concluded that poverty was the cause of their resorting to unlicensed prostitution.[66] Café owners also pressured waitresses to offer erotic services. As mentioned earlier, this occurred when the Depression stiffened competition for customers, but it was also attributed to an influx of capital from Osaka after the earthquake and with this, the spread of a flashier Kansai-style of café to Tokyo. Osaka cafés and waitresses were characterized as friendlier than Tokyo café waitresses; they did not put a distance between themselves and the customer. Proprietors had pushed this type of service, for example by having their waitresses stop wearing aprons so that they would be seen more as women rather than as workers and by telling them to chat with patrons and to behave like a friend or girlfriend.[67] Cafés in Dôtonbori, Osaka's main *sakariba*, were noisier and gaudier than cafés in Ginza. They thrived in the 1920s, challenging the popularity of the traditional theaters in the district with their dazzling lights and jazz music, especially after big cafés emerged in 1927 and 1928. Their dozens of waitresses, colored windows, brightly colored lights, and gramophone music lured patrons away from the traditional teahouses with geishas. The hit song from the musical *Dôtonbori March* in 1928 marked the heyday of cafés in Osaka.

Akai hi, aoi hi, Dôtonbori no
Kawamo ni atsumaru koi no hi ni
Nande kafê ga wasurareyoka

Yotte kudamakya abazure onna
Sumashi gao surya kafe no kyuin
Dôtonbori ga wasurareyoka

Sukina ano hito mô kuru jibun
Nafukin tatamôyo utaimashô yo
Oo natsukashi no Dôtonbori yo.

Red lights and blue lights in Dôtonbori
The lights of love that gather on the river.
How can I forget the café?

What a bitch when you're drunk and babble!
The queen of the café when you look prudish.
How can I forget Dôtonbori?

Nearly time for my loved one to come.
Let's fold napkins and let's sing a song.
My dear old Dôtonbori.[68]

The Ginza cafés established by Osaka capital included the previously described Ginza Palace. Other big ones were Café Akatama and Grand Ginza, owned by the same person. They not only introduced the new ideas about architectural design and decor, but also intensified *ero* service and devised new kinds of advertising that Tokyo cafés had never thought of before. Placing one waitress to a patron, for example, meant that no man would miss out on the seductive experience. In the publicity area, Bijinza Kafê (Café of Beauties) created a sensation by flying in thirty waitresses from Osaka by plane, a rarity in 1930, and the Nichirin (The Sun) added to the dazzling glamor of cafés by opening in October with the entire building covered with neon lights.[69] Some, such as Ginza Kaikan, introduced Osaka local color by having Osaka waitresses who spoke Osaka dialect.[70]

The women who worked in these big cafés numbered among the few who earned a lot of money from the commodification of their beauty and alluring behavior, but Marxist social critics viewed them, as well as their poor counterparts in smaller cafés, as proletarianized workers merely being used by capitalists. Gonda Yasunosuke regarded café waitresses as "formal" rather than genuine representatives of "modern life," no more than workers in the "modern life industry."[71] In such views the women had lost, not gained, freedom, and the "wretched" salarymen who patronized them did so because they lived in a period of no hope for the future.[72] According to Gonda, "modern life" was a way of living divorced from any productive work or concerns other than consumption and therefore led to the enjoyment of "perverse tastes" in the streets and their extensions, the cafés.[73] The association of cafés and café waitresses with erotic-grotesque-nonsense was seen as symptomatic of the final stage of capitalism.[74]

Police repression at the end of the 1920s shows that government authorities shared with left-wing critics the association of cafés and café waitresses with decadence and moral degeneracy. Restrictions on dancing and dance halls presaged the crackdown on cafés. In 1925 Osaka authorities banned dancing in places serving food and drinks, then in 1927 brought in strict control regulations on dance halls, such as limits on their hours and a ban on students. Repression gradually increased until they were prohibited in December. A proposal to impose restrictions on cafés came in August 1929. By measures such as prohibiting the sale of strong kinds of alcohol, limiting opening hours and dim lighting, and stopping the spread of cafés to new areas, government authorities hoped to control the immoral behavior of waitresses and limit the harmful effects of cafés on public morals. Some café owners responded by voluntarily introducing restrictions similar to those proposed, but some waitresses responded by presenting their own demands, including the abolition of *kisoku* and charges for damages to furnishings. Several hundred other waitresses attempted to form a city-wide union, but police warnings to the leaders prompted them to give up their plans. They were admonished to stop being prostitutes instead of trying to create a union.

In October the proposed regulations went into effect. They were responsive to waitresses' demands in that they included a ban on *kisoku*. However, owners managed to compensate for fines no longer collected by raising their charges for meals and drinks. In addition, the restrictions advantaged large cafés over small ones, especially those in entertainment areas which were allowed to stay open longer and to have jazz and stage dancing. Many small cafés gave up and turned themselves into soda fountains, candy stores, or pure restaurants. Those that tried to survive resorted to selling their waitresses as a sexual commodity.[75] Similar restrictions, including bans on *desen*, were imposed on Tokyo cafés the same year and with similar effects. Arrests of café waitresses, dance hall women, and "delinquent modern boys and girls" added force to the repression.[76] Further morals campaigns, supported by middle-class Protestant reform groups, followed during the 1930s.[77] Nevertheless, as we have seen, the big cafés (many capitalized by Osaka entrepreneurs) thrived during the early 1930s. Small cafés still numbered in the thousands along the back streets, but relied more and more on plying erotic service.[78] Miriam Silverberg refers to such café owners' introducing "the underground" or "subway service" which allowed a customer to slip his hand through a slit in the waitress's skirt. Others provided an *"orugan sābisu"* (organ service) which had a waitress drape herself across the laps of a few customers and provide the "keyboard" for them to play upon. When the men touched different parts of her body, she would sing notes ranging from bass to soprano.[79]

Conclusion

Murobushi and others saw the cafés and modern life as grounded in the petit bourgeoisie, but it appears to have been the big bourgeoisie that profited from them. Here
we have an image of modernity in 1920s and 1930s Japan full of loneliness and
despair as well as decadence and immorality. This was the "dark side" of modernity
which colored the image of the modern in popular songs and novels as well as socialist
and Christian critiques of the era:

> *Watasha yoru saku sakaba no hana yo*
> *Akai kuchibeni kinsha no tamoto*
> *Neon raito de ukarete odori*
> *Samete samishii namidabana*

> *Watasha kanashii sakaba no hana yo*
> *Yoru wa otome yo hiruma wa haha yo*
> *Mukashi kakushita namida no tamoto*
> *Fukete omoi wa tsuyu ja nai*

> *[I am a flower in the bar that blooms at night*
> *With red lipstick and silk kimono sleeves.*
> *I dance merrily under the neon light.*
> *When sober, it's a lonely flower of tears.*

> *I am a sad flower in the bar.*
> *A young girl by night and a mother by day.*
> *In the past, I hid my tearful sleeves.*
> *When the night wears on, it's not the dew that makes them heavy.]*[80]

As in this "Jokyū no uta" (Song of a Café Waitress) and Hayashi Fumiko's *Hōrōki*, the
eroticized, commodified, and victimized representation of the café waitress dominates
the "dark side" of modernity. Out of her context of the café also emerge glimpses of
economic stagnation and depression for the new white-collar middle class in images of
the "wretched" unemployed or poorly paid salarymen who comprised the majority of
patrons. Alternatively, images of patrons buying erotic services evoke a new era of
decadent mass consumerism and selfish indulgence. The café from this point of view
appears to be a sphere divorced from politics and foreign policy, but we are reminded
of the state's growing intrusiveness in daily life, its incorporation of the social into the
political, by the introduction of governmental regulations on cafés and the arrests of
students and café waitresses that began in the late 1920s and continued throughout
the 1930s.

The cafés of the 1930s did not, however, represent the last stage of capitalism after all, although Japan was soon to go through a disastrous period in its history. They represented a more complex modernity which was not all decadence, gloom and doom, or "*ero-guro-nansensu.*" For the "bright" side of modernity we can return to Murobushi Kōshin's celebration of the café's liberating effects for both women and men, but his view is just as blinkered as that of the damning and pessimistic critics.

If we put aside the value judgments in the discourse of the café, what else did the modern connote in post-earthquake Japan? Japanese observers failed to agree either on a definition of the café or on its meaning. They were not even agreed on whether it was Japanese or a superficial imitation of the United States. But they all felt very strongly that it must mean something. So, perhaps it is not inappropriate to evoke the contested nature of the site, and end here with a string of nouns and adjectives, following the penchant of the period for catchy words and phrases — speed, noise, light, bright, liberation, love — but also perverse, tawdry, decadent, cheap, oppressed, lust. And for whom? The masses.

Acknowledgments

I would like to acknowledge the opportunity to work on this project provided by the Extended Research Secondment scheme of the Research Institute for Humanities and Social Sciences, The University of Sydney, during the second half of 1998. All illustrations are reproduced with permission of the author, Hatsuda Tohru, from Kafē to kissaten, INAX Album 18, *INAX Shuppan, 1993.*

Notes

1   Steve Bradshaw, *Café Society: Bohemian Life from Swift to Bob Dylan*, London, Weidenfeld & Nicolson, 1978.
2   Murobushi Kōshin (Takanobu), "Kafe shakaigaku," *Chūō kōron*, September 1929, pp. 189–90.
3   Ishikado Harunosuke, "Ginza kaibōzu: Dai 1-pen Ginza hensenshi," in Minami Hiroshi (ed.), *Kindai shomin seikatsushi*, vol. 2, *Sakariba to uramachi*, Tokyo, San'ichi Shobō, 1984, p. 311.
4   For a list of members, see Hatsuda Tōru, *Kafē to kissaten*, INAX Album 18, Tokyo, INAX Shuppan, 1993, p. 13; or Fujimori Terunobu, Hatsuda Tōru, Fujioka Hiroyasu, *Ushinawareta teito Tōkyō: Taishō Shōwa no machi to sumai*, Tokyo, Kashiwa Shobō, 1991, p. 76.
5   Ishikado, *Ginza kaibōzu*, p. 311.
6   Hatsuda, *Kafē to kissaten*, p. 16.
7   Ishikado, *Ginza kaibōzu*, p. 311.
8   Murashima Yoriyuki, "Kanraku no ōkyū — kafe" (originally 1929), in Minami (ed.), *Kindai shomin seikatsushi*, vol. 10, p. 373.
9   Dōke Saiichirō, "Baishunfu ronkō" (originally 1928), in Minami (ed.), *Kindai shomin seikatsushi*, vol. 10, p. 279.
10   Tōkyō Hyakunenshi Henshū Iinkai (ed.), *Tōkyō hyakunenshi*, vol. 5, Tokyo, Tōkyō Hyakunenshi Henshū Iinkai, 1979, p. 86.
11   ibid., p. 271.
12   Seidensticker quoting Tanizaki Junichirō, Edward Seidensticker, *Tokyo Rising*, Cambridge, Mass., Harvard University Press, 1991, p. 57.
13   Shun'ichi Watanabe, "Metropolitanism as a Way of Life: The Case of Tokyo, 1868–1930," in Anthony Sutcliffe (ed.), *Metropolis 1890–1940*, London, Mansell, 1984, p. 408.
14   Edward Seidensticker, *Low City, High City*, Cambridge, Mass., Harvard University Press, 1983, pp. 58–61.
15   Andō Kōsei, "Ginza jidai" (originally 1930), in Minami Hiroshi (ed.), *Gendai no esupuri — Nihon modanizumu*, no. 188, March 1983, p. 132.

16   Seidensticker, *Low City*, p. 111.
17   Seidensticker, *Tokyo Rising*, p. 30.
18   ibid., p. 31.
19   Gonda Yasunosuke, "Modan seikatsu to hentai shikōsei," *Kaizō*, vol. 11, no. 6, June 1929, p. 32.
20   ibid., p. 33.
21   For example, Andō, "Ginza jidai," p. 131; Uchida Roan, "Modan o kataru" (originally 1928), in Minami (ed.), *Gendai no esupuri*, p. 16. Shunya Yoshimi employs the same metaphors in *Toshi no doramaturugi — Tōkyō, sakariba no shakaishi*, Tokyo, Kōbundō, 1987, but derives them from Walter Benjamin.
22   Andō, "Ginza jidai," p. 132.
23   Shunya, *Toshi no doramaturugi*, p. 222.
24   Ishikado, *Ginza kaibōzu*, p. 286. For comparisons between Asakusa and Ginza, see Shunya, *Toshi no doramaturugi*, Chapter 3.
25   Hori Makoto, "Gendai jokyūron" (originally 1931), in Minami (ed.), *Gendai no esupuri*, p. 189.
26   Seidensticker, *Tokyo Rising*, pp. 71, 111–15.
27   Watanabe, "Metropolitanism," p. 422.
28   According to the 1930 census, 308,000 people commuted from the suburbs to the city, while only 35,000 commuted in the other direction. Watanabe, "Metropolitanism," p. 423.
29   ibid.
30   On the growth of commercial and entertainment areas around railway terminuses, see Katō Hidetoshi, "Service-Industry Business Complexes — The Growth and Development of 'Terminal Culture'," *The Japan Interpreter*, vol. 7, no. 3–4, Summer–Autumn 1972, pp. 376–82.
31   "Paradise" was in English, as was "Fruits Parlor" in the name of the greengrocer Takano Fruits Parlor near the station. Seidensticker, *Tokyo Rising*, p. 50.
32   ibid., p. 53.
33   Tōkyō Hyakunenshi Henshū Iinkai, *Tōkyō hyakunenshi*, vol. 5, p. 86. Seidensticker also concludes that although sometimes busier than Ginza, Shinjuku was "still second-rate Ginza. The high life of the years after the earthquake centered upon the cafés. In these Ginza was preeminent, the place that other places looked up to. The early interwar period was the full summer of the cafés, and this word almost demands the qualification 'Ginza'." Seidensticker, *Tokyo Rising*, p. 53.
34   Seidensticker, *Tokyo Rising*, p. 51.
35   Hori, "Gendai jokyūron," p. 189.
36   Matsuzaki Tenmin, "Shinjuku no inshōki, 2" (originally 1930), in Minami (ed.), *Kindai shomin seikatsushi*, vol. 2, p. 350.
37   See photographs in Hatsuda, *Kafē to kissaten*, pp. 20–2.
38   Thanks to Ikuko Sorensen for the translation of the lyrics for this and other songs. Asahi Shinbunsha (ed.), *Tōkyō no uta*, Tokyo, Asahi Shinbunsha, 1968, p. 183.
39   "Akai hi, aoi hi" became a catchphrase of the early 1930s. Ibid., p. 182.
40   Hatsuda, *Kafē to kissaten*, pp. 33–9.
41   ibid., p. 31.
42   Murobushi, "Kafe shakaigaku," p. 190.
43   ibid., pp. 190–1.
44   Matsuzaki Tenmin, *Ginza*, Tokyo, Shinsensha, 1986, p. 82.
45   Murashima, "Kanraku no ōkyū," pp. 319–21.
46   ibid.
47   Matsuzaki, *Ginza*, p. 80.
48   Murashima, "Kanraku no ōkyū," pp. 319–20.
49   ibid., p. 322; Matsuzaki, *Ginza*, p. 83; Murobushi, "Kafe shakaigaku," p. 191.
50   On middle-class working women, see Margit Nagy, "Middle-Class Working Women During the Interwar Years," in Gail Bernstein (ed.), *Recreating Japanese Women*, Berkeley and Los Angeles, University of California Press, 1991, pp. 199–216; Susan Newell, "Women Primary School Teachers and the State in Interwar Japan," in Elise K. Tipton (ed.), *Society and the State in Interwar Japan*, London, Routledge, 1997, pp. 17–41.
51   According to a Central Employment Agency survey, "because the money is good" was the second most common reason given for becoming a café waitress. Murashima, "Kanraku no ōkyū," p. 323. On actresses opening cafés, see p. 374.

52   Ôbayashi Munetsugu, *Jokyū seikatsu no shin kenkyū*, in the series *Kindai fujin mondai meichō senshū*, *Shakai mondai hen*, vol. 3, Tokyo, Nihon Tosho Sentā, 1983, p. 85.

53   See Sheldon Garon, *Molding Japanese Minds*, Princeton, NJ, Princeton University Press, 1997, Chapter 3.

54   Miriam Silverberg, "The Café Waitress Serving Modern Japan," in Stephen Vlastos (ed.), *Mirror of Modernity*, Berkeley and Los Angeles, University of California Press, 1998, pp. 208–25.

55   Murashima noted this relative freedom compared to the situation of geishas and licensed prostitutes as a reason for the popularity of the café waitress's job among young women. Murashima, "Kanraku no ôkyū," pp. 319, 329.

56   Hayashi Fumiko, *Hayashi Fumiko zenshū*, vol. 1, Tokyo, Bunsendô, 1977, pp. 319–20. For another reference to this novel, see Tomoko Aoyama's chapter in this volume.

57   Ôbayashi, *Jokyū seikatsu*, pp. 73–4.

58   Hayashi, *Hayashi zenshū*, pp. 406–7.

59   Murashima, "Kanraku no ôkyū," p. 331.

60   ibid., p. 327; Tôkyô Hyakunenshi Henshū Iinkai (ed.), *Tôkyô hyakunenshi*, vol. 5, p. 262. Ôbayashi's survey found the most common average monthly income to be 30–35 yen. Only a few waitresses in the big cafés in the central district made 150–200 yen in a month. Ôbayashi, *Jokyū seikatsu*, pp. 97–8.

61   Murashima, "Kanraku no ôkyū," p. 337.

62   ibid., p. 323; Ôbayashi, *Jokyū seikatsu*, p. 81.

63   Ôbayashi, *Jokyū seikatsu*, pp. 39–40.

64   Since most café waitresses were in their late teens, it is less surprising that 57.42 percent were unmarried. Ibid., p. 64.

65   Murashima, "Kanraku no ôkyū," pp. 336–7.

66   This was the main conclusion of a 1930 study of café waitresses and prostitutes conducted by Kusama Yasô, an official with the Social Affairs Bureau of the Tokyo Metropolitan Government. Kusama Yasô, *Jokyū to baishôfu*, in the series *Kindai fujin mondai meichō senshū zoku hen*, vol. 9, Tokyo, Nihon Tosho Sentā, 1982.

67   Murashima Yoriyuki, "Osaka kafê dan'atsushi" (originally 1929), in Minami (ed.), *Gendai no esupuri*, pp. 171–2.

68   Hibi Shigejirô, "Dôtonbori doori" (originally 1930), in Minami (ed.), *Kindai shomin seikatsushi*, vol. 2, p. 222.

69   Hatsuda, *Kafê to kissaten*, p. 19.

70   Fujimori et al., *Ushinawareta teito*, p. 86.

71   Gonda, "Modan seikatsu," p. 34.

72   Takada Tamotsu, "Kafe, chian Nihon" (originally 1929), in Minami (ed.), *Gendai no esupuri*, p. 167.

73   Gonda, "Modan seikatsu," pp. 33–5.

74   For example, Hori, "Gendai jokyūron," pp. 184–90.

75   Murashima, "Ôsaka kafê," pp. 175–83.

76   Garon, *Molding Japanese Minds*, p. 107. Arrests of 150 modern girls and boys in Ginza cafés had already taken place in August 1927. *Shôwa Day by Day – Shôwa nimannichi no zenkiroku*, vol. 1, Tokyo, Kôdansha, 1989, p. 142.

77   ibid., pp. 107–8.

78   Silverberg, "The Café Waitress," p. 217.

79   Mori Hideto, *Taishū bunkashi*, Tokyo, Kabushiki Kaisha Sanpô, 1964, p. 191.

80   Lyrics by Saijô Yaso, music by Shiojiri Seihachi, 1930. Tôkyô Hyakunenshi Henshū Iinkai, *Tôkyô hyakunenshi*, vol. 5, pp. 269–70.

CHAPTER EIGHT

An Alternate Informant
Middle-Class Women and Mass Magazines in 1920s Japan

Barbara Hamill Sato

Introduction

As the development of an urban culture — reflected in the way of life of the expanding middle class, growing mass-production industries, and especially the media — gained momentum following World War I (1914–18), the elements of a mass society emerged and changed the shape of Japanese society. Particularly conspicuous were the multi-faceted images of women. On the one hand, culture (*bunka*), a term popularized in the 1920s, was linked to the intellectuals' concern with spirituality and considered the fruit of a select group of sophisticated scholars. On the other hand, "mass" culture (*taishū bunka*), under the sway of Western symbols, emerged against the backdrop of Japanese social *modanizumu* (modernism), a predominantly urban lifestyle in which women figured as prominent icons and stood out in contradiction. In exploring the interaction between changing gender definitions and social *modanizumu*, this chapter focuses on urban middle-class women — what occupied their interests, what shaped their actions — and the role of mass women's magazines, a propelling force in the construction of new female identities in 1920s Japan.

The publication of *Fujin sekai* (Woman's World) beginning in 1906, followed by *Fujokai* (Woman's Sphere) in 1910, *Fujin kōron* (Woman's Review) in 1916, *Shufu no tomo* (The Housewife's Companion) in 1917, and *Fujin kurabu* (Woman's Club) in 1920, brought to the fore a new and novel media product in the form of mass women's magazines. Editors' efforts to increase circulation ensured that many young women who were not in the habit of reading joined the ranks as regular subscribers. In rural hamlets, housewives accessed information about "modern" lifestyles utterly different from their own, a factor that contributed to the diffusion of new female images. With the rise of sophisticated family articles (*katei kiji*), fashionable articles (*ryūkō kiji*), and confessional articles (*kokuhaku kiji*), women in city and country alike were in a position to articulate their feelings while being privy to alternative views that detailed the lives of other women.

By the 1920s, mass women's magazines had become an influential site in the cir-culation of information. Nevertheless, almost no one accorded them a positive role in effecting those changes in outlook which, figuratively if not literally, thrust the average Japanese woman into wider society. Although women's magazines comprised a large portion of the mass magazines of the period, from the outset they were connoted by the labels "conservative" (hoshuteki) and "unscientific" (hikagakuteki).[1] Novelist and literary critic Uchida Roan (1868–1929), who wrote a series of essays between August 1922 and May 1928 for the popular women's magazine Josei (Woman), summed it up in these words:

> Inasmuch as women's magazines are concerned with a woman's domain, they publish many articles on topics like cooking and sewing ... The fact that the opinions and ideas relate to personal experiences is not bad, but experience which is not based on scientific principles, while it may have inspired the writer, is not beneficial for others.[2]

Even today, many scholars in the field of Japanese journalism continue to censure pre-war women's magazines for their editorial conservatism and frivolity of tone.[3] No doubt such criticisms reflect the fact that even in the 1920s mass women's magazines projected a discourse prevalent in Meiji period (1868–1912) women's magazines.[4] Almost every issue of Shufu no tomo contained articles such as "Suitable Sidework Even for Girls" ("Joshi kodomo nimo dekiru yūri na fukugyō," March 1917), and "Readers' Recommendations for Becoming a Model Wife" ("Risōteki fujin no suisen happyō," January 1926), which urged women to persevere under the most adverse circum-stances and instructed them on how to live virtuous lives.

Nevertheless, not all women readers found offensive articles which promoted a doctrine they had been taught to respect from childhood. The editorials and feature stories carried in mass women's magazines show that many parents, and the general public as well, supported the "good wife, wise mother" (ryōsai kenbo) philosophy of education on which the "official" morality for women had been made to rest from 1898. The reason was not because of its intrinsic values, but because it was familiar.[5] The intellectuals' dismay resulted both from the media's tendency to promote out-moded values, and the complacency of women readers to accept what some intellect-uals deemed the status quo. Uchida, well-attuned to the woman problem, interpreted it this way:

> When I see women on subways and trains who look like intellectuals (sōtō na chishiki kaikyū no fujin rashii) really enjoying reading women's magazines, which are an even lower level than the gossip magazines (kodan zasshi), it makes me utterly disappointed.[6]

The appeal of a mass-directed media naturally promoted circulation figures while it molded changes in media content. Shufu no tomo turned to monthly themes like health tips for women (June 1919), birth control methods (January 1922), and

Western clothes and the proper way to wear them (June 1923) as calling cards for beckoning new readers. From 1918, another successful ploy included the periodic inclusion of supplements (*furoku*) ranging from ten to fifty pages in length.[7] As the fight for readers intensified, a greater propensity for mixing the old with the new surfaced, a factor that appeared to minimize the individual differences between magazines. Tsugawa Masashi, the editor of *Fujokai*, argued that:

> all the [women's] magazines have their own special features, but because of their subtle-
> ties, a cursory reading leads one to think there are no differences. The reason is that the
> magazine editors are basically aiming at the same reading public, the masses (taishū),
> and the pressure to achieve circulation goals is tremendous.[8]

Although standardization, rather than individuality, defined the temper of women's magazines at this time, not all articles were uninspired or dull. Compared to the women's magazines of the early 1900s, which stressed education and ethical training in order to achieve "civilization and enlightenment", mass women's magazines in the 1920s could not have attracted readers if the information they disseminated dwelt only on time-worn subjects like female morality. By the mid-twentieth century, these women's magazines were informed by a pastiche of articles. Much like Noma Seiji's declaration, when he founded the popular magazine *Kingu* (King) in 1925, that there "be something for everyone," the topics covered ranged from the conventional to the latest in foreign, particularly American, trends and popular customs. No doubt this policy led to the assumption that editorial direction was wanting.

Among the "new" articles, the family articles (*katei kiji*) and practical articles (*jit-suyō kiji*) informed the character of women's magazines in reinforcing and propelling women away from time-worn lifestyles. Because the discourse centered on basic concerns like cooking, housework, and family relationships, women readers could evaluate the direction in which their own lives were moving. Accordingly, the magazines fostered a social concern for women's cerebral changes as well as their materialistic desires, with consumerism as the go-between. More than whether one had the wherewithal to purchase new commodities was how great an impression was made by the allure of goods promised through the print medium.[9]

Setting the stage for mass women's magazines in the 1920s

By the early 1900s, the motivation behind women's magazines was no longer to satisfy the interests of young elite schoolgirls. Instead, women's publications were evolving from passive to competitive, profit-making ventures. In 1880 compulsory education, which originally had been fixed at four years by the Ministry of Education in 1871 and reduced to sixteen months during the decentralization of education in 1879, was extended without regard to gender to three years, and then to the original four years. By 1906 it had been increased to six years. With the foundation firmly laid for

Fig. 1 A visit to the bookstore, 1920s.
Permission of Endo Noriaki

elementary school education, families began to recognize that females, too, were entitled to schoolroom learning. The choices narrowed considerably after that, but girls did have the option of entering a women's higher school (*kōtō jogakkō*). Chronologically, the women's higher school was equivalent to the boy's middle school (*chūgakkō*), which went from grades seven to eleven. Qualitatively, the differences were vast.[10] Clearly, women's magazines became mass magazines as part of the developing urban culture and a general publishing boom, but the spread of women's education cannot be overlooked (Fig. 1).[11] Neither of these elements had matured sufficiently during the Meiji period for this to occur.

In 1887, 285 of all girls of elementary school age were receiving an elementary education, and 2363 students were attending the eighteen government-controlled *jogakkō* then in operation. In 1898, 1–2 percent of girls continued their education beyond the elementary school level. A total of only 8500 girls were enrolled in women's higher schools across Japan.[12] This was due both to the commonly accepted notion that higher education for women was unnecessary, and also to economic conditions that blocked their way. Women's magazines operated under a similar set of economic restrictions. At a time when middle-class families were still limited, the female readership encompassed a minimal number of elite households. Moreover, the cost of the *Ōsaka asahi shinbun* (Osaka Asahi Newspaper) in 1891 was 0.28 yen, equivalent to approximately 600 yen in today's currency.[13] As a result, the social class of girls who subscribed to women's magazines overlapped with that of those who entered a women's higher school. This explains why the discourse promoted by most late nineteenth-century women's magazines was largely geared to higher-school students with refined tastes and why they were crammed full of fiction. Naturally, these earlier magazines were far removed from the young women who entered the labor force after their graduation from elementary school.

Indeed, *Fujin sekai*'s debut in 1906 caused little more than a ripple. Most people considered it just another mainstream women's magazine. It, too, catered to schoolgirls and young unmarried women, exhibiting a high regard for "traditional" culture. Only one year after its founding, however, in addition to articles on education, school life, plans for the summer holidays, or preparations for married life, particularly conspicuous was the emphasis on the woman's world after marriage. Even the short pieces that publicized the lifestyles of famous families targeted married women. Also notable was the amount of space allotted to entertainment. With popular writer and noted gourmet Murai Gensai (1863–1927) as editor, *Fujin sekai* addressed Murai's personal interests in popular literature, housekeeping, and food.[14] Based on early Shōwa journalist and critic Kimura Tsuyoshi's analysis, not a single page of *Fujin sekai* would have interested a male reader.[15] As the female reading public entered a transitional stage, the shift in *Fujin sekai*'s editorial policy mirrored the expansion in numbers and diversification taking place among readers (Fig. 2). Although *Fujin sekai*'s management policies could not compete with those of *Fujokai*, *Fujin kōron*, *Shufu no tomo*, and *Fujin kurabu*, it was called "a prototype for the next generation of family magazines."[16] This accounts for the editor's decision to incorporate practical family-oriented articles into *Fujin sekai*'s schedule of regular features. Generally, *Shufu no tomo* is credited with being the first magazine to set its sights on young married women as readers. In actuality, *Fujin sekai* deserves the distinction. Its editorial policy served as a model for Ishikawa Takemi (1887–1961), *Shufu no tomo*'s founder.

Although Ishikawa Takemi looked to unmarried as well as married women, he defied critics with a title that singled out the housewife as the cornerstone of the magazine's readership (Fig. 3). Insistent that a woman's life began only after marriage, the "mountain of things" a woman must learn and be taught became *Shufu no tomo*'s mission.[17] According to the Tokyo City Office Survey of 1922, out of 2000 women interviewed, 1184 were magazine readers, and 845 of that number read women's magazines — almost 80 percent of the total.[18] The large numbers of young married women and working women who formed the readership during the 1920s spurred the growth of the new women's magazines. The information housewives gleaned from readers' columns also became a vital factor in the rise in circulation figures.[19]

With Japanese publishing companies reluctant to make public their circulation, however, the figures reported are unreliable. In 1931, *Shufu no tomo* boasted a monthly circulation of 600,000 and a rate of 0.5–1 percent in unsold, returned magazines, *Fujin kurabu* reported 350,000 and a return rate of 25 percent, *Fujin kōron* 200,000 and a return rate of 15 percent, and *Fujin sekai* 120,000 with a 45 percent return rate.[20]

Fig. 2 Fujin sekai (Woman's World), 1911, cover

Fig. 3 Shufu no tomo (*The Housewife's Companion*), January 1923, cover. Permission of Shufu no Tomosha

A turning point in women's journalism

Although the restrictions on education are closely linked to the positioning of women, by 1912, 97.6 percent of those eligible had registered in elementary school. A total of 208 government-sponsored *jogakkō* operated throughout the country, with a recorded enrollment of 75,128 students.[21] In the 1910s and 1920s the increasing literacy among women, characterized by a degree of economic latitude, allowed greater numbers of women to purchase magazines. Conscious of the connection between marketing and the potential occasioned by this new reading public, most women's magazines published from the 1910s followed *Fujin sekai*'s example and aimed at becoming mass magazines. Of the 2000 working women interviewed for the Tokyo City Office Survey of 1922, over 40 percent received a monthly salary of 26–30 yen, or approximately 60,000 yen today; the second most common salary was 31–35 yen, or approximately 70,000 yen today.[22] The average monthly income for male government employees, based on figures compiled in 1921, was 96 yen and for office workers 98 yen or approximately 190,000 yen today.[23] Since the price of *Shufu no tomo* was 17 sen, or 0.17 yen (340 yen today), which amounted to approximately 0.5–1 percent of a working woman's monthly salary, even women with low-paying jobs probably could have afforded to purchase one magazine.[24]

Editors quickly recognized the advantages of winning the trust of these untapped women readers. In an article in the March 1927 issue of *Kaizō* on the status of women's magazines, proletarian literature activist and social critic Hirabayashi Hatsunosuke (1892–1931) wrote:

> *I don't think there is another foreign country that has achieved the success Japan has in marketing women's magazines ... the main reason is the peculiar structure of Japan's family system. In Japan, a housewife's work is clearly defined in its separateness from a man's work, and it is also extremely time consuming. Consequently, the bulk of the articles address a variety of topics like bringing up children, information related to illnesses, cooking, sewing, knitting, flower arranging and other artistic pursuits, and proper etiquette. In a country where a family system like Japan's prevails, these are the things that a housewife must know.*[25]

Shufu no tomo's fundamental strategy involved perfecting family articles. Different from the family articles in *Fujin sekai*, *Shufu no tomo* subdivided its articles into socalled practical or *jitsuyō kiji*, and fashionable or *ryūkō kiji*. Even *Fujin kōron* (Fig. 4) determined to reject the family article approach in the early years of publication, reconsidered, and followed *Shufu no tomo*'s lead. Although family articles varied depending on the publication and editor's stance, the motivation was the same — to offer housewives helpful hints pertaining to home and family.[26] Although *Shufu no tomo* came out at approximately the time of World War I, one could easily have read the magazine unaware that a war was raging in Europe.[27]

Practical articles or *jitsuyō kiji*

Domestic concerns remained the mainstay of *Shufu no tomo*'s practical articles, similar to those articles published in *Fujin sekai*. But Ishikawa added another component. Information now involved relaying advice to women on the latest, most diverse methods of homemaking (Fig. 5). A look at the practical articles found in the first issue of *Shufu no tomo* (March 1917) is telling. "Building a Convenient House on a Low Budget" ("Anka de tateta benri na ie") introduced the concept of an eat-in kitchen and also taught that by limiting entry to the front hall or kitchen, locking the house would be simplified. Health-related articles like "Fool-proof Home Remedy for Gastrointestinal Disorders" ("Kanarazu naoru ichōbyō no kateiryōhō") filled most mass women's magazines, but abounded in *Shufu no tomo*.

Journalist Nii Itaru encapsulated the problem when he wrote that "large numbers of women read women's magazines, but that doesn't necessarily mean they became

Fig. 4 Fujin kōron (*Woman's Review*), *April 1921, cover*

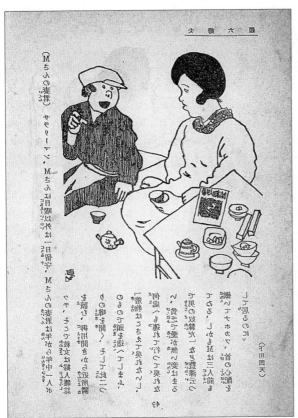

Fig. 5 *A housewife's informants —*
women's magazines and the delivery
man, Onna no sekai-gendai manga
taikan, *vol. 9, Chūō Bijutsusha,*
1928, p. 49.

any more intelligent."[28] Nii's misgivings that household tasks alone did not make up the "total" woman was apparent. Attitudes similar to Nii's among other intellectuals earned *Shufu no tomo* the blot of "ultra-conservative." Yamakawa Kikue's devotion to socialism and a genderless society led her to bemoan the fact that mass magazines induced women to "look inward" rather than "outward."[29] Yamakawa's article, "Discussion on the Present State of Women's Magazines" ("Gendai fujin zasshi ron") unharnessed the following criticism: "Women are made to feel self-satisfied with their present status which is really slave in the bedroom and slave to the family. [Women] become ostentatious and hedonistic."[30] Regarding the contents of the journals, Yamakawa lamented:

> the jitsuyō kiji *that are concerned with women in the home are practical articles without any practical value. And the articles on sex are nothing more than wordy descriptions about the coquettish behaviour of prostitutes ... Jitsuyō kiji, like doctors' statements on child-rearing and caring for the sick, are filled with generalities ... It seems frighteningly crude and unkind that no warning is given about the dangers of these articles.*[31]

Nii added that "perhaps *jitsuyô kiji* have the potential for being useful, but what is their basis scientifically and economically?"[32] Even if the modus operandi deployed by the majority of mass women's magazines presumed a fixed role for women in society, by introducing women to alternative thought patterns through family articles, they unintentionally opened the way for domestic unrest. Articles such as "An Economical, Attractive *Hakama* for School Girls" could hardly have been inflammatory. But other articles, such as "Women Decide their Fate," did provide determination for some women to envision disruptions in their lifestyles. The pursuit of rationalization (*gôrika*) became an important force in shaping changes in female attitudes exhibited in modes of behavior women's magazines helped create.[33]

Using World War I as an impetus, the government launched the Daily Life Reform Movement, or *Seikatsu kaizen undô*, one of the first organized attempts to assure efficiency by eliminating wasteful spending and simplifying everyday living.[34] Directives from within the Ministry of Education (Monbushô), and later its Social Education Agency (Shakai Kyôikukyoku) set up for this purpose, urged people to safeguard their time, refrain from irrational customs like exchanging costly year-end gifts, and pay heed to the health dangers presented by a predominantly white rice diet. Although the impetus for reform emanated from the state, two private organizations, established in Tokyo and Osaka in 1920 and 1921 respectively, lent their support to the movement.[35] The wife of a jurist devoted to the cause commented:

> *the need for this type of research finally has been recognized. All of us living in today's world — men and women alike, regardless of occupation — have to get together and find a way to make our lives rational [gôriteki] and economical as quickly as possible. We must strive to eliminate the tremendous waste around us and the old-fashioned lifestyle that we have come to know ...*
>
> *Among the many things we should learn from the American family's lifestyle, most important, I think, is that the housewife's duty is to make her home a happy and beautiful place to live.*[36]

Housewives were preached to by the state, but less direct channels like mass women's magazines obliquely encouraged the more haphazard process of thinking and reassessing values. Of course, not all practical articles met with success, just as not all things "modern" gained acceptance. *Shufu no tomo* celebrated the nutritional value of the tomato in the hope of promoting a more balanced diet.[37] But tomato tempura (deep-fried tomatoes) and tomato *udon* (a tomato noodle) never titillated the Japanese palate. Still, editorial boldness in inspiring women to try the untried, even in the kitchen, should not be underestimated. The ramifications for women were greater than the editors might have imagined.

Fashionable articles or ryūkō kiji

More than the practical articles, it was the timely, fashionable features known as ryūkō kiji that articulated the "modern." The ryūkō kiji gave readers a taste of in-vogue fashions, hairstyles, and accessories, as well as the latest dance steps. "Make-up Becoming a Housewife" ("Shufu rashiki okeshōhō," March 1917), and "How to Convert Unused Kimono into Western Style Clothing for Women" ("Fuyō no wafuku o fujin yōfuku ni shitatekata," February 1925) illustrate the types of fashionable articles carried in Shufu no tomo. Other women's magazines deployed similar techniques, although the titles varied slightly. For example, Josei published pieces such as "A Study of Women's Clothing and Hairstyles Suitable for the New Age" ("Shin jidai ni tekiō suru fujin no fukusō to riyō [rihatsu] no kenkyū," March 1923), which discussed Japanese dress versus Western dress, how to make over clothes, hairstyles for the future, and "The Popularity of the Shawl" ("Shōru no ryūkō," October 1927), called a symbol of "today's modanizumu" (social modernism). Detailed, step-by-step diagrams instructing women that they, too, could reproduce fashionable clothing for the entire family, create alluring hair-dos like the stars, or dance the tango and foxtrot, were featured in most mass women's magazines.

The department store, yet another icon of "modernity," also generated new life into "fashionable articles." By 1921 the doors of Mitsukoshi, Matsuyama, Takashimaya, Daimaru, and Isetan, major department stores, opened promptly at 10 a.m. Now, one could see at first hand, and perhaps even purchase, what was being written about and photographed in the magazines.[38] But the strategy for publishing these "fashionable articles" was not to refashion a new role for women in society. In that regard, they, too, deserved the label "conservative." Yet, like the practical jitsuyō kiji, these articles presented a perspective on everyday practices that women up until then may have desired, but never imagined existed within their grasp.

Confessional articles or kokuhaku kiji

Shufu no tomo's expertise for charming women readers extended beyond the inclusion of family articles. Another resourceful formula was the solicitation of letters and other short pieces called confessional articles or "kokuhaku kiji", which were written by the readers themselves and later published in each issue.[39] Fujin kōron, also anxious to win over women readers, followed a similar editorial policy. Relying on monthly themes like "Pride or Embarrassment" ("Hokori ka haji") or "Educated Women and Marital Problems" ("Kyōyō aru fujin to kekkon nan," June 1924), the magazine requested contributions from readers that focused on those subjects. In 1923, Shufu no tomo added an advice column to address women's quotidian concerns ranging from marital difficulties to worries consonant with the complicated web of Japanese-style human relations.[40] Although earlier confessional articles had been penned by intellectuals and famous personalities, the magazine's shift in policy represented an attempt to move closer to its readers. Gradually, almost all women's magazines employed comparable editorial ploys. Even *Fujin sekai*, the pioneering force behind the family articles, capitalized on *Shufu no tomo's* technique, and from 1924 sponsored round-table discussions with women readers as the main participants.[41]

Among the commercial magazines put out in the 1920s, women's magazines became the first to devote space to readers' letters and confessional articles. This same practice continues today. The popularity of these letters hinged on the circumstances directing many Japanese women's lives — especially women with conventional roles. Men used the workplace and after-work activities for forming liaisons with fellow workers and friends, but women's chances to mingle socially remained limited.[42] Household management consisted both of performing domestic tasks and childcare. Cultivating a life outside the home required time, a commodity most women lacked. Shortly after the Great Earthquake, Shimanaka Yūsaku, editor of *Fujin kōron*, remarked that if women joined the labor force, ideally they could bear the burden with men in time of an emergency. But in reality, he admitted, men were not amenable to such a role for women.[43] If one assumes that a domestic setting implied a woman's sphere, the influence of women's magazines may have loomed even larger in rural areas than in the cities. The following letter describes one woman's feelings:

> *Shufu no tomo is my one and only friend. For someone like me tucked away in this mountain hamlet it is the only friend I have to teach me about all the new things going on in the world and to tell me interesting stories.*[44]

Women's magazines filled a void in the lives of some country women and formed an integral part of their daily existences.

By the early 1920s, the new mass women's magazines were drawing on a broad stratum of women readers, many of whom had only the equivalent of an elementary school education. For Hirabayashi Hatsunosuke, the success of these magazines was preordained. Because Japanese women were less educated than men and intellectually unprepared to read challenging articles, he felt justified in assuming that women rarely picked up anything other than a magazine.[45] Be that as it may, up until this time most of these women, whether housewives or still unmarried, had not relied on print communication to articulate hopes and disappointments. Nor was it even considered a site of information. True, the *Yomiuri shinbun* (Yomiuri newspaper) became the first national paper to include a women's section in 1914, but the one-page section was dis-continued in August of the following year.[46] Not surprisingly, a genre that devoted its energies to the average woman evoked a positive response from the outset. The authorities, however, thought differently. By 1913 the government already had deter-mined that women's magazines posed a veritable threat to the so-called traditional morality. On April 20 of that year the Ministry of Education issued a statement that

magazines which opposed the "good wife, wise mother" philosophy were unfit reading. The sale of the February issue of Seitô and the May issue of Jogaku sekai both were
banned, but obviously this decree was not effective.[47]

Confessional articles can be read more than merely in terms of helping to increase
circulation figures. They also helped transform the social function of women's magazines. The light reading and short stories, though entertaining, and the practical
articles, all offered one-sided information furnished by women educators, critics, and
intellectuals. With the addition of letters and articles written by women readers themselves, a readers' forum developed. A flow of information between the readers and the
magazines prevailed which initiated a new balance with the media. The information
women internalized from readers' contributions formed an indispensable departure
point from their "traditional" behavioral patterns. Emotionally, women learned they
were not alone in their uncertainty. Slight though it may seem, women, whose involve-
ment in greater society was marginalized, began to recognize the significance of self-
management. Isolated young housewives formed attachments to other women
through their contributions to women's magazines. The ability to escape the social
mores that constrained their other female friendships can be interpreted as a welcome
response to often perverted conditions. Literary critic Maeda Ai commented on the
"personal style of communication" apparent in Shufu no tomo with the inclusion of
readers' letters and confessional articles:

> For housewives who had been shut up at home with no place of their own where they
> could communicate, personal accounts [shuki] provided a communication style to
> which they could easily relate. It was closely akin to the style of communication
> promoted by the advice column.[48]

Mass women's magazines provided an opportunity for women to confront their
problems and learn about other women's problems, affording women the courage to
contemplate change — a kind of practical handbook or window on the world outside
their home.[49]

Despite the gradual increase of women in the workforce, many middle-class
women still felt pressured into staying at home after marriage. Besides domestic
duties, most pressing among their concerns were finding a mate and adjusting to married life in the face of the challenges posed by the Japanese family network. Magazines
were not loath to use sex and racy articles as a stimulus to lure women readers and fuel
their fantasies. But in most cases, women received the brunt of the negative publicity,
which attests to the pervasiveness of the restraints placed on them for behavior which
did not necessarily deserve condemnation as a social aberration.[50] Sensational coverage foretold the media's limitless potential to capitalize on women and sex.

Publicizing the affairs of socially elite women put female readers in contact with a
class of women whose world differed from their own, but whose marital and romantic

problems struck a not unfamiliar chord. These women, held up as paragons of ideal Japanese womanhood, actually had the courage to break loose and exercise their own will. Many readers realized that there were already women in society who did not abide by the conventional standards that governed marriage and married life. Prompted by incidents featured in the pages of women's magazines, these women seemed all the more willing to share their own experiences, as shown by the vast number of letters and articles they submitted to the magazines.

Conclusion

By the 1920s, women's magazines no longer sought merely to educate and fill women's lives with cultural refinement. Gathering momentum with their sensational stories aimed at expanding circulation, mass women's magazines of the 1920s paid tribute to a wide range of readers comprising of factory workers, sales clerks, young women in rural communities, in addition to urban middle-class wives and higher school students and graduates. The popularization of women's magazines — damned by some, praised by others — coincided with significant social change, the growth of a new urban culture called *modanizumu*.

While most intellectuals of the left and the right criticized the editors of mass women's magazines for their conservatism, many women readers themselves harbored a distrust of overly radical change. But that is not to say that women opposed all change. Articles about the family lives and romantic liaisons of other women, for example, stirred an awareness in women that often raised their own self-images. Even women from conservative families, too timid to exert themselves at home, recognized from stories about women at home and abroad the possibilities of lifestyles different from their own. Among the wide range of discourses that became the identifying features of the mass magazines, indeed, the familiar topics addressed in family articles, practical articles, and confessional articles articulated the everyday needs of these new women. Yamakawa Kikue, who misread the role some women would assume in the labor movement, admitted that even young women who worked in factories or as domestics and were members of the proletariat succumbed to the foolish bourgeois topics carried in mass women's magazines like *Shufu no tomo*, rather than actively voicing concern for socialist causes.[51] Just as it would be inappropriate to sound overly optimistic when discussing the alteration of everyday practices, so too would it be amiss not to suggest that many women, in their own way, were ready to seize the opportunities open to them through mass women's magazines and their narratives.

Notes

1   See Uchida Roan, "Onna no zasshi no genzai to shōrai," *Uchida Roan zenshū*, vol. 3, Tokyo, Yamani Shobō, 1987, p. 95. Regarding the growth of mass women's magazines, see Maeda Ai, "Taishō kōki tsūzoku shosetsu no tenkai — fujin zasshi no dokusha-sō," *Bungaku*, July 1968, reprinted in *Maeda Ai chosakushū*, vol. 2, Tokyo, Chikuma Shobō, 1989, p. 161.

2   Uchida, *Uchida Roan zenshū*, vol. 3, p. 95.

3   In Oka Mitsuo's opinion, *Shufu no tomo* had a tendency to maintain the status quo and could not take a stand against a lifestyle that treated women as inferior to men. Oka Mitsuo, *Fujin zasshi jānarizumu*, Tokyo, Gendai Jānarizumu Shuppankai, 1981, p. 102.
   Fujitake Akira commented that women's magazines "made women compliantly conform to a set of moral standards that governed an entire country." Fujitake Akira, "Taishō bunka no seiritsu," *Kōza gendai jānarizumu*, vol. 1, Tokyo, Jiji Tsūshinsha, 1981, p. 102. Both Oka and Fujitake's arguments are in keeping with the argument set forth by Matsushita Keiichi in his landmark article on mass culture in the postwar period. Matsushita Keiichi, "Taishū kokka no seiritsu to sono mondaisei," *Shisō*, no. 389, November 1956.

4   Many Japanese intellectuals then and now share a view of popular culture similar to that of Theodor Adorno of the Frankfurt School. When Adorno commented on popular music (jazz included), he said that it is "patterned" and "predigested," and "serves within the psychological household of the masses to spare them the effort of that participation (even in listening or observation) without which there can be no receptivity to art." Theodor W. Adorno (with George Simpson), "On Popular Music", *Studies in Philosophy and Social Science (Zeitschrift für Sozialforschung)*, vol. 9, 1941, pp. 17–48.

5   Pathbreaking examples that represent a new direction in Japanese gender history on *ryōsai kenbo* appear in the work of Mitsuda Kiyoko, "Kindaiteki boseikan no juyō to henka — 'kyōiku suru hahaoya' kara 'ryōsai kenbo' e," in Wakita Haruko (ed.), *Bosei o tou — rekishiteki hensen*, vol. 2, Tokyo, Jinbun Shoin, 1985, pp. 100–29; Koyama Shizuko, *Ryōsai kenbo to iu kihan*, Tokyo, Keisō Shobō, 1991; Kathleen Uno, "The Origins of 'Good Wife, Wise Mother' in Modern Japan," in Erich Pauer and Regine Mathias (eds), *Japanische Frauengeschichte(n)*, Marburg, Forderverein Marburger Japan-Reihe, 1995. Also see, Ulrike Wöhr, *Hiroshima City University Bulletin*, Hiroshima City University, 1997.

6   Uchida, *Uchida Roan zenshū*, vol. 3, pp. 96–7.

7   *Shufu no Tomosha no gojūnen*, Tokyo, Shufu no Tomosha, 1967, p. 14.

8   Tsugawa Masashi, "Fujin zasshi no henshū," *Sōgō jānarizumu kōza*, vol. 10, 1931, pp. 56–7. Hereafter cited as *Sōgō jānarizumu*. Although the editors were male, there were some positions open to women as reporters.

9   Robert Bobcock makes the point that "desires appear in a state of flux ... They are related to sexual potentialities of the human body as this has become articulated in images, symbols and representations in the decades since the invention of the cinema, magazines and colour photography ... The desires of the unconscious, however, remain untamed." Robert Bobcock, *Consumption*, London and New York, Routledge, 1993, p. 93.

10 Ann M. Harrington, "Women and Higher Education in the Japanese Empire (1869–1945)," *Journal of Asian History*, vol. 21, no. 2, 1987, p. 170; Susan Newell, "Women Primary School Teachers and the State in Interwar Japan," in Elise K. Tipton (ed.), *Society and the State in Interwar Japan*, London, Routledge, 1997, pp. 18–21. For a discussion of the social impact on education in the Meiji period, see Carol Gluck, *Japan's Modern Myths: Ideology in the Late Meiji Period*, Princeton, NJ, Princeton University Press, 1985, pp. 163–74.

11 On technological advancements and the growth of mass magazines see Sugimura Sojinkan, "Nihon jānarizumu no gensei — shinbun jānarizumu," *Sōgō jānarizumu*, vol. 12, 1931, pp. 17–27.

12 Fukuda Sumiko et al., *Kōto jogakkō shiryō shūsei — kōto jogakkō no kenkyū*, vol. 2, Tokyo, Ōzorasha, 1990, appendix, p. 29.

13 In 1920 the cost of a morning and evening set was 1.20 (2400) yen. See *Nedan no Meiji, Taishō, Shōwa fūzoku shi*, Tokyo, Asahi Shinbunsha, 1981, p. 161.

14 Okano Takeo, *Nihon shuppan bunka shi*, Tokyo, Hara Shobō, 1981, pp. 248–9. Murai was the author of the best-selling novel *Shokudōraku*.

15 Kimura, *Sōgō jānarizumu*, vol. 5, p. 253.

16 Inoue, *Sōgō jānarizumu*, vol. 5, p. 7.

17 *Shufu no Tomosha no gojūnen*, pp. 40–1. Although Ishikawa was known to the general public as Ishikawa Takemi, the correct reading of his given name was Takeyoshi.

18   Tōkyō-shi Shakaikyoku (ed.), *Shokugyō fujin ni kansuru chōsa,* taken in 1922 and published in February 1924. In 1925 this survey was published under the name *Fujin jiritsu no michi* and reprinted in *Kindai fujin mondai meicho zenshū zokuhen,* vol. 7, Tokyo, Nihon Tosho Sentā, 1982. Hereafter cited as Tokyo City Office Survey of 1922, p. 107.

19   For information regarding early women's magazines in Britain, see Margaret Beetham, *A Magazine of HER OWN?: Domesticity and Desire in the Woman's Magazine, 1800–1914,* London and New York, Routledge, 1996, particularly Parts III and IV. Frank Luther Mott's *A History of American Magazines, 1741–1930,* vols 1–5, Cambridge, Mass., Harvard University Press, 1938–39, though dated, is still a detailed source on early women's magazines in the United States.

20   Minemura Toshio, "Kigyō fujin zasshi keitai ron," *Sōgō jānarizumu,* vol. 5, pp. 26–7.

21   "Joshi shōgakkō shūgaku ritsu" and "Joshi chūtōgakkō kōtōgakkō-tōkeihyō," in Kokuritsu Kokkai Toshokan Chōsa Rippō Kōsakyoku (ed.), *Meiji-ikō kyōiku bunka tōkei,* 1957, reprinted in Ōhama Tetsuya and Kumakura Isao, *Kindai Nihon no seikatsu to shakai,* Tokyo, Hōsō Daigaku, 1989, pp. 72–3. On early women's higher schools, see Fukuda et al., *Kōtō jogakkō shiryō shūsei — kōtō jogakkō no kenkyū,* pp. 3–13.

22   Tokyo City Office Survey of 1922, Introduction.

23   See Chimoto Akiko, "Nihon ni okeru seibetsu yakuwari bungyō no keisei," in Ogino Miho et al., *Seido toshite no onna — sei, san, kazoku no hikaku shakaishi,* Heibonsha, 1990, p. 192. Also see Iwasaki Jirō, *Bukka no sesō hen,* Tokyo, Yomiuri Shinbunsha, 1982, pp. 60–l.

24   *Shufu no Tomosha no gojūnen,* p. 53.

25   Hirabayashi Hatsunosuke, "Fujin zasshi kanken," *Kaizō,* March 1927, p. 70.

26   Inoue Matsuko, "Ryūkō to katei kiji ni tsuite," *Sōgō jānarizumu,* vol. 5, pp. l–2.

27   *Shufu no Tomosha no gojūnen,* p. 46.

28   Nii Itaru, "Fujin zasshi ron," in *Sōgō jānarizumu,* vol. 7, p. 276. Yosano Akiko also expressed skepticism of women's magazines from early on. "Fujin zasshi no dakyōteki keikō," January 1919 and reprinted in *Teihon Yosano Akiko zenshū,* Tokyo, Kōdansha, 1980, vol. 17, p. 315.

29   Yamakawa Kikue, "Fujin zasshi no hizokusei," *Fujin to sesō* (1937), *Yamakawa Kikue shū,* vol. 5, Tokyo, Iwanami Shoten, 1982, p. 137.

30   "Gendai fujin zasshi ron," *Keizai ōrai,* November 1930, in ibid., vol. 5, p. 298.

31   ibid., pp. 293–4.

32   Nii, *Sōgō jānarizumu,* vol. 7, p. 275.

33   In the 1910s, articles featured in American magazines such as *Ladies' Home Journal* and *House Beautiful* introduced so-called minimal houses which were designed to simplify a woman's household tasks, giving her time to get out and hold a job or do volunteer work. "Rational plans, efficient technology, and easily cleaned surfaces seemed the key." See Gwendolyn Wright, "Prescribing the Model Home," in Arien Mack (ed.), *Home: A Place in the World,* New York, New York University Press, 1993, p. 217.

34   *Kan'i seikatsu* (Simple Life), a magazine reflecting the ideals for social reform advocated by Sakai Toshihiko, Ōsugi Sakae, Kōtoku Shūsui, Kamitsukasa Shōken (the magazine's publisher), and others, was published from 1906 to 1907. American writer Charles Wagner's book *The Simple Life* was already translated into Japanese at this time.

      Atina Grossman points out that in Germany during Weimar "the pivot of the new rationalized domestic culture was the 'modern superwoman'; a health- and nutrition-conscious consumer and socializer of children, gainfully employed, and a willing and active sex partner." "The New Woman and the Rationalization of Sexuality in Weimar Germany", in Ann Snitow, Christine Stansell and Sharon Thompson (eds), *Powers of Desire: The Politics of Sexuality,* New York, Monthly Review Press, p. 158.

35   See the special issue of *Fujokai* (*Seikatsu kairyō*), May 1918, which deals with the question of daily life reform; Morimoto Shizuko, "Nichibei katei seikatsu no hikaku kenkyū (l)," *Fujin kōron,* March 1920, and "Shakō to settai — nichibei katei seikatsu hikaku kenkyū (2)," *Fujin kōron,* May 1920, pp. 53–8, 70–7; "Katei seikatsu no kaizen ni chikuonki o riyō seyo — katei seikatsu kaizen no tame ni," *Fujin kōron,* July 1920, pp. 26–30; Nishikawa Junsei, *Fujin shin undō,* Tokyo, Kōkyō Shoin, 1920.

      The directive warning against white rice no doubt was a result of the Rice Riots (*kome sōdō*) (1918) and the rising cost of rice. Sukemori Kinji, one of the original members of the Seikatsu Kaizen Dōmeikai (1920), refers to problems related to rationalization of the lifestyle tackled by the organization in his textbook *Joshi shinsahō* (Kinkōdō, 1928) which was in its seventieth printing at that time. See Appendix entitled "Seikatsu kaizen dōmeikai chōsa kettei jikō," pp. 1–14.

36   Morishita Shizuko, "Nichibei katei seikatsu no hikaku kenkyū (1)," *Fujin kōron*, March 1920, pp. 53, 55.

37   *Shufu no tomo*, July 1918.

38   Regarding the new-found popularity of consumer goods, see Ogi Shinzō, Haga Tōru, and Maeda Ai, *Tokyo kūkan —1868–1930, Modan Tokyo* (3), Tokyo, Chikuma Shobō, 1986, pp. 78–9. See aso "Modan raifu — zadankai," *Bungei shunjū*, January 1928. On the birth of the department store, see Hatsuda Tōru, *Hyakkaten no tanjō*, Tokyo, Sanseidō, 1993.

39   Inoue, *Sōgō jānarizumu*, vol. 5, p. 202; on this same subject see Sato Nobuko, "Fujin zasshi no henshū to kiji no torikata," *Sōgō jānarizumu*, vol. 7, p. 200.

40   From 1918 *Shufu no tomo* regularly solicited contributions from readers about their own problems. Murakami Nobuhiko saw this as a two-sided policy. Although Murakami believed it originated as a way for the magazine to lower its editorial expenses, he also considered it a means for "Ishikawa [Takemi] to make contact with the readers." Murakami Nobuhiko, *Nihon no fujin mondai*, Tokyo, Iwanami Shinsho, 1978, p. 124.

41   Maeda Ai, "Kindai dokusha no seiritsu," *Maeda Ai chosakushū*, vol. 2, Tokyo, Chikuma Shobō, 1989, p. 161.

42   It has been noted that an important change in women's role came in Meiji with a more affluent lifestyle. See "Shōwa shoki no mura ni okeru haha yakuwari kihan no henyō — zasshi *Ie no hikari* o tōshite," *Joseigaku nenpyō*, no. 11, November 1990. See also Ogi Shinzō, Kumakura Isao, and Ueno Chizuko (eds), *Nihon kindai shisō taikei — fūzoku sei*, Tokyo, Iwanami Shoten, 1990, pp. 362–5.

43   "Joryū shinsaigo danwakai," *Fujin kōron*, November 1923, in *Nihon fujin shūsei — seikatsu*, vol. 7, pp. 221–38.

44   *Shufu no tomo*, September 1928, quoted in Kimura Ryōko, "Fujin zasshi no jōhō kūkan to josei taishū dokushasō no seiritsu," *Shisō*, 812, February 1992, p. 245.

45   Hirabayashi Hatsunosuke, "Fujin zasshi kanken," *Kaizō*, March 1927, *Hirabayashi Hatsunosuke bungei hyōron zenshū*, vol. 2, Tokyo, Bunsendō, 1975, p. 70.

46   On April 4, 1914, the *Yomiuri* added a women's page to the newspaper. By 1921 other newspapers like the *Asahi, Kokumin, Jiji, Miyako, Hōchi*, and *Mainichi Evening News* followed suit and ran a women's page. For a more detailed discussion, see Inoue, *Sōgō jānarizumu*, vol. 5, p. 199.

47   *Kindai Nihon sōgō nenpyō*, Tokyo, Iwanami Shoten, 1968, p. 214.

48   See Maeda, *Maeda Ai chosakushū*, vol. 2, Tokyo, Chikuma Shobō, 1989, p. 185.

49   In her chapter on "Everyday Media Use," Joke Hermes remarks that "reading women's magazines, even if it is not important in itself, may still have its place or its importance in the structure of everyday routines, and thus lose its meaning while not disappearing entirely from readers' memories." Joke Hermes, *Reading Women's Magazines*, London, Polity Press, 1995, p. 19.

50   Oka, *Fujin zasshi jānarizmu*, pp. 68–70.

51   Yamakawa, *Yamakawa Kikue shū*, vol. 5, p. 290. In their concluding remarks, Rayna Rapp and Ellen Ross ("The 1920s: Feminism, Consumerism, and Political Backlash in the United States") took a stance similar to that of Yamakawa: "Looking at the twenties, we were struck by the contrast between the opening up of lifestyle opportunities for some women and the weakening of feminism as an organized, political movement to transform all of 'woman's condition'." *Women in Culture and Politics: A Century of Change*, p. 59.

Writer and intellectual Miyake Yasuko criticized fellow intellectuals like Yamakawa for placing their expectations in popular women's magazines, which she believed were read purely as entertainment and in no way reflected the intellectual level of women. Miyake Yasuko, *Gozen kuji*, Tokyo, Jitsugyō no Nihonsha, 1928, p. 39.

CHAPTER NINE

The Divided Appetite
"Eating" in the Literature of the 1920s

Tomoko Aoyama

This chapter sets out to examine literary texts of the 1920s which include as an important element the representation of food or eating. The reason for this focus on food is that it may well allow one to examine a cross-section of literature and society of the time, revealing issues which conventional literary history has ignored or concealed. It may also contribute usefully to our examination of modernism, modernity, and the modern.

The definition of "modern" in modern Japanese literature involves several major factors: political and social changes after the Meiji Restoration (1868), the Sino-Japanese War (1894–95), and the Russo-Japanese War (1904–05); the great influx of Western thought and theory; the creation of a "modern" Japanese literary language; the emergence of "modern" literary topoi such as landscape, "self," and sexuality; the development of media; and the establishment of the so-called *bundan* (socio-literary world). Depending on which of these factors one chooses, one can think of "modern" Japanese literature as beginning at a variety of moments between 1868 and 1906.[1]

The 1920s have been regarded in literary history as the period when the so-called *watakushi shōsetsu* (or *shishōsetsu*[2] — often translated as the "I novel") occupied a central position. The precise description of this genre, and even the question as to whether it does in fact constitute a genre in its own right, has long been debated by scholars, novelists, and critics.[3] It is usually described as an autobiographical narrative concentrating on the everyday life of the author, and the everyday life depicted varies from destitution to harmonious upper-class life. This latter sub-genre, if it is one, exemplified by the work of Shiga Naoya, is given another name, *shinkyō shōsetsu*, which Donald Keene explains as "mental attitude novels — a variety of the 'I novel' which usually involves meditation on some aspect of nature."[4] Despite its name, the *watakushi shōsetsu* may not necessarily have a first-person narrator, but what is important is that the reader's knowledge of the extra-textual relationship between the author and the protagonist is taken for granted. Tayama Katai's *Futon* (The Quilt, 1907) is usually identified as the first *watakushi shōsetsu* text. It was only in the 1920s, however, that the term began to appear frequently in literary debate.[5]

The *watakushi shōsetsu*, then, became an accepted genre, if vaguely defined, in the literary world of the 1920s. The same decade, especially its second half, however, saw the rise of other types of literature, such as proletarian writing, modernist or avant-garde writing, and popular literature such as detective stories and "sword" novels. Against this background the dichotomy between "pure literature" and "mass litera-ture" was created. Suzuki Sadami points out that the view that sees the "tradition" of *watakushi shōsetsu* as the core of "pure literature" was not a product of the 1920s but was "invented" by later critics such as Kobayashi Hideo, Yamamoto Kenkichi, Itō Sei, Nakamura Mitsuo, and Hirano Ken.[6] A thematic of food may turn out to be a useful tool in the deconstruction of this "invented" literary history.

Roland Barthes,[7] as is well known, saw food as a semiotic system whose language comprises:

1. rules of exclusion (alimentary taboos);
2. signifying oppositions of units;
3. rules of association, either simultaneous or successive; and
4. rituals of use.

Part of his *Empire of Signs* is devoted to the analysis of the Japanese culinary system, which is ill-suited to a discussion in Lévi-Straussian terms — that is, "the raw and the cooked." Barthes also claims that, unlike the system of clothing-as-sign, culinary lan-guage is not decided by a minority group but "evolved only from a broadly collective usage, or from a purely individual speech."[8] This difference between the two systems may indeed have existed until relatively recently, when food increasingly has become treated like fashion. This tendency for a minority group to decide the culinary language, however, was already appearing in the 1920s, as we shall see.

Food in written texts must be understood as a combination of the culinary system and a linguistic system determined by generic requirements. Kaikō Takeshi, who is undoubtedly one of the most ardent writers on food in literature, laments in many essays that eating, unlike drinking, has been regarded as "low" and hence has been absent from literature in Japan. There are, of course, exceptions. And although he does not make an issue of the time-frame, the exceptions he cites in his essay "Nihon no sakkatachi no shokuyoku" (The Appetite of Japanese Writers) all date from the 1920s.[9] It is from this period that I have chosen the texts for discussion, and they include various types of fiction and poetry. Food seems to be used in these texts essen-tially as a division marker. The division may be a social, ethical, aesthetic one, or one based on gender, and the text may take an affirmative or neutral stance toward the division, may be complicitous with the division, or may advocate opposition to it. Some texts depend on the metonymy of food and eating, while others deliberately undo the familiarized relation between the signifier and the signified and reverse the roles of the agent (the eater) and the object (food).

Food marking class distinction

We might begin with the representation of food as a sign for class distinction. This kind of representation is prominent not only in the canonical texts of proletarian literature but also in other types of texts, written from the viewpoint of the privileged class. The division between those who can afford to eat and those who cannot has, of course, been a theme in literature regardless of time and place. As far as Japanese Marxist or socialist literature is concerned, the most notable difference between the food representation of the 1920s and that of the previous decade[10] involves the contemporaneous shift in focus from primary industry to secondary industry.

In Kobayashi Takiji's *Kani kōsen* (Crab Cannery Boat, 1929), laborers are exploited in the food processing industry. Symbolically, these workers are recruited from primary industries such as mining and agriculture, which have failed to provide enough food to them. People made redundant are thrown off the land just like "peas fried in a pan."[11] Food is frequently used in this text to depict the brutal milieu on the crab boat, and the recurring metaphor is of workers being eaten.

The living quarters of the workers below decks are called *kusotsubo* (a shit pot) because of their airless and unsanitary atmosphere. It is so cold that "living creatures shiver in it as if they had been mistaken for salmons and trout and thrown into a refrigerator."[12] When they eat, they need to be careful not to drop their snot onto their hot rice. The situation of other workers is no better: construction laborers in the "new colony" Hokkaidō are called "octopuses" because they "eat their own limbs in order to survive," and miners are sliced like tuna in explosions.[13] The crab cannery workers are eaten alive by fleas, lice, and bedbugs and eat their extremely humble meals below decks, while their superiors and their visitors feast above them in the saloon on the ship.

The first two-thirds of the novel is full of such food metaphors and metonymy. When the workers start to act against the inhumane management through strikes and sabotage, however, food suddenly disappears from the text and remains absent until the concluding chapter. The exploited workers, now united, become aware of "who their enemies are, and how those enemies are connected to each other."[14] Their enemies are the industrialists, who exploit them on the pretext of "a mission to solve the problems of over-population and food shortage,"[15] the military that protect the industrialists rather than the workers, and the imperial family to whom the company makes a presentation of its product every year. The awareness of the workers is evident: "We make [the presentation cans] with our real flesh and blood. I bet they taste good. Lucky if they don't get stomach ache."[16]

The exploitation of food industry workers is depicted in many other proletarian texts, including Sata Ineko's short story "Kyarameru kōjō kara" (From the Caramel

Factory, 1928). The thirteen-year-old[17] heroine Hiroko barely has time for breakfast, which is an indispensable source of energy for her long hours of work and the only source of warmth on the cold winter morning. This is because the factory gate closes at seven sharp to exclude any latecomers and deny them their badly needed wages for the day. The tram she takes to the factory is full of workers, its atmosphere reeking of their hurried breakfasts. "Hiroko squeezed herself in between adult legs. She, too, was a worker — a fragile, little worker, like grass to be eaten by a horse."[18]

Hiroko has had to leave school where she was in grade five and doing well. In the factory, however, she suffers the humiliation of being one of the least efficient. Her income dwindles to one-third of what she started with, when the factory abolishes the fixed wage system. Girls in the factory are allowed to eat broken fragments of caramel, but their afternoon snack (always sweet potatoes) is paid for out of their meager salaries. Just like the men on the factory boat, these child laborers are seen as being devoured by the capitalists. Hiroko's own father[19] joins the exploiters by sending her to the factory while he apparently makes no effort to find a job for himself. At the end of the story Hiroko is allowed to leave the factory, but not for school, simply for another menial job at a noodle shop. Although this story is based on Sata's own experience as a child, this move from secondary industry to the service industry (both related to food) interestingly parallels the direction of capitalism. At the same time, as depicted in many women's autobiographical texts of the period, working in restaurants and cafés was one of the few ways for women to earn a living, however meager, in the rapidly growing cities.[20]

That class divides appetite is also clearly presented in Shiga Naoya's celebrated short story "Kozō no kamisama" (The Errand Boy's God, 1920). The division is between the working class, represented by the young shopboy Senkichi, and the upper class, represented by the member of the House of Peers, called A in the story. A witnesses Senkichi's embarrassment at a sushi stall — the boy has no other choice but to return the piece of sushi he has picked because it costs more than he has in his pocket. (Sushi, by the way, was regarded not as an expensive delicacy but as commoners' food in prewar Japan.[21]) Having heard from a parliamentary colleague (referred to as B) how a real connoisseur eats sushi with his fingers, and not in a proper restaurant but at a stall, A is curious to try it himself. The food and film critic Ogi Masahiro has suggested in connection with this story that around the time of World War I it began to be fashionable among "snobs" to eat dangerous, lower-class food.[22] Food was already becoming an object of fashion in the urban society of the 1920s. Just as A's curiosity is instigated by his peer's talk, the boy Senkichi's desire to taste good sushi is aroused when the topic arises in a conversation between his senior shop assistants. While A can easily indulge such a whim, however, the child cannot afford even one piece.

Unlike the two proletarian texts mentioned above, Shiga's story does not deal with extremely harsh living conditions; Senkichi, about Hiroko's age, is hungry but not starving. Neither does it express any anger or frustration over social injustice; instead, it focuses primarily on A's feelings, beginning with pity for the boy and finishing with the "strangely lonely, unpleasant feeling" that is recurrent in Shiga's narratives and his sense of guilt about making Senkichi's dream come true. A has not the "courage" to rescue the child from his embarrassing situation, but when he has another chance meeting with Senkichi, he takes the boy from his shop to a sushi restaurant without revealing his intentions or identity. The benevolent A leaves the child in the restaurant, which happens to be the one mentioned favorably in the shop assistants' conversation, telling him that he can eat as much as he likes. Senkichi eats three helpings alone in a private room, "like a starved thin dog with unexpected food."[23] Unaware of A's identity, the boy wonders if A was a god, and from then on the thought of this mysterious benefactor brings him hope.

The story concludes with the device of misekechi (showy erasure; canceling what is written and still visible): the "author" decides not to follow his initial plan to end the story with Senkichi visiting the address of his benefactor only to find a small shrine, because "it seems a little cruel to the shopboy."[24] One wonders, however, if it is not more cruel to leave the boy believing in his "god." A's scruples after his philanthropic deed may simply look like the guilt and embarrassment of the privileged, but they can also be interpreted as coming from his encounter with the naïve, unfettered appetite of the child worker, to be satisfied only in a closed room without A's presence.

It should be noted that the publication of this text coincided with another new development: children's literature. Suzuki Miekichi founded the magazine for children Akai Tori (The Red Bird) in 1918. As Karatani Kōjin points out,[25] children were "discovered" just as landscape had earlier been discovered by writers. It is no surprise that not only Shiga and Sata but also many other writers depicted children's appetite.[26]

Food marking gender division

"Kozō no kamisama" implies another kind of division, though it is rather less obvious than the class division. In her parody-critique of the story, Ogino Anna draws our attention to A's wife, whom she calls a "kakure kozō" (hidden errand boy).[27] The character appears twice in the story, both times expressing her wish to have some sushi home-delivered. Her husband, though loving and considerate, seems to be too absorbed in his thoughts to take any notice of this repeated request. Upper-class men may try out lower-class food at a street corner; their wives may not, even at home.

Another canonical text of the 1920s, Kawabata Yasunari's Izu no odoriko (The Izu Dancer, 1926), also involves the encounter of a privileged male with marginalized people. Food is by no means central in this text, which has been widely described as a pure and beautiful love story between a student and a young itinerant dancer. Nevertheless, food and drink play a significant role in it, as markers of class and gender divisions. Unlike Shiga's text, this story contains several scenes where the middle-class male protagonist accepts food or drink humbly offered by lower-class people. Only one of these scenes is directly related to the love story: when the dancer Kaoru brings the student a cup of tea, her face is flushed and her hand trembles so visibly that her brother's mother-in-law frowns at the girl's budding sexuality. Other scenes mark class–gender divisions and the student's longing to break the crust of his solitude. Traveling entertainers are regarded as outcasts and are denied entry to some villages. Women are ranked lowest in the troupe; hence the mother-in-law apologizes twice to the student for his having to share food or drink with "unclean" women.[28] In the final scene, though parted from the dancer, the student sheds joyful tears on the journey home when he finds himself accepting the food and kindness of a younger male student. This is not the beginning of a homosexual love story; the whole story is, as Arashiyama Kōzaburō sees,[29] a journey of escape from solitude rather than a love story. The student may seem at least temporarily to succeed in straddling the divisions, but it is all in his solitary mind rather than in the actual relationship.

The preparation of food is, not surprisingly, heavily gender-oriented. As Barthes remarks, "[m]ythologically, food is men's business; woman takes part in it only as a cook or as a servant; she is the one who prepares or serves but does not eat."[30] In some autobiographical texts by proletarian women writers such as Sata Ineko and Hirabayashi Taiko, this division is evident.[31] It was taken for granted that women provided food and other necessities for their husbands and lovers who were imprisoned for their illegal political activities. These men may be regarded within their circles and by later generations as martyrs to their principles, but the support of their partners, who themselves were involved in the same kind of activities, did not receive recognition until much later.

Among all these texts of the 1920s, perhaps no other captures the ferocity which the gender–sex division could take on as vividly as *Suzumushi no mesu* (Female Bell-Cricket, 1929) by Nakamoto Takako. Tomoko, depressed and miserable at the beginning of the story, gains in power, beauty, and weight at the expense of her admirer Miki, who gives her all the food he can, while he himself is starving. Living with this glorious female finally led Miki to idolize and worship her. Tomoko only despised him even more, laughing at his hopeless romanticism. She coldly watched as this male bell-cricket became emaciated with the approach of autumn, ready to be eaten by his female.[32]

Unlike the female protagonist of Hayashi Fumiko's *Hōrōki* (A Vagabond's Story, serialized in 1928, published in book form in 1930), who finds it intolerable to be supported ("fed", as the Japanese has it) by a man and decides to work as a waitress,[33] Tomoko snatches Miki's food without compunction and uses her sexual attraction to gorge herself on richer and better food. In this sense, Tomoko is strikingly similar to the "modern girl" Naomi in Tanizaki Jun'ichirō's *Chijin no ai* (A Fool's Love, 1924–25, translated by Anthony Chambers with the title *Naomi*); both thrive by taking food and other offerings from the men they disdain.

Food marking relational division

It is well known that eating has a social(izing) function.[34] A warm family meal has long been a symbol of happy union. Although that union may be structured within a patriarchal and hierarchical family system, it still connotes happiness and harmony. Because of such associations and expectations, food is often used to depict a relationship that is either dysfunctional or socially unacceptable. In Satô Haruo's poem "Sanma no uta" (Song of the Mackerel Pike, 1921), for instance, a man desperately addresses himself to the autumn winds:

> *O! Autumn winds,*
> *If you have any heart,*
> *Go and say to*
> *The wife whose husband has not yet deserted her*
> *And the little girl whose father has not yet gone away*
> *That a man is sitting here*
> *Alone at his supper table*
> *Eating broiled pike,*
> *And letting fall salty tears.*[35]

It is generally understood that the "man" is Satô himself and that the "wife" he loves is Tanizaki Jun'ichirô's first wife, Chiyoko. Tanizaki, who had long neglected his wife and had a sexual relationship with her sister (and model for Naomi), refused to divorce, which made Satô break off communications with the Tanizakis in 1921. It was nearly a decade later when Chiyoko finally obtained a divorce and married Satô. This extra-textual information, or more precisely gossip, regarding this famous *ménage à trois* usually accompanies any commentary; it is by no means essential to a reading of the poem, which became extremely popular. Its charm for the reader must surely lie in the way it skillfully mixes the commoners' fish, mackerel pike, with an elegant and old-fashioned diction and with the romantic convention of the ode. This amalgam creates the pathetic and yet humorous tone.

Problematic relationships between family members are significant elements in many autobiographical texts. Eating scenes, such as the one that appears in the prologue of Shiga Naoya's *An'ya kôro* (A Dark Night's Passing, 1922–37),[36] can poignantly illustrate family conflict. Miyamoto Yuriko's novel *Nobuko* (1928) has several examples of relational disunity marked by food. Nobuko's husband, Tsukuda, refuses to join in the family meal or tea at her parents' home. This refusal seems partly to stem from the class difference between the couple: Nobuko is an upper-middle-class daughter, while her husband is from the working class. More importantly, it is caused by their personal incompatibility. When Nobuko realizes that the marriage is unworkable, the metaphor of eating appears:

to Nobuko, who was at the height of her inner growth, an artistic atmosphere was just as essential as food; the lack of this deeply tormented her.[37]

And again:

His kind of happiness did not need Nobuko. Should she watch the satisfied husband eat his happiness, with a smile on her face and with nothing to eat for herself? She was the type of person who wanted to eat. She felt hunger acutely. She was someone who could not help eating. She realised that she had to find or create what she wanted by herself. If she asked him, he would give her some. Only she could never eat his; she wanted something cleaner.[38]

Food here represents the intellectual and artistic fulfillment which the heroine sees lacking in her relationship with her husband.

Food marking ethical division

Just as food can highlight class, gender, and relational divisions, it can mark moral and ethical differences. Nogami Yaeko's *Kaijinmaru* (*The Neptune*, 1922) presents an extreme case of ethical conflict by dealing with the subject of survival cannibalism. Unlike Swift or Sade, or her contemporary Lu Xun (1881–1936),[39] Nogami (1885–1985) does not use the subject for satirical purposes. Neither does her text depict the act of cannibalism itself; the act is attempted but stops short. The *Kaijinmaru*, a schooner with four people on board, drifts for weeks after severe storms. After many days of starvation one of the crew, Hachizō, becomes obsessed with a craving for the slender, supple flesh of Sankichi, the captain's nephew and ship's cook. Hachizō pressures the simple-minded Gorosuke to help him, and the two murder the young man. The captain manages to retrieve the body of his nephew before it is eaten, thanks to Gorosuke, now full of terror and remorse.

The captain, a believer in the guardian deity of seafarers, Kumbhira, is depicted as personifying moral fortitude. Hachizō, on the other hand, represents unchecked physical appetite. Between these two extremes sways the simple Gorosuke. Upon this allegorical structure Nogami builds realistic details of the violent storms, the interior of the ship, and the physical and psychological sufferings of the crew. *Kaijinmaru* is widely recognized as an important and pioneering text dealing with cannibalism. In literary history, however, it has largely been neglected, perhaps because it cannot be assigned to the genre *watakushi shōsetsu*, or to proletarian literature, or to any other genre.

As we have seen, workers being eaten was a recurring motif in proletarian literature. We have also seen in Nakamoto's text the metaphor of a female bell-cricket eating her mate. Human beings eaten by other human beings or animals appears in a wide range of texts of the period. If *Kaijinmaru* represents the high ethic that forbids the consumption of human flesh, Edogawa Ranpo's early work, *Yami ni ugomeku* (Squirming in the Darkness, 1926), certainly deals with the other end. Ranpo, whose pen name was taken from Edgar Alan Poe, is known as a pioneer of detective stories of a grotesque eroticism. An artist goes to a remote hot springs resort with his girlfriend. She goes missing and he is trapped with two other men in a cave underneath the hotel, where they find the remains of the bodies of people murdered – in order to eat them – by the hotel owner. They realize that this hotel owner must be responsible for the mysterious disappearance of the young woman and that of other people in the village. The hotel owner's cannibalism began as a means of survival after shipwreck and it has become an addiction. The cannibalism spreads in turn to the three men in the cave, who eat half-rotten flesh in order to survive their confinement.

Ranpo's text not only presents the obverse of the ethical decision in Nogami's text; its style, too, is dramatically different from Nogami's realism, for all that the latter is allegorical. Ranpo, as Suzuki Sadami remarks,[40] mixes scientific knowledge with the garrulous narrative style of leading *watakushi shōsetsu* writer Uno Kōji and the rich decadence of Tanizaki[41] and Kitahara Hakushū, as well as the narrative tradition of Western detective stories. It is not just the storyline that is intriguing in his text; its intertextuality, too, lures the reader into the maze.

Eating marking the transformation of the mundane into fantasy

Despite Ranpo, most of the food representations we have seen so far relate to social issues of everyday life. Eating, however, can mark an escape from the mundane and the mechanical, and there are just as many and varied examples of this as realistic representations. Ranpo's text is an example of eating depicted as passage to dark grotesque fantasy. Tanizaki's short story "Bishoku kurabu" (The Gastronome[42] Club, 1919) also treats eating as a quest for unknown delicacies. This quest does not overtly include cannibalism, but it has scenes that blur the division between the eater and the eaten. Detective-story-like suspense is combined with a detailed analysis of sense-impressions. Count G and four other members of the Gastronome Club seek stronger and stronger stimuli. Compared with the mild curiosity of the aristocrat A in Shiga's story about commoners' food, these members are already satiated with common delicacies.

> They were naturally tired of Japanese food; there was nothing new in Western cuisine, unless one actually went to Europe; even the last fortress, Chinese food — renowned as the best developed, and the most diversified in the world — began to taste to them as disappointing and insipid as plain water.[43]

The cultural division between Japan and the West, with China seen either as independent, as in the above case, or as a substitute for the West, as we shall see below, is another common theme found in texts to do with eating. Also recurrent is the close association of gastronomic pleasure with eroticism. In "The Gastronome Club" it is predicted that the members will sooner or later go insane or die of some gastric disease, which suggests to the reader the analogy of the sexual libertine succumbing to syphilis. One of the dishes comprising the members' sumptuous feast is preceded by a thorough massage of their faces, inside and out, by female hands. This gastronomic foreplay is then followed by Chinese ham and cabbage — only, Member A wonders how the taste of ham seems to come from his own saliva activated by the massage, and how the cabbage seems more like a cross between Chinese cabbage and human female fingers.[44] The aesthetics of the slimy is, as many commentators have pointed out,[45] one of Tanizaki's specialties. The following remarks made by Barthes in his reading of Brillat-Savarin fit nicely for our reading of "The Gastronome Club:"

Added to the good food, the convivium produces what Fourier (whom we always find close to B.-S.) called a composite pleasure. The vigilant hedonism of the two brothers-in-law inspired them with this thought, that pleasure must be overdetermined, that it must have several simultaneous causes, among which there is no way of distinguishing which one causes delight; for the composite pleasure does not derive from a simple bookkeeping of excitations, it figures a complex space in which the subject no longer knows where he comes from and what he wants — except to have his voluptuous pleasure —jouir.[46]

Just as Nogami's text is essential reading in any study of cannibalism in Japanese literature, Tanizaki's certainly set an example for the gastronomic novel. At the time of its publication it inspired not only writers like Ranpo but also gourmands like Kitaôji Rosanjin (1883–1959), who named his gourmet circle after the title of this story.[47] In literary criticism, however, this text was neglected for nearly six decades before the "gourmet boom" of the 1980s rediscovered it.[48]

Another text of the period, Miyazawa Kenji's story "Chûmon no ôi ryôriten" (The Restaurant of Many Orders, 1924), not only blurs the division between food and the eater but reverses the roles. Two snobbish gentlemen on a hunting excursion visit a restaurant called Yamanekoken (Wildcat House) and unwittingly prepare themselves to be eaten by the proprietor and the staff of the restaurant. Eating lures these gullible philistines out of the safety and order of everyday life. Like Ranpo's, this story is set in remote mountains, and like Ranpo's hotel, the restaurant is in Western style. The West as fashion plays an important role in both stories. Ranpo's protagonist paints Western-style paintings in his Western-style studio, while the two men in Kenji's story are attired "completely like English officers."[49] Unaware of what lurks beneath the modernity and sophistication, the visitors in both stories fall straight into the waiting lethal trap. Kenji's story was advertised at the time of its first publication as reflecting "the antagonism felt by children of villages with little food towards urban civilisation and the self-indulgent classes."[50]

In 1922 Kenji wrote a short "operetta," *Kiga jin'ei* (The Camp of Starvation), for his students at Hanamaki Agricultural School. The self-indulgent classes are represented in this play by General Bananan, who returns to his camp stuffed with food and drink, while his men are all starving. However, when his desperate sergeant and soldiers have eaten his precious banana epaulettes and medals made of sweets, the General, inspired by some divine revelation, invents the "production exercises," a new kind of physical exercise that would produce fruit for everyone.[51] The military, identified in Kobayashi Takiji's text as one of the three enemies of the workers, is given a second chance in this musical fantasy to change starvation into harvest.

Thus the alternative world to do with food or eating is not always destructive. Some of Hagiwara Sakutarô's poetry, such as "Hibari ryôri" (The Skylark Dish) and "Kanga na shokuyoku" (The Elegant Appetite), clearly represent elegant, blissful eating.[52] Sexual desire and eroticism are again combined with eating in "Sono te wa kashi de aru" (Her Hands Are Cakes) and "Katakoi" (Unrequited Love).[53] Unlike Tanizaki's greasy, slimy delicacies, food in these poems is simple and ethereal. While Chinese cuisine is the center of focus in "Bishoku kurabu,"[54] Hagiwara garnishes his heavenly dishes with a Western flavor. When specifically Japanese food appears in his poems, it is almost always associated with solitude and futility.[55]

The cultural division between Japan and the West is elaborated in many texts by Tanizaki. *Tomoda to Matsunaga no hanashi* (The Story of Tomoda and Matsunaga, 1926) is about a man leading a double life. The identity of the protagonist alternates every few years between the Japanese country gentleman Matsunaga and the decadent cosmopolitan Tomoda, alias "Tom." As his taste and lifestyle change from one extreme to the other, his weight, too, sways dramatically between 41kg (while he is Matsunaga) and 75kg (as Tomoda). Tanizaki's dichotomy of light (West) and shadow (Japan) is well known.[56] In this text he suggests another analogy: anorexic Japan and the bulimic West. China is regarded in this text as part of the West; Shanghai, Tientsin, and Hong Kong are, like the cosmopolitan Yokohama and Kôbe, Tomoda's territories, while Matsunaga lives in the old province of Yamato.

Food appears in many poems of the young Dadaist Takahashi Shinkichi. As the following sample shows, it is used to question or deny all the accepted demarcations and associations:

Can anyone declare that Dadaists are inedible? Are they not lickable?
All is food; and food is anarchists.[57]

Dish dish dish dish dish dish dish dish dish dish dish dish dish dish dish dish dish
ennui
passion with earthworms crawling on the forehead
Do not wipe the dishes
with the rice-coloured apron
Woman with a black nest of a nose
humor smokes there

>*in the pot of cold stew*
>*with life dissolved in water*
>*tedium is floating*
>*Break a dish*
>*If you break one*
>*it will make the sound of weariness*[58]

The same kind of (imagined) explosive moment appears in many other modernist texts. Toda Tatsuo's poem "Shokuyoku" (Appetite, 1924), for instance, ends with the poet's determination to throw into the fire all the forks, plates, cups, apples, and his "troublesome appetite."[59] In Kajii Motojirō's short story or prose poem "Remon" (The Lemon, 1925), too, a lemon placed on a pile of art books at the Maruzen bookshop in Kyoto becomes in the narrator's mind a golden bomb capable of blowing away his melancholy.[60] Maruzen, dealing with imported European books and goods, was to many writers and would-be writers a gateway to Western civilization.[61] Dennis Washburn keenly observes:

> The narrator wants to destroy not only Maruzen, with its luxurious goods and books that arouse in him desires that can never be fulfilled, but also the constraints that the conventions of the artistic tradition represent to him. The lemon becomes his source of self-liberation; it soothes him physically, and it becomes a symbol for the destructive impulse of his own art.[62]

Coincidentally, in Akutagawa Ryūnosuke's short story "Mikan" (The Mandarines, 1919), the eponymous fruit thrown by a girl out of the window of the moving train to her younger brothers allows the first-person protagonist to forget for a moment his "indescribable fatigue and ennui, and the impenetrable, vulgar boringness of life."[63]

Conclusion: Toward merging appetite

As we have seen, the representation of food was a significant component in the formation of the new literary genres and movements in the 1920s. For proletarian literature, food functioned as a sign of class struggle. For the newly emerged group of women writers, food was a constant reminder of the gender division and obstacles to women's liberation. While these class and gender divisions are certainly discernible in other types of texts, proletarian and women writers stepped further to identify the source and the mechanism of social injustice and exploitation. In popular literature, especially in the genre of detective stories, eating was a source of mystery and/or a quest for the bizarre and the exotic. Food was used not only to represent the materialistic and mechanistic in modern society, but also to defamiliarize mundane, everyday life or to cross the border between reality and fantasy, and between Japan and the West. The desire to eat, which in some texts is closely associated with sexual desire, may be regarded, like its counterpart, as a basic human need or as a dangerous trap leading to deviancy and destruction.

The varying perceptions of food and eating determine the form and rhetoric of representation; metaphor, allegory, and symbolism are used in both realistic and fantastic narratives for different purposes. Cannibalism, for example, is a metaphor for the gender or class struggle in some texts, while in others it is an allegory for a religious or ethical taboo, a metaphor for the ultimate hedonism, or a satirical device targeted at cultural snobbery. Just as the gustative sensation varies individually and culturally, some writers polished the aesthetic of the slimy, while others pursued the aesthetic of simplicity. Fragmented, explosive language was developed to question and invert cultural and linguistic conventions.

The desire or curiosity to transgress boundaries that appears in many texts parallels the cross-generic participation of writers. Tanizaki in the 1920s was not only writing for literary magazines but was also involved in the early days of Japanese cinema. Women wrote autobiographical stories and proletarian texts as well as detective stories, avant-garde poetry, and children's stories. We have already mentioned the intertextuality in Ranpo's text. Meandering through back alleys is found across the board, in texts by Tanizaki, Ranpo, Shiga, Kajii, and many others. All these seem to suggest two things about the literature of the 1920s: the awareness of the divisions, and the desire for transgression or destruction of those divisions. And it may well be said that these two are the driving force, as well as the critique, of modernity.

Before concluding our survey of food in literary texts of the 1920s, we must mention the exceptional case of Takamura Kōtarō, whose poems clearly propose powerful, all-inclusive eating, as is evident in the following excerpt from "Yonekyū no bansan" (Dinner at Yonekyū, 1921):

> *An August evening steams up now in Yonekyū*
>
> *I and my friends — in a trance,*
> *Praising the nutritious, mountainous beef at Yonekyū,*
> *Hearing in this vigorous human appetite and bestiality the irrepressible voice of nature,*
> *Feeling the unfathomable mind of the one who gave such a blind element to the motive power of this world,*
> *With tears at each little omnipresent sight of pure and beautiful human nature,*
> *Even to the serenely world-wise reticent greetings of the old head-waitress*
> *Sending our embraced and embracing love,*
> *Showering as members of this crowd our sincere passion over their carefree heads,*
> *With mysterious energy growing inside us — calmly left our table.*
>
> *An August evening steams up now in Yonekyū.*[64]

Thus the poem, "the best *sukiyaki* song ever written," as Kaikō puts it,[65] captures happy, energetic, and uninhibited eating, free of fear, anger, guilt, or morbid obsession. Kōtarō maintained his "vigorous human appetite" even during and after the war, which itself is unique in the history of modern Japanese literature. That, however, is a topic for another day.

Acknowledgments

This chapter is a part of the project on food in modern Japanese literature funded by the Australian Research Council Small Grant. I should like to thank the organizers and the participants of the "Modernity, Modernism and the Modern" symposium for their support and valuable comments. Thanks also to Vera Mackie and Gennifer Weisenfeld, who drew my attention to Nakamoto Takako and the Mavo poems respectively.

Notes

1   The year 1906 is when Shimazaki Tōson's *Hakai* (The Broken Commandment) was published. The novel is regarded as the first major naturalist work.

2   In the 1920s the reading of the three characters used for the term was "*watakushi shōsetsu*;" "*shishōsetsu*" became more commonly used after World War II. See Suzuki Sadami, *Nihon no "bungaku" o kangaeru*, Tokyo, Kadokawa Sensho, 1994, p. 42.

3   Studies on this issue include: Edward Fowler, *The Rhetoric of Confessions: Shishōsetsu in Early Twentieth-Century Japanese Fiction*, Berkeley and London, University of California Press, 1988; Irmela Hijiya-Kirschnereit, *Rituals of Self-revelation: Shishosetsu as Literary Genre and Socio-cultural Phenomenon*, Cambridge, Mass., Harvard University Press, 1996; and Tomi Suzuki, *Narrating the Self: Fictions of Japanese Modernity*, Stanford, Stanford University Press, 1996. See also the *zadankai* "'Watashigatari' no gensetsu ni tsuite" with Hijiya-Kirschnereit, Kamei Hideo, Suzuki Tomi, Fujii Sadakazu, and Munakata Kazushige in *Bungaku*, vol. 9, no. 2, Spring 1998, p. 226.

4   Donald Keene, *Dawn to the West: Japanese Literature in the Modern Era*, vol. 1, New York, Henry Holt & Company, 1987, p. 1244.

5   Some of the writers involved in the debate were Kume Masao, Nakamura Murao, and Akutagawa Ryūnosuke.

6   Suzuki Sadami, *Nihon no "bungaku" o kangaeru*, pp. 39–44.

7   Roland Barthes, *Elements of Semiology*, trans. Annette Lavers and Colin Smith, New York, Hill & Wang, 1967, pp. 27–8.

8   ibid., p. 28.

9   Kaikō Takeshi, *Saigo no bansan*, Tokyo, Bunshun Bunko, 1982, pp. 127–53. The three examples cited by Kaikō are Takamura Kōtarō's "Yonekyū no bansan," Satō Haruo's "Sanma no uta," and Tanizaki Jun'ichirō's "Bishoku kurabu," all of which are discussed in this chapter.

10   Examples include Mayama Seika's *Minami Koizumi-mura* (1907–09) and Nagatsuka Takashi's *Tsuchi* (1910).

11   Hayama Yoshiki, Kobayashi Takiji, and Nakano Shigeharu, *Hayama Yoshiki, Kobayashi Takiji, Nakano Shigeharu shū*, *Gendai nihon bungaku zenshū*, vol. 67, Tokyo, Chikuma Shobō, 1967, p. 147.

12   ibid., p. 150.

13   ibid., p. 163. The metaphor of an octopus eating its own limbs also appears in Hagiwara Sakutarō's prose poem "Shinanai tako" (Itō Shinkichi et al. (eds), *Nihon no shiika*, vol. 14, Tokyo, Chūō Kōronsha, 1968, pp. 352–3).

14   Hayama et al., *Hayama Yoshiki, Kobayashi Takiji, Nakano Shigeharu shū*, p. 182.

15   ibid., p. 148.

16   ibid., p. 182.

17   This, in Western terms, is twelve years old.

18   Sata Ineko and Tsuboi Sakae, *Sata Ineko Tsuboi Sakae shū*, *Nihon gendai bungaku zenshū*, vol. 83, Tokyo, Kōdansha, 1964, p. 207.

19   G.T. Shea calls this father "an unsympathetic and indolent step-father" (G.T. Shea, *Leftwing Literature in Japan: A Brief History of the Proletarian Literary Movement*, Tokyo, Hosei University Press, 1964, pp. 298–9), but it is her mother who died and her father's second marriage which broke up. Nowhere in the story is it

suggested that the father is a stepfather. Shea's description of a letter from Hiroko's teacher is also misleading; it does not say "that trying to get money for school expenses is unimportant, that it is good enough if one has only finished elementary school" (ibid., p. 299), but urges her to find someone to pay for her school expenses, which, in the teacher's opinion, should not be too difficult, and to finish at least primary school.

20   See Elise Tipton's chapter in this volume.

21   See Ogi Masahiro's *Rekishi wa gurume*, Tokyo, Chūkō Bunko, 1986, pp. 194–6.

22   ibid., p. 196.

23   Shiga Naoya, *Shiga Naoya shū*, *Gendai bungaku taikei*, vol. 21, Tokyo, Chikuma Shobō, 1963, p. 367.

24   ibid., p. 370.

25   Karatani Kōjin, *Nihon kindai bungaku no kigen*, Tokyo, Kōdansha Bunko, 1988, pp. 155–87.

26   See, for instance, Miyamoto Yuriko's "Mazushiki hitobito no mure" (1916), which begins with a scene of poor peasant children fighting with each other for food.

27   Ogino Anna, *Watashi no aidokusho*, Tokyo, Fukutake Shoten, 1991, p. 60.

28   Kawabata Yasunari, *Kawabata Yasunari shū*, *Gendai nihon bungaku zenshū*, vol. 66, Tokyo, Chikuma Shobō, 1967, pp. 23, 24.

29   Arashiyama Kōzaburō, *Bunjin akujiki*, Tokyo, Magajin Hausu, 1997, p. 272.

30   "Reading Brillat-Savarin," in Roland Barthes, *The Rustle of Language*, New York, Hill & Wang, 1986, p. 253.

31   See, for example, Sata Ineko's *Haguruma*, in Sata and Tsuboi, *Sata Ineko Tsuboi Sakae shū*, pp. 46, 65, 98, 100, 109, 118.

32   Nakamoto Takako, "The Female Bell-Cricket," in Yukiko Tanaka, *To Live and to Write*, Seattle, WA, The Seal Press, 1987, p. 141.

33   Hayashi Fumiko, *Hayashi Fumiko shū*, *Shōwa bungaku zenshū*, vol. 19, Tokyo, Kadokawa Shoten, 1953, p. 23.

34   See Barthes, *The Rustle of Language*, pp. 267–8.

35   The translation cited is from James Kirkup, trans., A.R. Davis (ed.), *Modern Japanese Poetry*, St Lucia, University of Queensland Press, 1978, p. 36.

36   *Shiga Naoya shū*, p. 7.

37   Miyamoto Yuriko, *Gendai nihon bungaku zenshū*, vol. 64, Tokyo, Chikuma Shobō, 1967, p. 157.

38   ibid., p. 165.

39   About cannibalism in literary texts, see Nakano Miyoko, *Kanibarizumu ron*, Tokyo, Fukutake Bunko, 1987.

40   Suzuki Sadami, *Nihon no "bungaku" o kangaeru*, p. 177.

41   In *Yami ni ugomeku*, Ranpo alludes to Tanizaki's food fetishism. *Ankokusei, Yami ni ugomeku*, Shun'yōdō, 1988, p. 161.

42   Tanizaki uses the rare form "Gastronomer" in his text. Tanizaki Jun'ichirō, *Tanizaki Jun'ichirō zenshū*, Tokyo, Chūō Kōronsha, vol. 6, 1973, p. 167.

43   ibid., pp. 144–5.

44   ibid., pp. 182–6. I have mentioned this scene in my paper "Cannibalism, Gastronomy, and Anorexia: A Short History of Eating in Modern Japanese Literature," presented at the 19th Biennial Conference of the Japanese Studies Association of Australia, in July 1997.

45   Arashiyama, *Bunjin akujiki*, pp. 186–96; Kaikō, *Saigo no bansan*, p. 152.

46   Barthes, *The Rustle of Language*, pp. 267–8.

47   Kitaōji Rosanjin, *Rosanjin midō*, Tokyo, Chūkō Bunko, revised edition, 1995.

48   Kaikō Takeshi, for example, writes that this text is "neither a very famous work nor a widely known short story" (Kaikō, *Saigo no bansan*, p. 144). For discussions of the story, see Arashiyama, *Bunjin akujiki*, pp. 186–96, Takahashi Gen'ichirō, *Bungakuō*, Tokyo, Kadokawa Bunko, 1996, pp. 55–9.

49   Miyazawa Kenji, *Kōhon Miyazawa Kenji zenshū*, vol. 11, Tokyo, Chikuma Shobō, 1974, p. 28.

50   ibid., p. 389.

51   ibid., pp. 325–40.

52   Hagiwara Sakutarō, *Hagiwara Sakutarō*, Itō Shinkichi et al. (eds), *Nihon no shiika*, vol. 14, Tokyo, Chūō Kōronsha, 1968, pp. 26, 136–7.

53   ibid., pp. 95–7, 160–2.

54   Kawamoto Saburō discusses a new China boom among Taishō writers including Tanizaki, Akutagawa, and Satō Haruo. See Kawamoto, *Taishō gen'ei*, Tokyo, Chikuma Bunko, 1997, pp. 165–201.

55   See, for example, "Aoki no kozue o aogite" and "Akiya no banshoku," in Itō Shinkichi et al. (eds), *Nihon no shiika*, vol. 4, pp. 61–2, 258–9.

56   The best known, and most elaborate manifesto, is his collection of essays entitled *In'ei raisan* (In Praise of Shadows, 1933–34).

57   Excerpt from "Dangen wa dadaisuto" (Declaration is Dadaist, first published in 1922). Itō Shinkichi et al. (eds), *Nihon no shiika*, vol. 20, p. 197.

58   This poem, perhaps the best known among Takahashi's poems, is numbered 49 with the subtitle "Sara" (Dishes) in the section entitled "1911nen shū" (The 1911 [sic] Collection). Ibid., pp. 205–6.

59   Toda Tatsuo, "Shokuyoku," *Mavo*, no. 2, July 1924, [n.p.].

60   Kajii Motojirō, Miyoshi Tatsuji, and Hori Tatsuo, *Gendai nihon bungaku zenshū*, vol. 43, Tokyo, Chikuma Shobō, 1954, pp. 5–7.

61   See, for example, Tayama Katai's *Tōkyō no sanjūnen*, Tokyo, Iwanami Bunko, 1981, pp. 168–73.

62   Dennis Washburn, *The Dilemma of the Modern in Japanese Fiction*, New Haven and London, Yale University Press, 1995, p. 235.

63   Akutagawa Ryūnosuke, *Akutagawa Ryūnosuke zenshū*, vol. 3, Tokyo, Iwanami Shoten, 1977, p. 61. This kind of positive image of food is exceptional in Akutagawa's texts, in which food usually marks strong disillusionment (e.g. "Imogayu" and "Negi").

64   Takamura Kōtarō, *Takamura Kōtarō zenshū*, vol. 1, Tokyo, Chikuma Shobō, 1957, p. 332.

65   Kaikō, *Saigo no bansan*, p. 131.

CHAPTER TEN

The Past in the Present
War in Narratives of Modernity in the 1920s and 1930s

Sandra Wilson

If modernity is characterized by economic, political, and social transformation, it is equally a matter of beliefs, values, and human consciousness. One of the features of modernity may well be a pronounced emphasis on the future as "a primary orientation for both imagination and activity."[1] It is also true, however, that a public consciousness of the past is essential to modernity — that is, there must be a shared story or stories about how we came to be the way we are, and hence how we came to be modern.

This necessarily produces a paradox, since modernity is a relative concept, implying a time when we were not modern, as well as perhaps the parallel existence of others who are not modern even now. It therefore implies a rupture with and indeed a repudiation of the past, as was often seen in the Japanese context in a blanket rejection of anything which could be labeled "feudal," or an "evil custom of the past," in the words of the Emperor's Charter Oath of 1868. At the same time, the modern requires a usable past, or a sort of pedigree, to legitimate and explain it. It is this pedigree of modernity in the case of Japan in the 1920s and 1930s that will be discussed here, and in particular, the function of the wars fought by Japan after 1868 in the construction of the narrative of modernity.

Official versions of modernity

By the 1920s and 1930s, Japan was widely perceived by its own articulate elite as "modern." Many of the indicators of this modernity related to issues discussed by other contributors to this volume: the rise of a mass society, continued growth of cities, expansion of the press, absorption of Western ideas, and other domestic factors. But issues to do with Japan's place in the contemporary world were also important. By the 1930s the image of the modern nation stressed vitality, growth, high levels of industrial production, large territory, and a prominent role in world affairs. In Japan, I would argue, it included a perceived capacity to go to war and a willingness to use war as a political instrument.

By this time, too, "modern Japan" had a known pedigree which was often recited by officials, journalists, and others. It began with Matthew Perry's arrival in 1853, progressed through the international treaties of the later 1850s (without always mentioning that those treaties had been foisted on an unwilling Japan), the Meiji Restoration of 1868, and the granting of a constitution in 1889; it was amply illustrated and much strengthened by victory over China in 1895 and Russia in 1905; and was both symbolized and reinforced by the equal alliance signed with Great Britain in 1902, by Japan's role in the Versailles Conference in 1919, and by subsequent founding membership of the League of Nations. By the 1920s all these events were seen as landmarks on the road stretching from feudal isolation and domestic stagnation to a modernity which included taking a prominent and active role in world affairs.

A particular version of the wars in which Japan had been involved was crucial to notions of modernity. Indeed, after 250 years of peace, the idea of warfare in itself probably helped to divide the modern from the premodern. At the same time, however, Japan's modern wars appeared as landmarks in rival discourses as well, suggesting both the power of war in the formation of public memory, and the ambiguity of wars in terms of their contributions to national "stories."

Certainly the "memories" of past wars that were current in the 1920s and 1930s differed often from the ways in which the same wars were perceived at the time they were being fought — as is common with wars everywhere. Retrospective interpretations of Japan's wars, for example, usually inscribed them as positive, rather than negative or ambiguous, experiences. It is precisely the question of which aspects were selected as reflections of or contributions to modernity that is important here.

The "dominant narrative" of Japan's modernity, including the role of warfare in achieving that modernity, was presented in many forums. It was, of course, deployed chiefly by an articulate elite, but the elite was a comparatively broad one, comprising not only government and bureaucratic leaders, but also ideologues outside of government, molders of opinion everywhere from the press to teachers and local bureaucrats.[2] Furthermore, given rising literacy rates and the remarkable growth of the press — both in themselves markers of modernity — molders of opinion were addressing more and more people as time went on, thus raising the stakes for competing versions of the same events. So the pedigree of Japan's modernity was recited to the Japanese population and to foreigners, and was used to justify a variety of actions, policies, and opinions. Within this narrative, modern war had a particular place.

Rival discourses

The terrain of the recent past, however, was fertile ground, and for those who looked backward in the 1920s and 1930s there was more than one way to chart the way Japan had come to its present. Even within Japan's elite, not all endorsed the same versions of Japan's past. The state itself was not a monolithic entity, and there was considerable fragmentation among and within its constituent parts. To give one example, civilian bureaucrats might well disagree with the army about the significance of past and present wars, preferring not to place emphasis on matters for which they had little responsibility and for which they could claim little credit.[3] Outside of government, business elites, too, tended to stress the gradual expansion of trade and participation by Japan in world economic networks rather than the role of armed conflict in promoting modernity. Amongst dissident groups, the socialists recounted a different version of the past again, emphasizing, instead of the standard landmarks, the rise of capitalism, the concomitant growth of the industrial working class, and the increase in class consciousness as signs that society was "progressing." For the socialists, war had more negative than positive connotations. Not only did it sacrifice workers in the interests of capitalists; it also placed great burdens on those who stayed at home. In later years the Russo-Japanese War of 1904–05 held a particular place in socialist memory in Japan as a time of marked repression of left-wing criticism of the government and its war.

Other influential discourses about the past considered outcomes that apparently had little to do with modernity. As will be shown below, Japan's wars appeared again in narratives which stressed the enduring nature of Japanese tradition despite modernization and change, emphasizing not the gradual acquisition of modern characteristics but rather the supposedly immutable characteristics of the Japanese people. Another important alternative narrative featured the construction of Japan as a sort of international victim: a precursor, perhaps, of the "victim consciousness" (*higaisha ishiki*) which many observers have noted as Japan's dominant historical memory of World War II. The landmarks in the prewar version of this narrative are naturally rather different from those on the road to modernity, though wars again featured prominently. The story of Japan-as-victim cited the Triple Intervention of 1895, when diplomatic pressure by three European countries forced Japan to give up territory it had won by "legitimate" means in the war with China; the failure to insert a clause proclaiming racial equality in the Versailles Treaty after World War I; the passage of the US Immigration Act of 1924, which made further Japanese emigration to the United States virtually impossible; and the anti-Japanese movement in China in the late 1920s and early 1930s.[4]

Dominant narratives — in this case, those promoted or sanctioned by the state — compete not only with rival public discourses but also with more private memories of past events. Moreover, they do not emerge fully formed at a given point in time and continue unchanged. Private memories of Japan's wars existed, and continue to exist, in a complicated relationship with each other and with state-sanctioned narratives.

The gap that could exist between official versions of Japan's wars and memories of the same conflicts among ordinary people is suggested by a tantalizing piece of evidence from 1938. The Thought Police (Tokkō) reported that a 61 year-old unemployed man had been arrested late the previous year in Toyama Prefecture for making anti-war remarks. One of his complaints was that Japanese newspapers reported only victories in the new war with China, even when Japanese troops were losing. He also observed that while Japanese now laughed at Chinese soldiers because they supposedly had to be forced into battle by their own comrades, exactly the same thing had happened in the Russo-Japanese War more than thirty years earlier, when Japanese soldiers trying to flee or retreat risked being shot from behind by a disciplinary corps of the Japanese army.[5] Such "memories," whether first-hand or passed on by others, stand in stark contrast to the official discourse, propagated widely in the decades after 1904–05, of brave Japanese soldiers full of fighting spirit and eager to lay down their lives in battle, suggesting that even decades of consistent propaganda had been unable to eliminate a sub-stratum of negative memories of the war.

Modernity and Japan's wars

Nevertheless, despite the continued existence of other versions of Japan's past, the standard story of modernity undoubtedly exerted a powerful influence in the 1920s and 1930s. In constructing and elaborating that story, ideologues of all kinds drew inspiration from the full gamut of Japan's modern conflicts: from the wars leading up to the Meiji Restoration, or more accurately the victory of the group which in theory returned the emperor to power; the wars against China in 1894–95 and Russia in 1904–05; Japan's participation in the suppression of the Boxer Rebellion of 1900 and in the World War I; and from the invasion of Manchuria in 1931–32 and the Sino-Japanese conflict in Shanghai in early 1932. Arguably the most important was the Russo-Japanese War, because, as a war against a European power — one said to have the largest army in the world at that time — it produced in a sense the greatest victory; and because it provided crucial justification for the later project of gaining direct control of Manchuria, even though that had not been the prime purpose of the war originally.

The wars functioned as a source of inspiration in four main ways: first, and most obviously, militarily successful wars provided evidence of Japan's power and prowess, exhibited through the use of modern technology by a modern army and navy; second, they produced territory as part of the victory settlements, and possession of substantial territory in itself was seen as a hallmark of the modern nation; third, they could be made to furnish proof of Japan's equality and diplomatic cooperation with the major Western nations; and fourth, they were regularly raised as laudable examples of national unity — in itself, again, a concept intimately associated with notions of modernity.

(i) Power

The view that Japan's successes in war provided evidence of power and prowess, and showed Japan's modernity in military terms, was so widespread as to be a commonplace among foreign as well as Japanese observers. Murat Halstead, an American war correspondent, made this typical comment about Japan's victory in 1905:

> *The gigantic struggle in which an Oriental nation for the first time was successful in*
> *warfare with the most populous and one of the most powerful European Powers ...*
> *brought into the family of nations a lusty giant from the East that henceforward will*
> *become one of the factors to be reckoned with in the development, progress and adjust-*
> *ments of civilization.*[6]

The specific connection with modernity was often made clear. One very long verse treatment of the war included these lines near the beginning:

> *On modern lines Japan now wages war;*
> *'Tis well that Europe should quite grasp this fact ...*[7]

The emphasis on "modern lines" was in the original.

In Japan and overseas there was great celebration of the modern ships used against Russia, the daring maneuvers implemented by Admiral Tōgō in the famous Battle of the Japan Sea, "the gigantic artillery of the modern siege batteries" used by Japan,[8] and so on.

The modernity of the Japanese military and of society itself was also stressed in contemporary and later treatments of the Sino-Japanese War of 1894–95: woodblock prints like the one in Figure 1 show a marked contrast between the modern, Western-style uniforms of the Japanese soldiers and the elaborate but loose-fitting, old-fashioned costumes of the Chinese, emphasizing a Japan advanced in modernization replacing a conservative and outmoded China. In contrast to older, more respectful Japanese views of Chinese civilization, the Chinese were now portrayed as contemptible and easily defeated; various epithets were coined linking the Chinese with pigs.[9] Murat Halstead commented ten years later that Japan had beaten China because it was more modern, in terms of society as well as the military: unlike China, Japan had "welcomed modern education and manners" in addition to "organiz[ing] and equip[ping] her army and navy according to the latest and most approved methods of warfare." In China, on the other hand, the admirable efforts of "a few bright minds" to modernize the military "were practically nullified by the prejudices and hatred of the masses against modern civilization, and by the deep corruption existing among almost all those in authority, great and small." The moral was made clear in a heading: "The Vast Hordes Do Not Always Win."[10]

(ii) Territory

The acquisition of territory was of particular importance for some observers. Since the early Meiji period, it had been obvious to Japan's leaders that the great, powerful, and modern nations in the world were colonizers, and that Japan should aim for the same status. Wars gave Japan territory — first Taiwan, won in 1895, but both the Sino-Japanese and the Russo-Japanese wars also contributed very significantly to the extension

Fig. 1 *The Sino-Japanese War in Korea, The Fall of Heijō (Pyonyang),1895, Japanese woodblock print.*
Victoria and Albert Museum, London. From Richard W. Van Alstyne, The United States and East Asia, *London,*
Thames & Hudson, 1973, p. 67.

of Japanese control over Korea, which culminated in colonization in 1910. The prominent journalist Tokutomi Sohō was one of those who were convinced of the connection between modernity and territory. He believed that emigration to other countries was
essential if Japan was to have influence in the modern age, and that modern nations:

> *backed by powerful military establishments and supported by citizens united for the*
> *purpose of promoting their common destiny, were all engaging in imperialistic expan-*
> *sion, wantonly conquering more backward civilizations in quest of the wealth and*
> *power that came from controlling overseas territories and populations.*[11]

Rights over territory were absolutely central to the retrospective construction of the
Russo-Japanese War in the late 1920s and early 1930s because the earlier war provided one of the principal justifications for Japan's moves to gain control of
Manchuria, which culminated in the covert invasion of Manchuria in 1931 and the
creation of the supposedly "new nation" of Manchukuo in 1932.

(iii) Equality

A major reason for the positive portrayal of the Russo-Japanese War was the convic-
tion expressed by many influential people that through its victory in 1905, Japan had

at last joined the ranks of the great powers. It is also true, however, that the same claim had been made before. One foreign observer, for example, already felt in 1903 that Japan, by its participation in the war against the Boxers in China two years earlier, to which it contributed about half the total number of foreign troops, had "confirmed her claim to recognition as a world power," and that the conclusion of the alliance with Great Britain in 1902 had encouraged Japan "to continue steadfast in the paths of progress along which she has been moving so rapidly."[12] Tokutomi Sohō had written that defeat of China in the 1890s "marks a new epoch in Japanese history," bringing Japan "in one leap from a national existence to a world existence."[13] By victories against Russia, he wrote ten years later, "we are dispelling the myth of the inferiority of the non-white races. With our power we are forcing [our] acceptance as a member in the ranks of the world's great powers."[14] This tentative sense of acceptance by the dominant countries of the world was strengthened when Japan was given a seat at the Versailles Conference of 1919 as one of the five major victors in the World War I, despite the very small role it had in fact played in that war.

Hara Kei (Takashi), Prime Minister of Japan from 1918 until his assassination in 1921, extended the idea that Japan now had a new place among the great powers. His 1920 view was that the Russo-Japanese War had been a sort of contribution to regional stability and international cooperation; it had been fought by Japan in self-defense in the face of Russian pressure. Foreigners now, in 1920, mistakenly believed that Japan was a militaristic country, he wrote, but informed people in Britain, which had greatly assisted Japan financially (in the form of loans) and diplomatically during the war, and in the United States, which did much for peace in the Far East by mediating the peace negotiations, knew very well what a difficult defensive war Japan had fought. At the time of the conflict, too, the Powers and their populations had shown their whole-hearted approval of the fact that the consequences of the war — which were, according to Hara, Japanese administration of Korea, Sakhalin, Manchuria, and so on — in one fell swoop removed the obstacles to peace in the Far East and indeed guaranteed permanent peace in East Asia. Thus Hara, in 1920, constructed the Russo-Japanese War as part of the history of both Japan's acceptance by and its cooperation with the Western powers. Hara went on to claim that Japan had made a large and unselfish contribution to World War I, which was a gross exaggeration by any measure.[15]

(iv) Unity

The wars with both China and Russia, as well as the invasion of Manchuria in 1931–32, were always recalled as times of national unity, though the extent to which such claims were justified is dubious,[16] and the frequency with which they were made suggests a real and abiding concern with lack of unity. Thus, in the immediate aftermath of the invasion of Manchuria in 1931, readers of a magazine aimed at villagers were presented with a story from the Sino-Japanese War in which a poor villager is reluctant to go to war because he will leave behind a sick wife and two children. On the eve of his departure his despairing wife commits suicide, leaving a note implying that he should kill the children and telling him to go and die on the battlefield, since the family has no chance of happiness in this life. The father, whose earlier appeals to the landlord for help have fallen on deaf ears, is about to carry out his wife's wishes when the village policeman, who has previously helped and encouraged the father, steps forward to take the children into his own care. The father duly goes off to war. The editorial comment is aimed at the situation in the present rather than in the past: "Japan will win victory only if, as in this story, all our compatriots work together — those who fight and those who do not fight. Let us defend our homeland, Japan."[17]

At first, assertions that in war the nation was united represented a claim to modernity to be contrasted with the premodern past, which was characterized by a fragmented, stratified society. Katsura Tarō, Prime Minister during the war with Russia, emphasized the theme of national unity from the time of the conflict itself. This war, he argued, differed from those of the past because it was everyone's war, rather than a matter only for the warrior class (*bushi*). All the people were now in a sense soldiers, implying a contrast with earlier periods when the duty to fight was the preserve of the aristocracy. Now there was no distinction between town and country either.[18] So "national unity" for Katsura meant that Japanese society in spirit was no longer stratified, hierarchical, and therefore backward. Rather, it was a society united by common goals and common striving: *national* goals, not goals related to village or region or class interest in the old sense.

In later years, however, calls for "national unity" seem to imply not an assertion of modernity but a need to repair the damage already wrought by modern trends. Modernity, for many observers, had come to mean not unity but new kinds of social division, especially division based on class in the Marxist sense, and differences created by or reflected in party politics, in which "parties" were synonymous with "partisan" interests. The past was now constructed not as fragmented but as a time of social unity. That unity still potentially existed among the Japanese people, but it was apparently a fragile thing, in need of regular bolstering. Thus the need to "reawaken" national unity and national spirit was a frequent theme in various kinds of discourse in the 1920s and 1930s. Times of crisis were often said to be the occasion of such "reawakening."

In the years after the Russo-Japanese War, Home Ministry bureaucrats, for example, invoked that conflict as a time marked by a sense of nation and a spirit of public service and cooperation.[19] It was a theme that tended to arise whenever a particular observer felt that social cooperation was lacking in the present. By this time, the earthquake of 1923 had been added to the wars in the list of events that had called forth such praiseworthy national unity. For one observer writing in 1933, the significance of the earthquake was that "we returned to our original selves," discovering a spirit of neighborliness (obviously excluding Koreans) that previously had lapsed. On the tenth anniversary of the earthquake, however, he lamented that the spiritual revival of 1923 had died away, and Tokyo, though outwardly magnificent in its prosperity, now lacked all spiritual substance. One recent consequence, according to this writer, had been the attempted right-wing *coup d'état* of May 15, 1932: the young terrorists, appalled at the corruption of the political parties, *zaibatsu*, and government, had tried to save their country by administering a shock to Tokyo as great as that of the earthquake, in order to generate an equal spiritual revival.[20]

Some private citizens recalled the war with Russia in similar terms. The publisher Noma Seiji, discussed by Barbara Sato in chapter 8 of this volume, reminisced in idealistic terms in 1934 that "while Tsarist Russia was divided in its counsels, Japan was united from highest to lowest."[21] The crisis over Manchuria from September 1931 onward was often said to be having the same effect, though clearly not sufficiently to impress the writer on the earthquake, discussed above, who felt that Tokyo had not awakened from its lethargy until May 1932. It was not uncommon for other observers to assert that the Japanese people had lost their sense of national purpose until it was rekindled in group acts of sending off soldiers and making up packages to send to the front during the fighting in Manchuria in 1931–32.[22] Thus, past wars were used to hold up an idealized model of social cooperation, often, as noted above, because that cooperation was seen to have been diluted by modernization. In effect, a "memory" of national unity was being used to foster national unity. But by the early 1930s the implication was not so much that national unity was necessary to overcome the divisions inherent in a feudal society. Rather, national unity meant overcoming the divisions inherent in *modernity* — that is, petty and selfish differences within the population produced by new social conditions were now collectively to be forgotten.

By the same token, it is ironic that the wars could produce a quite different rhetorical point. At the very time that Prime Minister Katsura Tarô was extolling the virtues of national unity in 1904–05, one of his harshest critics, the famous socialist Kôtoku Shûsui, was making the opposite point on the basis of another modernizing ideology, that of socialism. For Kôtoku, the fundamental point about the war was that it benefited capitalists to the detriment of workers, and thus it was a nonsense to say that the meaning of the war was the same for all Japanese.[23]

Remembering and forgetting

So, Japan's modern wars, in the hands of an articulate elite, became part of a narrative of national identity, forging links between past experience and present concerns. Representation of past wars in the dominant discourse was, of course, selective: as Benedict Anderson points out, forgetting can be as important as remembering in the construction of historical memory.[24] The Russo-Japanese War, for example, had originally been fought over the issue of control of Korea: as the declaration of war said, "the safety of Corea [sic] is in danger, the vital interests of Our Empire are menaced."[25]

Within a few years, however, the reconstructed Russo-Japanese War appeared to have been about Manchuria first and foremost, not Korea at all. The reason was undoubtedly the desire to weave the conflict with Russia into a narrative which would justify a Japanese invasion of Manchuria, either prospectively or retrospectively. By 1931–33, readers of daily newspapers and popular magazines were continually being told that Manchuria "belonged" to Japan by virtue of the blood and treasure expended there twenty-five years earlier, when Japan had made such sacrifices on behalf of Manchuria. "Manchurian March," one of a number of patriotic songs written in the aftermath of the Manchurian Incident, was typical in its emotive linking of the two wars through the common ground of Manchuria and through the theme of sacrifice:

> The bones of the brave warriors of the long-past battles between
>   Japan and Russia are buried here.
> Look up at the monument to the war dead.
> Bathed in the evening sun which is stained with red blood,
> Set on a thousand miles of plain, it soars high into the sky.[26]

In both official and popular discourse, the centrality of Korea to the earlier war was almost completely forgotten, now that Korea was a colony and control of Manchuria was the aim.

Similarly, the fact that Japan's victory in 1905 had been a precarious and ambiguous one, gained at enormous cost, was also "forgotten." Although in 1905 the terms of the peace treaty with Russia were so unsatisfactory to the public at large as to provoke major civil disturbance in Tokyo and other cities, by the 1920s and 1930s it was simply a great victory for Japan, and established Japan's claim to Manchuria. The "costs" of the war were certainly stressed again and again. But, in a curious way, the human and financial costs were remembered only in a positive light, as irrefutable evidence of Japan's right to control Manchuria. The negative connotations of these costs — which had placed enormous strain on all sectors of Japanese society and had led military and political leaders to seek peace quickly in the knowledge that Japan could not keep fighting much longer — were, again, forgotten. Such reshaping of the war experience was no accidental process; the devices used to aid it included not only written texts, speeches, and popular songs such as those alluded to here, but the many war memorials built throughout Japan after 1905, and the increasing emphasis on the national monument, Yasukuni Shrine, which in the 1930s became more and more prominent in daily civilian life.[27]

"Japanese spirit"

Japan's wars were thus ideal sources of inspiration for an elite seeking to construct a pedigree of modernity. In the final analysis, however, the legacy of the wars was ambiguous, and modernity was not the only lesson that could be learned. The wars

Fig. 2 *Matsui Noboru*, The Keepsake, *Imperial Household Collection, 1895. From Tan'o Yasunori and Kawada Akihiza,* Imeeji no naka no sensō, *Iwanami Shoten, 1996, p. 19.*

also contributed powerfully to one of the strongest discourses about Japaneseness in the prewar period: the discourse of *yamato damashii*, or Japanese spirit.

In the conflicts with both China and Russia, the idea that the unique "Japanese spirit," as exhibited by battle-front bravery and home-front sacrifice (see Fig. 2[28]), was the crucial factor behind Japanese victories was a pervasive one.[29] Such analyses were also widely accepted by foreign observers. The wars were often used as sources of inspiring exemplary stories, whether real or fabricated, for children and adults. Thus, children in the early 1930s were told stories of brave Japanese soldiers captured by the Russians twenty-five years earlier and who faced death resolutely rather than divulging any information; of a soldier who through his resourcefulness out-witted the Russians and engineered the capture of 160 enemy officers; of a battalion commander who, unable to commit *seppuku* (ritual suicide) because of his wounds, nevertheless heroically shot himself because his forces were in a seemingly hopeless position.[30] Kiguchi Kōhei, the heroic bugler of the Sino-Japanese War who was supposedly found dead on the battlefield with the bugle still pressed to his lips, endured in school textbooks and elsewhere for many years (see Fig. 3).[31]

Even World War I, in which Japan had played a very limited military role, could apparently provide examples of *yamato damashii*. One story recounted the episode of the captain of the *Hitachi maru*, an unarmed merchant ship challenged and then attacked by a German cruiser in the Indian Ocean in 1917. Crew and passengers were arrested by the Germans and the Japanese ship was sunk. Taking responsibility for the disaster, the captain leaped into the ocean before the enemy ship on which he was a captive reached port. Every word of the two letters he left behind, it was said, provided moving testimony to the *yamato damashii* which impelled him to this action.[32]

In such ways, retrospective versions of Japan's wars strongly reinforced a dis-course about qualities that were essential, not progressively acquired; qualities that were transcendental, immutable, and which stood outside of historical processes. In this sense the discourse of *yamato damashii* appears to have undermined the narrative of modernity, even while traversing the same historical territory. On the other hand, however, as proponents of *Nihonjinron* (theories of the Japanese) implicitly argued

Fig. 3 *Suzuki Kason,* The Valiant Bugler *from vol. 3 of* Picture Scroll of the Sino-Japanese War, *woodblock print, March 1895. From* Tan'o and Kawada, p. 9.

again in the 1970s and 1980s, there is no reason why "Japanese spirit" should not have contributed to Japanese modernity. Some in the 1920s and 1930s also claimed that it could. One writer, for example, called for a transfer of "Japanese spirit" from the army to the industrial front in order to combat the economic crisis of the early 1930s.[33]

Conclusion

The links between modernity and the interpretations of past wars had particular implications for the 1930s. Public attitudes to war are a prominent case in point. Articles in popular magazines in the 1930s, for example, show both a pride in Japan's physical capacity to wage war and a marked lack of any instinctive abhorrence for war in general. Such attitudes are very difficult to imagine in a mainstream publication of the same period in countries like Britain or France, or even the United States, where the memory of war was very different. World War I was certainly glorified, but even within the major victor nations, influential sections of opinion nevertheless retained an abhorrence for war for decades after 1918 — of which the policy of appeasement in the 1930s is one manifestation.

In popular publications in Japan in the 1930s, notwithstanding an emphasis on "Japanese spirit," the material side of warfare was by no means neglected, and journalists could be astonishingly blasé about the offensive use of war weapons. Articles about military weapons, particularly airplanes, appeared quite frequently, often with photographs. Thus, one magazine article aimed at rural readers in 1933 enthusiastically explained the latest developments in the technology of searchlights, anti-aircraft guns, automatic rifles, warships, and other weapons. Pride of place went to the airplane, because "modern warfare has become unthinkable without airplanes."[34]

As Peter Fritzsche has noted in another context, "[a]viation, perhaps better than any other field of technology, clarifies the links between national dreams and modernist visions" in the first half of the twentieth century.[35] That the military airplane in particular signified modernity for Japanese readers was clear. Thanks to the fighting between Japan and China in 1931, one article explained, the capacity of the airplane had been revealed to the world; at that time:

> [the airplane's] power — its effectiveness in actual battle conditions — was amazing, beyond even the wildest dreams of the air forces of the world Powers at the time of the great European war [1914–18].[36]

Photographs of war weapons came with captions which gloried in the destructive power of the latest technology. Thus the explanation accompanying a photograph of a large cannon mounted on a train read: "A large cannon like this, moved around on top of a train, rapidly drives away the enemy."[37]

Warfare itself was portrayed in a similarly positive way:

When the interests of nations conflict and diplomatic negotiations end in failure, the final means of telling right from wrong is war. War!! Once war breaks out, it is necessary to exert all efforts and win.[38]

Another article, aimed at young girls at New Year in 1932, constituted a virtual incitement to war against the Western powers. The author argued that now was the most suitable time for Japan to insist on the justice of its position in Manchuria, because at this point Japan was in a much more favorable position militarily than it would be in five years' time, when the United States would be better equipped for war, the Soviet Union would have reaped the benefits of its Five-Year Plan, and, in contrast, Japan's warships would be that much older.[39]

Thus, to many Japanese writers in the 1930s, military weapons were not horrifying but rather were exciting, fascinating, and modern. Furthermore, it was acceptable or even desirable to run the risk of war in pursuit of national objectives. Japan, in short, entered the 1930s with a view of war as essentially a positive and profitable undertaking, with little public memory of the enormous burdens it could bring, and with an assumption that going to war was a *modern* thing to do.

Acknowledgments

I wish to thank Dr Stewart Lone, Ms Beatrice Trefalt, and Ms Iwane Shibuya for their comments on an early draft of this chapter.

Notes

1   Peter L. Berger, *Facing up to Modernity: Excursions in Society, Politics, and Religion*, Harmondsworth, Penguin Books, 1979, p. 104.

2   On the process of disseminating officially-sanctioned ideologies, see Carol Gluck, *Japan's Modern Myths: Ideology in the Late Meiji Period*, Princeton, NJ, Princeton University Press, 1985.

3   See Sandra Wilson, "Bureaucrats and Villagers in Japan: *Shimin* and the Crisis of the Early 1930s," *Social Science Japan Journal*, vol. 1, no. 1, April 1998, pp. 121–40.

4   See, for example, "Kojin dōtoku to kokusai dōtoku," *Fujo shinbun*, March 13, 1932, p. 1.

5   Matsumura Sazo and Akashi Hirotaka, *Shōwa tokkō dan'atsushi 5: shomin ni taisuru dan'atsu*, Tokyo, 1975, quoted in Ōe Shinobu, *Nichiro sensō to Nihon guntai*, Tokyo, Tachikaze Shobō, 1987, p. 167.

6   Murat Halstead, *The War Between Russia and Japan, Containing Thrilling Accounts of Fierce Battles by Sea and Land*, Sydney and Melbourne, Walter R. Hayes and Co., c. 1906, p. 632.

7   Jane H. Oakley, *A Russo-Japanese War Poem*, Brighton, Standard Press, 1905, p. 41.

8   Halstead, *The War Between Russia and Japan*, p. 246.

9   Tan'o Yasunori and Kawada Akihiza, *Imeeji no naka no sensō (Kindai Nihon no bijutsu 1)*, Tokyo, Iwanami Shoten, 1996, pp. 13–14.

10 Halstead, *The War Between Russia and Japan*, p. 256.

11 John D. Pierson, *Tokutomi Soho, 1863–1957: A Journalist for Modern Japan*, Princeton, NJ, Princeton University Press, 1980, pp. 43, 249.

12 Ernest W. Clement, *A Handbook of Modern Japan*, Chicago, A.C. McClurg and Co., 4th edition, 1904, pp. 153, 156.

13 Quoted in Pierson, *Tokutomi*, p. 235.

14 Quoted in ibid., p. 279.

15 Hara Kei, "Sekai ni gokai saretaru Nihon no kokuminsei (Nihon wa hatashite gunbatsukuni nari ya)," October 1920, in *Hara Kei zenshū*, vol. 1, Tokyo, Hara Kei Zenshū Kankōkai, 1929, pp. 1128–36.

16   See, for example, Stewart Lone, "Region and Nation in Wartime Japan, 1904–05," paper presented to Asian Studies Association of Australia Conference, Sydney, September–October 1998.

17   "Eiga monogatari: Dôinrei," Ie no hikari, December 1931, pp. 67–71.

18   Katsura Tarô jiden, Tokyo, Heibonsha, 1993, pp. 331–2.

19   Gluck, Japan's Modern Myths, p. 194.

20   "Kokoku Nihon no fukkô: daishinsai jûshûnen ni saishite," Fujo shinbun, August 27, 1933, p. 1.

21   Seiji Noma, The Nine Magazines of Kodansha: The Autobiography of a Japanese Publisher, London, Methuen and Co., 1934, p. 97.

22   "Kokumin undô," Fujo shinbun, December 13, 1931, p. 7; Hatoyama Ichirô (Minister of Education), "Kenkoku no seishin ni tsuite" (radio broadcast), Fujo shinbun, February 14, 1932, p. 4.

23   See Sandra Wilson, "The Russo-Japanese War and Japan: Politics, Nationalism and Historical Memory," in David Wells and Sandra Wilson (eds), The Russo-Japanese War in Cultural Perspective, Basingstoke, Macmillan, 1999, pp. 160–93.

24   Benedict Anderson, Imagined Communities: Reflections on the Origin and Spread of Nationalism, London and New York, Verso, revised edition, 1991, pp. 187–206.

25   Official translation, reprinted in Morinosuke Kajima, The Diplomacy of Japan 1894–1922, Vol. II, Anglo-Japanese Alliance and Russo-Japanese War, Tokyo, Kajima Institute of International Peace, 1978, p. 162.

26   Ôe Soten (journalist with Tôkyô asahi), "Manshû kôshinkyoku," Ie no hikari, March 1932, p. 182.

27   Ôe, Nichiro sensô, p. 172; Beatrice Trefalt, "War Monuments, War Memories and Nationalism," paper presented to the Asian Studies Association of Australia conference, Sydney, September–October 1998.

28   See Tan'o and Kawada, Imeeji no naka no sensô, p. 17, for rival interpretations of this picture.

29   On yamato damashii and the Sino-Japanese War see Stewart Lone, Japan's First Modern War: Army and Society in the Conflict with China, 1894–95, Basingstoke, Macmillan, 1994, pp. 51, 60; on the Russo-Japanese War see Wilson, "The Russo-Japanese War and Japan."

30   "Manshû gunji bidan," Ie no hikari, February 1932, Children's Section, pp. 172–8.

31   See Donald Keene, "The Sino-Japanese War of 1894–95 and its Cultural Effects in Japan," in Donald H. Shively (ed.), Tradition and Modernization in Japanese Culture, Princeton, NJ, Princeton University Press, 1971, pp. 145–51; Tan'o and Kawada, Imeeji no naka no sensô, pp. 8–10.

32   Mineda Hiroshi, "Isho ga monogataru yamato damashii," Ie no hikari, February 1932, pp. 12–13.

33   Kamata Eikichi, "Sangyôteki aikokushin," Ie no hikari, October 1932, pp. 20–1.

34   "Heiki to gunkan," Ie no hikari, January 1933, pp. 16–18.

35   Peter Fritzsche, A Nation of Fliers: German Aviation and the Popular Imagination, Cambridge, Mass., Harvard University Press, 1992, p. 3.

36   Iwasaki Sakae, "Hikô shôshi buyûden," Ie no hikari, June 1933, p. 43.

37   "Kôgun no iryoku atarashii heiki," Ie no hikari, June 1933, p. 200.

38   "Heiki to gunkan," Ie no hikari, January 1933, pp. 16–18.

39   Yamawaki Fusako, "Taibô no 1932 nen," Fujo shinbun, January 1, 1932, Girls' Section, p. 1. See also, for example, "Senran no Shina de iryoku o hakkisuru shinheiki no hanashi," Fujo shinbun, February 21, 1932, Girls' Section, p. 4.

CHAPTER 11

Modern Selves and Modern Spaces
An Overview

Vera Mackie

It is a commonplace of discussions of civil society to consider the role of the newspaper in forging an imagined community of readers, potential participants in a public sphere.[1] A striking representation of the importance of the newspaper for modern political action appears in Yanase Masamu's famous poster for the *Musansha Shinbun* (Proletarian News).[2] Against a background of black-and-white newsprint, a hand seems to reach out from the flat surface of the poster, attempting to link hands with the viewer of the poster and the potential reader of the *Proletarian News*. The hand and the injunction to "Read the *Proletarian News!*" (Musansha Shinbun o Yome!) are in the bright red ink of the socialist movement. Yanase's poster creates an alternative public — the readers of the *Proletarian News*.

Yanase's imagined community, however, is much more immediate and physical than the commonplace imagining of a series of isolated patriarchs, reading their morning newspapers in the dining rooms of the bourgeois household or on the suburban commuter train, in abstract communion with their fellow readers. By reading the *Proletarian News*, says Yanase's poster, you will be able to link hands with all of the other members of the proletarian community. When read alongside other socialist iconography, however, the poster says even more. The hands may beckon other workers, they may show the way to the socialist future, they may wield tools or they may brandish weapons.[3] The hands linked in solidarity may be transformed into the clenched fists of proletarian power — the fists which will overpower the overfed capitalists. Yanase's workers are also creatures of the streets, and they inhabit the streets as gendered subjects. The street is the space which mediates between the home and the factory; the street may be the space of consumption; and the street is also the space of political protest. Part of the construction of modern capitalist societies is the construction of spaces for political action and discussion — the space of civil society. Oppositional movements like the socialist movement and the women's movement, however, were often engaged in the construction of alternative publics and alternative spaces for political action and discussion.

Yanase's poster, then, can provide a starting point for considering the production of new selves in the cultures of early twentieth-century Japanese modernity. In this reflection on "being modern in Japan," I would like to focus on three aspects of the production of modern selves: that modern selves were embodied selves; that they were produced through embodied practices; and that these practices took place in the spaces of modern, urban Japan. In focusing on the bodies, practices, and spaces of urban Japan, I am not suggesting that rural Japan was untouched by modernity. On the contrary, it was the modern technologies of the newspaper, the wireless, the railway, and the automobile which allowed the integration of rural subjects into the national community. Indeed, the very opposition between "urban" and "rural" is one of the features of modernity. In this brief essay, however, I will focus on urban spaces and practices.

In another recent collection of essays on Japanese modernity, Dipesh Chakrabarty has challenged historians to write a history of "embodied practices of subjectivity."[4] An analysis of the urban cultures of early twentieth-century Japan provides an opportunity to explore the gendered dimensions of embodied practices and the struggles over these practices, and allows us to explore some of the questions raised by Chakrabarty:

> (a) what is the history of the embodied subject?, (b) how does it connect to the history of state-formation?, and (c) what are the moments where one history exceeds the other (for it is in these moments of excess that we glimpse the possibilities of other and alternative developments)?[5]

The body of modernity

Much of the work on the cultures of Japanese modernity has focused on the body of the "modern girl," and the anxiety produced by this figure.[6] Particular anxiety was focused on the place of the woman in public space. Women in public space were often seen as sexualized figures, whether they be prostitutes, café waitresses, or the "modern girls" of the 1920s who were the successors to the "new women" of the 1910s. Contradictory understandings of the woman in public space were dramatized in a series of cartoons in the satirical magazine, *Tokyo Puck*.

The cover of one edition in 1928 showed a young woman in bobbed hair and colorful kimono faced by a somberly-clad middle-aged woman from one of the Christian reformist organizations. The caption asked "Who is happier," the woman who loves the "earth," or the woman who loves "heaven"? Several illustrations from the year 1930 showed women as dangerous, sexualized figures: the "faces" of the year 1930 were a "modern girl" in flimsy dress, a working man in cap and serge overalls, and a *nouveau riche* man in suit, overcoat, and monocle. In another illustration it is the corrupt city which is represented by a rouged woman in transparent dress and stockings.

In another cartoon from 1930, the electoral process itself is represented by the body of a soiled woman. Diet members in suits surround a naked woman with scarred body bearing the word "election." The caption laments, "It's a laughing matter that the very people who pollute the election propose to clean it up."[7] While the focus of the satire is the politicians who have engaged in corrupt electoral practices and purport to be able to "clean up" the process, the use of the body of a disreputable woman to represent this corruption uncannily reveals the gendered political discourses which continued to exclude women from the political process, even after some moderate political reform.[8] Women could either be the sexualized figures of the whore, the café waitress, and the "modern girl," or the puritanical reformists who challenged masculine sexual behavior, censured the "modern girls," or attempted to "clean up" the political system.

As portrayed in the work of Yanase Masamu and other artists of the proletarian movement, the power of the working class was also expressed in bodily terms. The cover of the leftist journal *Senki* (Battle Flag) of May 1930 shows the muscular torso of the proletarian, the flagpole of his red flag being wielded like a spear.[9] One painting of the United States-based artist Ishigaki Eitarō entitled *Ude* (Arm, 1929) shows the muscular arm of a worker wielding the hammer which symbolizes the proletarian class. The word "*ude*" (arm, or hand) refers both literally to the arm portrayed in the painting, and metaphorically to the skills (*ude*) of the manual worker.[10] In other illustrations of the proletarian arts movement, it is the worker's boot which symbolizes power. The boot is shown kicking bosses, or dealing with the traitors of the proletarian movement.[11] Violence was sanctioned by the state when soldiers were trained to aim their weapons at the enemy of the day: China in the 1890s, Russia in the 1900s, rebellious Korean colonial subjects in 1919, China in the 1930s. The violence imagined by the workers was dangerous because it was aimed at the representatives of class privilege in Japan: the factory owners, the generals, and the Diet members.

The visual culture of urban socialist movements draws on the tropes of European socialist iconography in personifying capitalism as a fat and overfed factory owner, and personifying revolution through the bodies of muscular and violent male workers.[12] In the representations of working women, however, they are represented in Japanese dress in contrast to the more international style of their male comrades, implicitly placing the women in a more localized and feminized context, while reflecting the gendered dress styles of the urban working class. We can also see a difference in the representations of assertiveness for men and women: men's assertiveness is physically represented by the clenched fist and the kicking boot, but women are rarely shown in such violent postures. Rather, women's strength is expressed through solidarity. Women link arms, share the speaker's podium, or march through the streets together.[13]

While the body of the male worker is muscular and powerful, the body of the capitalist is fat and overfed, representing excessive consumption made possible by wealth produced at the expense of the workers' "blood, sweat, and tears." The excessive consumption of the capitalist class could be represented as vampirism or as cannibalism, enacted on the bodies of the workers. Indeed, the consumption, production, and serving of food is an important marker of social class, as analyzed in detail by Tomoko Aoyama in chapter 9 of this volume.[14]

Women, too, were seen to have the bodies of workers, but this was a further source of anxiety. Commentators of all political persuasions lamented the toll which factory work took on women's bodies, and struggled to come to terms with the reality of factory work which made it difficult for women to bear and look after healthy children. Anxieties about modernity and industrialization were expressed as anxieties about the bodies of potential mothers. Representations of working mothers bore huge symbolic weight. They are often shown as Madonna figures, suckling their children against a backdrop of factory chimneys. In a literal reading, these illustrations show the conflicts inherent in the lives of working women; in an allegorical sense, these women represent the values of caring and compassion which are seen to be absent from industrial capitalist society.[15] The cover of the 1925 edition of Hosoi Wakizō's classic documentary novel, *Jokō aishi* (The Pitiful Story of the Female Factory Workers) retreats from even attempting to represent the women workers. The cover is dominated by a semi-abstract representation of chimneys, steam, bricks, and stairs.[16]

The commodification of women's bodies achieved further refinement in the early decades of the twentieth century through the culture of the cafés, and the practices of *ero-guro-nansensu* (erotic-grotesque-nonsense). The subordination of women was reinforced through the bodily practices of the cafés, while the nude figure in art became another object of consumption. The unromantic portrayal of the naked woman in Yorozu Tetsugorō's *Nude with Parasol* was shocking to modern audiences, as described by Mizusawa Tsutomu in his contribution to this volume.[17]

State interest in the bodies of women focused on their reproductive capacities. Work practices which threatened the health of women of reproductive age could compromise their ability to reproduce boy children capable of becoming soldiers whose bodies could be deployed in the service of the nation. The "modern girls" who experimented with sexuality outside the marital home were seen to be threatening the family which, since the Meiji period, had been the privileged site for the symbolic reproduction of gender and class relations and the physical reproduction of nationalist subjects.

All of these women — the factory girl, the activist, the modern girl, the suffragist, the café waitress, and the prostitute — were implicitly contrasted with another new category of woman — the housewife. The housewife (*shufu*) was a category created through the increased nuclearization of families and the increased differentiation of the roles of men and women in society. The creation of the *shufu* was accompanied by a new market for consumer goods, a new audience for specialized housewives' magazines, and the construction of new domestic spaces. These domestic spaces are discussed by Jordan Sand, and the imagined spaces of the magazines are discussed by Barbara Hamill Sato, in this volume.[18]

The partner of the housewife was the salaried white-collar worker — the *sarari-iman*. While the proletarian was defined by his physical labor, and the soldier's body was placed in the service of the nation, the *sarariiman* was engaged in clerical, techni-cal, or service work; mental labor rather than physical labor. While the proletarian is associated with embodied work and embodied political practice, the *sarariiman* is associated with the international uniform of the business suit and white shirt, and with the practices of routinized work, of commuting by train from the suburbs to the workplace, and the commodified leisure of the modern city.

The body of modernity was thus a clearly sexed and gendered body, but there were limited spaces where these binaristic notions of gender could be challenged. Miriam Silverberg has documented advertising spaces where androgyny was toler-ated, and Jennifer Robertson has described the ritualized gender-bending masquerade of the Takarazuka Revue.[19] In mainstream cultures, however, there was little tolera-tion for such ambiguity. In Japan, as in other modern capitalist societies, gender is one of the basic organizing principles of the society, reflected in the gendered practices of the home and the workplace.

The practices of modernity

Modern selves were also constituted through the everyday performance of the prac-tices of work, leisure, and home life. By the 1920s, several generations of workers had engaged in factory work. The regular routines of daily factory labor were coming to be taken for granted, although the use of night shift continued to be opposed, particularly for women workers. Similarly, office and clerical work was increasingly naturalized, at least for men. Other new professions included the social worker, the factory inspector, and the commercial artist and designer. Each of these new occupations required new forms of training. Social Work departments were created in universities. New institu-tions specialized in art and design, as outlined by Kashiwagi Hiroshi and Gennifer Weisenfeld.[20] Women gradually moved into new professions such as teacher, clerk, switchboard operator, tram conductor, and bus conductor.

In of these occupations, new routines were constituted and new forms of dress became necessary. While the female factory workers wore simple kimono and white aprons, the tram conductors and bus conductors wore distinctive uniforms, and the dress of the café waitresses reflected changing fashions of hairstyling, and the changing values attached to kimono or Western dress. The cotton kimono of the factory workers was contrasted with the silken kimono or evening dress of the bourgeois wife or mistress. Salaried men were distinguished from manual workers by their white collars and neckties. Housewives took their aprons into the streets when they joined the Patriotic Women's Association and the National Women's Defense Association.

The regularization of working life was accompanied by the creation of specialized practices and spaces of leisure. Leisure could be expressed through the practice of "*ginbura*," "strolling along the Ginza"; through window-shopping in the new department stores; or through consuming the food, drink, and spectacle of the cafés. Cafés were the site of gendered practices of consumption and of leisure. *Ero-guro-nansensu* (erotic-grotesque-nonsense) placed men in the position of consumers of erotic spectacle (or physically embodied erotic services) and women as providers of such services. As described by Miriam Silverberg, this at times literally involved the customers playing with the bodies of the waitresses.[21]

New working patterns constituted individuals into new groupings with new identities. Occupational groupings were accompanied by the formation of class groupings and class-consciousness, which overlaid and gradually superseded earlier groupings based on caste, feudal status, or regional affiliation. New forms of working-class consciousness were expressed and produced through political practices. Some of these were the strike, the political demonstration, the political lecture meeting, and the production and selling of political publications. The workers who marched in May Day demonstrations and the women who celebrated International Women's Day in the 1920s were thus linked to international political movements.

New selves were also constituted through the routines of everyday home life. Housewives engaged in the rationalization of home life, through keeping a record of daily, weekly, and monthly expenses in the *kakeibo* (home budgeting notebooks) which were printed by the publishers of the magazines directed at housewives.[22] The home was also aestheticized, as women decorated their homes, often with objects they had made themselves. The family meal, encouraged by the writers of the early twentieth century, reinforced the nuclearization of families in urban areas, as described by Jordan Sand in this volume.

The home was also the space of consumption, mediated by the labor of the housewife. There was some potential for the linking of home-based consumption with broader political issues in the consumer cooperatives which developed in the 1920s and 1930s. One woman who tried to think through the political meanings of domestic consumption was Oku Mumeo, prewar suffragist and postwar consumers' advocate, as explained by Narita Ryūichi:

> In the latter half of the 1920s, Oku Mumeo concentrated on the domestic dimension of life as a working woman. She sought to minimize the burden of housework by means of communal consumption. Her attempt to grasp living patterns in terms of consumption and socialization was also linked to her claim that living patterns ultimately came down to making consumption rational and scientific. The horizons opened up by Oku corresponded to the development of consumer society in the latter half of the 1920s, pointing the way to a new fusion of the significance embodied in the linked concepts of women/

living patterns/consumption with that of men/labor/production, with the former cluster
of concepts serving as the axis. At the same time, however, Oku reinforced the links
between women, daily life, and consumption, without examining the principles
underlying this organization of consumer society.[23]

New audiences, communities, and publics were created through reading journals
and magazines addressed to specific audiences, through writing articles for them, and
through writing to the correspondence columns. Curiously intimate exchanges were
developed in the public spaces of these publications, with people receiving advice on
the most personal problems in the advice columns of newspapers and magazines.[24]
An intellectual community of artists, critics, and consumers was created through art
magazines. Not all readers and correspondents participated on equal terms, however,
with some commentators disparaging the lack of sophistication of the young women
who attempted to participate in the public discussion of art. Visiting art galleries was
one of the features of the new urban middle class.[25] Other publications imagined a
larger community which encompassed Japan and its colonies. Mainland publications
included articles on travel to the colonies, while specialized publications such as
Nippon took propaganda to the colonies, employing the latest techniques of graphic
art and photography, a feature of Japanese magazine publishing since the late Meiji
and early Taishô period, as outlined by John Clark in this volume.[26]

For many young men, their initiation into modernity was through their conscrip-
tion into military service. There, they were trained in military routine, in the aggres-
siveness and obedience required of the soldier, and even trained in the necessary
marshaling of emotion and sexuality. Chaste and sentimental relations were fostered
between soldiers and the young women of the patriotic women's organizations, while
sexuality was focused on sexualized and racialized others through the military prostitution system. The military brothels, then, were not simply about managing the sexuality of soldiers and preventing the spread of sexually transmissible diseases, the
practices of sexuality reinforced racial hierarchy and the conceptual divisions between
"us" and "them" which made militarism and colonialism possible.

The bureaucratic management of sexuality through the military administration
was the epitome of state rationalization of practices which are often thought to be rele-
gated to a putative "private sphere." The state was also involved in the management of
the sexuality of civilian male subjects, through the regulation of the licensed prostitution districts.[27] The same state agencies which attempted to crack down on *ero-
guro-nansensu* in the cafés gave tacit approval to the commodification of the sexual
practices of the licensed prostitution districts through zoning regulations, inspections,
and the levying of taxes.[28]

National identity was honed through the encounters on the battlefield and in
colonized spaces. Soldiers learned about the proper objects of their hatred and

aggression.[29] At a government level, the military provided a focus where the modernity of the nation could be proven in an international context through military victory, as discussed by Sandra Wilson in her contribution to this volume.[30] Military success was evidence of Japan's parity with the European powers and superiority over other Asian countries. This sense of Japan as a modern power was given limited international recognition through the Anglo-Japanese Alliance of 1902, the Versailles Treaty of 1919, and the London and Washington Naval conferences of 1922 and 1930. Military victory was proof of the superior rationality of the Japanese army — proof of the country's mastery of military technology, the practices of modern warfare, and of the medical practices which supported modern armies. The development of the modern profession of nursing for women was intimately connected with the development of modern military institutions.[31]

The state was linked with the embodied practices of everyday life through the training provided to military recruits, and through the activities of a series of organizations devoted to the improvement of daily life (seikatsu kaizen). The proponents of improvement attempted to intervene in questions of dress, the furnishing of homes, eating, and leisure, thus fostering an intimate link between daily life and state policies. The choice between sitting on tatami or using tables and chairs affected the purchase of furnishings, the design and decoration of homes, the serving of meals, and the training of bodies. This intimate link between daily life and state policy was a precursor of the total management of daily life for militarist ends under the total national mobilization policies of the 1940s.[32] Total national mobilization gradually extinguished the fragile spaces of public discussion which had been fostered in the 1920s and 1930s.

The spaces of modernity

As Tipton discusses in her chapter, cafés were seen to be the quintessential spaces of modernity, with one commentator giving them equal significance with the establishment of the Diet.[33] Cafés were spaces of consumption, one of the features of the modern city. The cafés were also sexualized spaces — the spaces of ero-guro-nansensu. For many women, however, the cafés were no more nor less than workplaces. It is here that we can see that the experience of such spaces as the café had gendered dimensions. For male customers these were the spaces of consumption of food and drink, and for consumption of the spectacle and the sexualized services of the café waitresses. For the waitresses, this was a workplace, and their work entailed enticing the customers to consume as much as possible. At times, members of the union federations which developed in the 1910s and 1920s recognized these activities as work, and attempted to set up "waitresses unions" (jokyū kumiai).

The cafés were the spaces for intellectual discussion, perhaps one of the "alternative" public spaces of the 1920s. Cafés provided a gathering place for artists, and were often depicted in the novels and paintings of the early twentieth century. The café waitress was the focus of artistic expression, the depiction of her direct gaze on the customer or artistic consumer being one of the features which distinguished her from the respectable housewife. Waitresses were often shown not only serving but consuming alcohol, another feature of their difference from respectable women. This link between women and alcohol was also made in the advertisements of the early twentieth century, such as the advertisements for Akadama wine.[34]

The café highlights the twin aspects of modern capitalist societies — production and consumption. While the café represented the space of consumption, the factory was the space of production. The factory worker was the classical proletarian worker; the café waitress engaged in a service industry. The curious nature of her workplace was captured in the phrase "passion factory" (jônetsu kôjô), used by one commentator to describe the cafés.[35]

The factory was the space of routine and rationalized mass production. Although the classic proletarian worker was imagined as a male worker in heavy industry, the majority of factory workers were in fact women in textiles and light industry. Cultural representations of factory work focus on the horrors of night shift, oppression by factory supervisors, and the physical toll taken on the bodies of workers, although some fictional representations also evoke the solidarity created between workers. It is often the external features of the factory which are focused on by artists and writers: the noises which penetrated into the streets, the smoke of the chimneys, and the gigantic chimneys themselves which overshadowed whole neighborhoods. Factory machinery also lent itself to the almost abstract geometric representations of cogs and wheels which drew on the influence of the Russian constructivists.[36]

For factory workers, streets mediated between the domestic space of the home and the space of the factory. Paintings and poetry dwell on the women walking from home to factory, usually before dawn or after dark. In one illustration from a textile workers' journal, a woman stands on a street corner while her children wave goodbye as she departs for the factory.[37] Other illustrations from the socialist press and proletarian arts movement show groups of women in Japanese dress and white aprons, returning from the factory by moonlight.[38] In Hata Teruo's painting Returning from the Night Shift, 1911, a group of women in grayish kimono blend into the darkness, in contrast to the lights of the factory they leave behind. In Chimney, also from 1911, the women workers are dwarfed by a massive factory chimney which cannot be contained in the frame of the painting.[39]

There were also hierarchies in the streets. Ginza represented the heights of conspicuous consumption and spectatorism, encapsulated in the phrase "ginbura," "to stroll along the Ginza." Streets like Ginza were also the site of the department stores and the plusher cafés, and Ginza was seen as the "stage" upon which modern life was performed. The department stores came to function as extensions of the streets as soon as it became possible to enter them in street shoes, unlike the older clothing stores where customers removed their shoes and stepped up onto *tatami*-matted areas. Department store caféterias also provided a space where respectable women could consume food outside the home.[40] In the backstreets away from Ginza were less celebrated spaces; the seedier cafés and bars were in the backstreets, and the streetwalkers were even more stigmatized than the café waitresses. The relatively innocent activity of strolling along Ginza in the daytime was contrasted with the less respectable pastimes of the backstreets at night.

As we have seen, women could not enter public space without arousing anxiety about their presence. Women in public space aroused anxieties about the dichotomies between the respectable women whose proper place was the domestic space of the home, and the waitresses and prostitutes of the streets and cafés. Some feminists, such as the Bluestockings who went sightseeing in the licensed districts, challenged these conceptual divisions; but the Christian reformers and suffragists who emphasized women's essential purity were actually reinforcing the ideologies which distinguished between respectable and unrespectable women.[41]

As women were denied access to the quintessentially masculine spaces of the Diet and political meetings, the streets were the place where they carried out demonstrations, where they stated their demands as strikers, where they collected signatures for petitions to the Diet, and where they sold their publications. The streets were also the space where the posters of artists such as Yanase enjoined workers to buy proletarian newspapers, join demonstrations, support strikers in current disputes, or attend the performances of the workers' theater troupes.[42] Several commentators in other national contexts have deployed Marshall Berman's concept of "modernism in the streets" to consider the multiple cultures of modernism.[43]

The streets were sometimes the spaces where resistance was crushed. The streets were the spaces of conflict between striking workers and the gangs employed by factory owners to suppress the activities of labor unions.[44] The streets were also the site for the performance of nationalist rituals. Soldiers departing for the battlefront paraded through the streets, and were farewelled by the women of the patriotic organizations, in their white aprons and sashes.[45]

Before leaving the streets of the 1920s, we should make some mention of the effects of the Great Kantô Earthquake of 1923. An observer who patrolled the streets in the aftermath of the earthquake would have seen evidence of some of the fissures in 1920s society. Geisha of the Yoshiwara district perished in the fires, unable to escape from the brothels where they were locked in. Korean immigrants were the victims of purges after rumors of their responsibility for looting and disease. Over a dozen labor activists were murdered by the secret police. One of the triumphs of modern architecture was the survival of Frank Lloyd Wright's Imperial Hotel, and the streets of Tokyo were soon embellished with new *art deco* buildings. The earthquake also occasioned some reflection on notions of community, and those who celebrated the volunteer activity in the aftermath of the earthquake rarely tried to reconcile this with the reports of the purges of Koreans and labor activists.[46]

The cafés, the streets, and the factories were all contrasted with the space of the home. As we have noted above, with the progressive nuclearization of the family, and the creation of the full-time housewife who provided domestic support for her husband's activities in the workplace, the domestic space came to take on new meanings. These new meanings involved both a rethinking of the family itself, and a rethinking of the living space allocated to the family. As Jordan Sand has explained, "home [katei] posited a space, with definite boundaries," in contrast to the extended temporal orientation of the feudal stem family and its associated household of kin, non-kin, and servants.[47]

> Normalizing the home in Japan required redrawing the contours of domestic space and reappointing its interior. Two fundamental spatial problems had to be solved in the invention of Japanese domesticity. First, to bind family and place, and give the bond normative significance, families had to be persuaded not merely to cohabit, but to exhibit family solidarity in some concrete form … Second, to articulate the priority of family over other social groups, a house design was needed that would segregate the cohabitant family from non-kin and the outside world. Here architects had a role to play.[48]

Another intermediate space between the home and the workplace was the railway. One way to consider the connections between the spaces and practices of the home and the workplace would be to write a history of commuting. Were the trains spaces of community, spaces of privatized reverie, or spaces of oblivion where workers tried to snatch a few extra minutes of sleep? What of the stations and their surrounding entertainment districts?[49] These are alluded to by Tipton in her discussion of such entertainment districts as Shinjuku, located at the terminus of a major suburban railway line. The railway companies made an important contribution to the cultures of modernity, through the department stores established by the railway companies at the junctions of the major private railway lines, and in the leisure facilities managed by these companies. An interesting dimension of the story of the Takarazuka Revue is the development of the Hankyū railway company which sponsored the Revue.

Two of the most significant buildings of the 1920s and 1930s are the Diet building and the Tokyo railway station building. Both of these buildings represented links between the Tokyo metropolis and the wider spaces of the Japanese nation and the Japanese empire. In the 1930s it was possible to go to Tokyo Station and obtain information about train timetables all over the empire.[50] Travelers could thus perceive a link between the Tokyo metropolis and the furthest reaches of the Japanese empire. As Sandra Wilson points out, modernity was also about the acquisition of territory, and the spaces of the battlefield and the colonies were important in the imagining of the modern nation.[51]

Colonial space was also at times an imaginary space. Customers of cafés in the metropolitan centers could consume the culture of colonialism in cafés decorated with Chinoiserie, and be served by waitresses in Korean and Chinese costume. In these spaces, as in the bars, cafés, and brothels of the colonies, the difference between the citizens of the metropolis and the subjects of the colonies was reinforced in the daily encounters between the customers and their sexualized and racialized "others."[52] Japan's modernity was a colonial modernity, and as in other colonizing nations "few who were educated could escape interpellation as colonizing subjects."[53] Japanese culture was imbued with the features of a colonial and imperial power, and the identity of Japanese people was the identity of imperial subjects: "imperial" in the twin senses of serving an emperor, and in being expected to provide support for an imperialist state.

Conclusion

Being modern in 1920s Japan involved the embodied practices of everyday life. Work, leisure, and home life constituted the hierarchies of gender and race, and the occupational hierarchies of the new class system. These activities were carried out in spaces which were newly constituted, or whose meanings changed though time. The décor of the cafés at times expressed longing for the prestigious culture of Europe, at times a celebration of modernist design, at times desire for the exotic spaces of the colonies. The streets could be the space of political contestation, of nationalist ritual, of stigmatized sexual commodification, or of the conspicuous consumption of the Ginza.

The embodied practices of everyday life were linked to processes of state formation in complex ways. The state became increasingly interested in the management of the daily consumption of food, and even in the management of sexuality, affect, and emotion. This involved the management of the sentimentality which linked the soldiers and the women of the patriotic women's organizations, and the management of the negative affect which allowed the soldiers to perform their aggressive roles on the battlefield.

What of resistance and excess? Were there moments when the state's attempts to manage affect and emotion were unsuccessful? When faced with the knowledge of the total national mobilization of the 1940s, it would be easy to assume that all resistance was either crushed or recuperated. Where should we look for the evidence of the excess sought by Chakrabarty? What were the emotions which were beyond the reach of state processes? This dimension of being modern in Japan deserves further study, and hints of other possibilities can perhaps be found in some of the artistic works of the period.[54] Artistic works may at least have opened up a space for critique, and the possibility of imaging alternative futures and alternative modernities.

Notes

1   See Benedict Anderson, *Imagined Communities: Reflections on the Origins and Spread of Nationalism*, London, Verso, 1983, p. 39.

2   Yanase Masamu, "Hold Hands with 50,000 Readers: Read the Proletarian Newspaper, Friend of the People," 1928, reproduced in Jackie Menzies (ed.), *Modern Boy, Modern Girl: Modernity in Japanese Art 1910–1935*, Sydney, Art Gallery of New South Wales, 1998, p. 102.

3   Yanase Masamu, cover of journal, *Taishū*, 1929; cover of journal, *Senki*, May 1930; poster for the Fourteenth Federation of National Farmers' Assembly, 1935, reproduced in Menzies, *Modern Boy, Modern Girl*, p. 103.

4   Dipesh Chakrabarty, "Afterword: Revisiting the Tradition/Modernity Binary," in Stephen Vlastos (ed.), *Mirror of Modernity: Invented Traditions of Modern Japan*, Berkeley, University of California Press, 1998, p. 295.

5   Chakrabarty, "Afterword," p. 295.

6   Miriam Silverberg, "The Modern Girl as Militant," in Gail Lee Bernstein (ed.), *Recreating Japanese Women: 1600–1945*, Berkeley, University of California Press, 1991, pp. 239–66.

7   See Yasumoto Ryōichi, "Who is Happier," cover of *Tokyo Puck*, vol. 17, no. 6, 1928; Ikeda Eiji, "Same Faces Again for the Year," cover of *Tokyo Puck*, vol. 19, no. 1, 1930; Yasumoto Ryōichi, "Ah, the Dirty Election," cartoon in *Tokyo Puck*, vol. 19, no. 2, 1930; Okamoto Tōki [Miura Toshi], "The City," *Tokyo Puck*, vol. 19, no. 3; reproduced in Menzies, *Modern Boy*, *Modern Girl*, pp.104–5.

8   Women were excluded from holding, attending, or speaking at public political meetings by the Law on Political Assembly and Association of 1890 and the Public Peace Police Law of 1900. Women were also one of the categories of people prohibited from voting in the Electoral Law of 1890. Some of the restrictions on women's attendance at political meetings were rescinded in amendments to Article Five of the Public Peace Police Law in 1922, but women were still prohibited from becoming members of political parties and were not included when suffrage was extended to all adult males without property qualifications in 1925, despite the fact that the suffrage was also extended to male colonial subjects resident in Japan.

9   Cover of journal, *Senki*, May 1930; reproduced in Menzies, *Modern Boy, Modern Girl*, p. 103.

10   Ishigaki Eitarō, *Ude*, 1929, reproduced in Menzies, *Modern Boy, Modern Girl*, p. 100.

11   Examples from author's collection of reproductions of prewar political posters.

12   cf. Joy Damousi's discussion of Australian communist iconography. Joy Damousi, *Women Come Rally: Socialism, Communism and Gender in Australia, 1890–1955*, Melbourne, Oxford University Press, 1994, pp. 162–83.

13   See the illustrations from journals directed at women workers in the 1920s, reproduced in Vera Mackie, "Liberation and Light: The Language of Opposition in Imperial Japan," *East Asian History*, no. 9, 1995, pp. 99–115.

14   On class exploitation as vampirism, see Vera Mackie, *Creating Socialist Women in Japan: Gender, Labour and Activism, 1900–1937*, Cambridge, Cambridge University Press, 1997, p. 123; on class exploitation as cannibalism, see Tomoko Aoyama, "The Divided Appetite: 'Eating' in the Literature of the 1920s," this volume.

15   Mackie, "Liberation and Light," pp. 99–115.

16   Yanase Masamu, cover of Hosoi Wakizō, *Jokō aishi*, Tokyo, Kaizōsha, 1925, reproduced in Menzies, *Modern Boy, Modern Girl*, p. 103.

17   Yorozu Tetsugorō, *Nude with Parasol*, 1913, in Menzies, *Modern Boy, Modern Girl*, p. 69; Nakamura Tsune, *Girl in Nude*, 1914, in Menzies, *Modern Boy, Modern Girl*, p. 67; Hashiguchi Goyō, *Woman after the Bath*, 1920, in Menzies, *Modern Boy, Modern Girl*, p. 116; Sakata Kazuo, *Study of a Female Nude*, 1924, in Menzies, *Modern Boy, Modern Girl*, p. 85; Ishikawa Toraji, *Repose*, 1934, in Menzies, *Modern Boy, Modern Girl*, p. 35; Yasui Sōtarō, *Artist and a Model*, 1934, in Menzies, *Modern Boy, Modern Girl*, p. 75; Mizusawa Tsutomu, "The Artists Start to Dance: The Changing Image of the Body in Art of the Taishō Period," this volume.

18   Jordan Sand, "The Cultured Life as Contested Space: Dwelling and Discourse in the 1920s," this volume; Barbara Hamill Sato, "An Alternate Informant: Middle-Class Women and Mass Magazines in 1920s Japan," this volume. See also: Nishikawa Yūko, "The Changing Form of Dwellings and the Establishment of the *Katei* (Home) in Modern Japan," *US–Japan Women's Journal*, English Supplement, no. 8, 1995, pp. 3–36; Jordan Sand, "At Home in the Meiji Period: Inventing Japanese Domesticity," in Stephen Vlastos (ed.), *Mirror of Modernity: Invented Traditions of Modern Japan*, Berkeley, University of California Press, pp. 191–207; Muta Kazue, "Images of the Family in Meiji Periodicals: The Paradox Underlying the Emergence of the 'Home',"

US–Japan Women's Journal, English Supplement, no. 7, 1994, pp. 53–71; Nakazawa Yôko, "Katei, Uchi, Kanai, Hômu," in Satô Kiyoji (ed.), *Kôza Nihongo no Goi*, vol. 9, Part 1, Tokyo, Meiji Shoin, 1983, pp. 222–7.

19   Miriam Silverberg, "Advertising Every Body," in S.L. Foster (ed.), *Choreographing History*, Bloomington, Ind., Indiana University Press, 1995; Jennifer Robertson, *Takarazuka*, Berkeley, University of California Press, 1998.

20   Kashiwagi Hiroshi, "On Rationalization and the National Lifestyle: Japanese Design of the 1920s and 1930s," this volume; Gennifer Weisenfeld, "Japanese Modernism and Consumerism: Forging the New Artistic Field of '*Shôgyô Bijutsu*' (Commercial Art)," this volume.

21   Miriam Silverberg, "The Café Waitress Serving Modern Japan," in Vlastos (ed.), *Mirror of Modernity*, p. 217.

22   Chimoto Akiko, "The Birth of the Full-Time Housewife in the Japanese Worker's Household as Seen through Family Budget Surveys," *US–Japan Women's Journal*, English Supplement, no. 8, 1995.

23   Narita Ryûichi, "Women in the Motherland: Oku Mumeo through Wartime and Postwar," in J. Victor Koschmann (ed.), *Total War and "Modernization*," Ithaca, Cornell University Press, 1998, pp. 144–5.

24   Sato, "An Alternate Informant," this volume.

25   Omuka Toshiharu, "The Formation of the Audiences for Modern Art in Japan," this volume.

26   John Clark, "Indices of Modernity: Changes in Popular Reprographic Representation," this volume.

27   Fujime Yuki, "The Licensed Prostitution System and the Prostitution Abolition Movement in Modern Japan," *Positions: East Asia Cultures Critique*, vol. 3, no. 1, Spring 1997, pp. 135–70; Fujime Yuki, *Sei no rekishigaku*, Tokyo, Fuji Shuppan, 1997.

28   On the state management of licensed prostitution, see ibid., and Sheldon Garon, "The World's Oldest Debate? Prostitution and the State in Imperial Japan, 1900–1945," *American Historical Review*, June 1993, pp. 710–32.

29   cf Ann Laura Stoler's discussion of modern states' deployment of emotion and affect. Ann Laura Stoler, *Race and the Education of Desire: Foucault's History of Sexuality and the Colonial Order of Things*, Durham, Duke University Press, 1995; Ann Laura Stoler, "Educating Desire in Colonial Southeast Asia: Foucault, Freud, and Imperial Sexualities," in Lenore Manderson and Margaret Jolly (eds), *Sites of Desire, Economies of Pleasure: Sexualities in Asia and the Pacific,* Chicago, University of Chicago Press, 1997, pp. 27–47.

30   Sandra Wilson, "The Past in the Present: War in Narratives of Modernity in the 1920s and 1930s," this volume.

31   Suzuki Sumuko, "Jûgun Kangofu," *Jûgoshi nôto*, no. 3, 1979, pp. 1–8.

32   On the daily life improvement movements, see: Kashiwagi Hiroshi, "On Rationalization and the National Lifestyle," and Sand, "The Cultured Life as Contested Space," in this volume; Sheldon Garon, *Molding Japanese Minds: The State in Everyday Life*, Princeton, NJ, Princeton University Press, 1997, pp. 11–13, 129, 132.

33   Murobushi Koshin (Takanobu), "Kafe shakaigaku," *Chûô kôron*, September 1929, paraphrased in Elise Tipton, "The Café: Contested Space of Modernity in Interwar Japan," this volume.

34   Mariko Inoue, "The Gaze of the Café Waitress: From Selling Eroticism to Constructing Autonomy," *US–Japan Women's Journal*, English Supplement, no. 15, 1998, pp. 86–9.

35   Inoue, "The Gaze of the Café Waitress," p. 91.

36   See Yanase Masamu, cover of Hosoi Wakizô, *Jokô aishi*, Tokyo, Kaizôsha, 1925, reproduced in Menzies, *Modern Boy, Modern Girl*, p. 103; and the covers of several socialist journals, particularly in the early 1930s.

37   Cover of the textile workers' journal, *Seigi no hikari*, no. 2, 1926.

38   Cover of the textile workers' journal, *Seigi no hikari*, no. 3, 1926.

39   Hata Teruo, *Returning from the Night Shift*, 1911; Hata Teruo, *Chimney*, 1911, both reproduced in Menzies, *Modern Boy, Modern Girl*, p. 98.

40   See Weisenfeld, "Japanese Modernism and Consumerism," and Tipton, "The Café" in this volume.

41   Such dichotomies of purity and corruption have been identified in representations of women in other national contexts, most memorably in Anne Summers's classic account of Australian women's history, *Damned Whores and God's Police*. One cannot assume a simple correspondence between modernist political discourse in European cultures and in Japan, but I would argue that the *Tokyo Puck* cartoons discussed above suggest that a similar dichotomy was operating in Japanese popular discourse in the late 1920s and 1930s.

42   Matsumoto Katsuhira, *Nihon shakaishugi engekishi: Meiji Taishô hen,* Tokyo, Chikuma Shobô, 1975.

43   M. Berman, "The Signs in the Street," *New Left Review,* 1984; M.Nava and A. O'Shea (eds), *Modern Times: Reflections on a Century of English Modernity*, London, Routledge, 1996.

44   See the descriptions of the "street war" which accompanied the Tōyō Muslin strike of 1930: Suzuki Yūko, *Jokō to rōdō sōgi*, Tokyo, Renga Shobō, 1989; Andrew Gordon, *Labor and Imperial Democracy in Prewar Japan*, Berkeley, University of California Press, 1991, pp. 243–5.

45   Fujii Tadatoshi, *Kokubō fujinkai*, Tokyo, Iwanami Shoten, 1985.

46   See Ishimoto Shidzue's account of the earthquake: Ishimoto Shidzue, *Facing Two Ways: The Story of My Life*, New York, Farrar & Rinehart, 1935 (reprint: Stanford, Stanford University Press, 1986), pp. 244–54. See also Gennifer Weisenfeld's discussion of artistic representations of the earthquake and Sandra Wilson's discussion of the valorization of the post-earthquake volunteer activity as a sign of national unity. Gennifer Weisenfeld, "Imaging Calamity: Artists in the Capital after the Great Kantō Earthquake," in Menzies (ed.), *Modern Boy, Modern Girl*, p. 127; Wilson, "The Past in the Present," this volume.

47   Sand, "At Home in the Meiji Period," p. 192.

48   ibid., p. 193.

49   See Kajiwara Hisako's painting, *Station Getting Dark*, 1918, which depicts a woman resting while she waits for the train home from work; reproduced in Menzies (ed.), *Modern Boy, Modern Girl*, p. 72.

50   William Coaldrake, personal communication.

51   Wilson, "The Past in the Present," this volume.

52   Miriam Silverberg, "Remembering Pearl Harbor, Forgetting Charlie Chaplin, and the Case of the Disappearing Western Woman: A Picture Story," in Tani Barlow (ed.), *Formations of Colonial Modernity in East Asia*, Durham, Duke University Press, 1997.

53   On colonial modernity, see Tani E. Barlow, "Introduction: On 'Colonial Modernity'," in Barlow (ed.), *Formations of Colonial Modernity*, pp. 1–20; on "interpellation as colonizing subjects," see Inderpal Grewal, *Home and Harem: Nation, Gender and the Cultures of Travel*, Durham and London, Duke University Press, 1996, p. 8.

54   cf. Menzies, *Modern Boy, Modern Girl*, passim.

Chronology
Japanese Printing, Publishing, and Prints, 1860s–1930s

John Clark

Printing Technology
Meiji

c. 1854–1859
: First photograph by a Japanese survives.

1857
: Kawakami Tōgai does illustrations for woodblock plates of translation of *Robinson Crusoe*.

1860
: First lithographic press received from the visiting Prussian mission. It is left unused until 1874.

1869–70
: Matsuda Rokuzan, second head of the copperplate print atelier Gengendō in Kyōto, moves to Tokyo to do work at the Ministry of Finance Printing Bureau.

1870
: *Yokohama Mainichi Shimbun* uses movable lead type. Wooden movable type is used in other newspapers until the mid-1870s. Most commercial printing using images such as matchbox labels is done offshore in Shanghai.

1874
: The first book illustrated by lithography, a drawing manual, is produced by Kawakami Tōgai with help from Lt Guerino, a French officer at the Army Officer's School, Numazu, where the Prussian lithographic press had been kept.

: From this year the later editions of the geographical compendium *Yochi shiryaku*, which had begun printing with woodblock illustration in 1870, includes lithographic and copperplate illustrations taken from European originals.

: Umemura Suizan invites to Japan two American lithographers, Smolik and Pollard, from the Bancroft Company in San Francisco. Lithographic stones are grained by grinding with sand or small stones in a technique called *suname* to give a half-tone effect when worked. Such graining is also applied to zinc and aluminum plate printing from the 1890s, where plates are used for half-tones, *amimeban*, until the HB photographic process becomes standard in the 1920s (see below).

1875
: Iwahashi Noriaki returns to work at the Printing Bureau after studying printing techniques at the Austrian Army Map School in Vienna.

1876
: Postage stamps are printed by the electro-membrane relief printing process.

1877
: A one-yen note (issued 1888) is printed in Tokyo by the Italian printer Chiossone from etched copperplates. Chiossone had previously worked for the banknote printers Dondorf in Frankfurt.

1879
: Chiossone does a mezzotint portrait of the statesman Ōkubo Toshimichi.

1880s
: Extensive Japanese translations from Jules Verne include Japan-produced etched copperplate versions of original French illustrations. Copperplates, and increasingly lithographs, are used for regional guidebook illustrations and trade advertisements. Lithographed monochrome and hand-colored views of famous places in Tokyo and of noted geishas replace Japanese polychrome woodblock prints in similar genres.

1885
: Ogawa Isshin, who had been in Boston from 1881 to 1884, returns from studies in the United States and starts collotype printing.

1886   Azuma Kenzaburô publishes the first Japanese art magazine, *Bijutsu zôshi*.

1887   Gôda Kiyoshi returns from studying end grain woodblock engraving in France. This technique flourishes for large-run printing of illustrations until about 1895, and is still used extensively for illustrations until about 1910.

     Some newspapers, like *Kaishin shimbun*, print serialized novels with colored illustrations.

1888   The first newspaper photograph appears in the *Bôeki shimbun* at Yokohama. By Hori Kinkichi from the Land Survey Department, he uses a French technical description, translated by his department head, to heat-treating photographic emulsion to a zinc sheet.

     Chromolithography is probably in use in Ôsaka and is exhibited at Fourth Exposition to Promote Domestic Manufactures in 1895. It is used around this time for tobacco labelling by Murai Kichihei using imported American machines.

1889   September: The magazine *Fûzoku gahô* (Customs Pictorial) is published by Azuma Kenzaburô, with reportage illustrated by Yamamoto Shôkoku, Terasaki Kôgyô, Kobayashi Eitaku, Matsumoto Fûko, and Tomioka Eitaku. From about 1892 the artists include Ogata Gakkô, Ichiryûsai Masanao, Kubota Kinsen, Kawasaki Senko, and Takeuchi Keishû. The last issue is in March 1916. The artist's underdrawing is transferred to a special paper and the lithographic plate then made. On the trial ink print from this the artist indicates colors which are then printed by a craftsman.

     Collotype photograph printing is used for the first issue of Ogawa Isshin's *Shashin shinpô*. In the same year he is also the printer of the art journal *Kokka*.

1890   A zinc relief plate with photographic emulsion is invented by Saitô Shôtarô for newspaper illustration.

1892   Tsujimoto Hidegoro imports the American Levy brothers' intersecting wire web screen for photographic plate-making.

1894   Ogawa Isshin begins to print using photographic copperplates (presumably a type of etching through a photographic emulsion exposed after fusion to a copperplate), and Hori Kinkichi does likewise with zinc plates.

1897   Ishikawa Iwao publishes a technique of photographic plate production which allows three-color printing.

     The first moving pictures of a horse tram are taken by Asano Shirô.

1898   A plate-making section is founded at the Tokyo Higher Industrial School, Design Section, under Yuiki Rinzô, who is later to study in Germany from 1902 to 1923. (see 1923, below).

1900   Printing on tinplate commences.
     Shinbi taikan, with photographic collotypes by Ogawa Isshin, wins a gold medal for printing at the Paris International Exposition.

1902   A three-color plate of 'Roses' in *Bungei kurabu* is first produced from a plate made by Ogura Kenji who had studied in Austria. He had been preceded in this by Ogawa Isshin in 1896, but Ogura's work had been more in the nature of research. Ôe Hiroshi also prints three-color labels for Ebisu Beer.

1903   The first chromolithographic poster is printed for Kirin Beer.

1906   *Shashin geppô* publishes a print made for Yuiki Rinzô from a plate using the 'scattered-dust' gravure process by Masako Tamotsu.

1911   Hashiguchi Goyô uses thirty-five litho plates in a poster for Mitsukoshi.

Taishô to early Shôwa

1914   The first offset litho printing in Japan is carried out by Shôsandô (Mizuno Gukichi). It had been invented in the United States in 1906 and then developed in Germany. It allows three-color printing, a clear impression even on poor paper, and economy in the use of printing ink.

     The rotating gravure press is developed.

1915   Tokyo School of Fine Arts starts a temporary Photography Section.

1920   The photographic polychromatic flat-plate HB process, invented by Huebner and Bleistein in the United States in 1909, is brought to Japan by Ichida Kôshirô for a syndicate of Tokyo printers.

This allows the reproduction of any kind of illustration from an original photograph, drawing or painting, without hand-processing of the image.

1922   The first gravure printing is included in a newspaper in Japan as a supplement to the New Year's Day edition of the *Ōsaka asahi shinbun*.

Photogravure printing is used to print a poster for *Akadama* Port Wine.

1923   The Konishi Photographic Technical School is established with Yuiki Rinzō as Director. It becomes the Tokyo Photographic Technical School in 1926.

1927   Hamada Shōjirō perfects a two-color offset process for which he had earlier invented an automatic paper feed. He later develops a three-color gravure process.

1929   April: *Fujin sekai* includes a full-color gravure illustration using a Swiss process.

Publishing and Prints
Meiji

1867   First appearance of an advertisement in printed matter, the newspaper *Bankoku shimbunshi*.

1884   Fukuzawa Yukichi distinguishes advertisements from signboards and handbills in a newspaper article in *Jiji shimpō*.

1887   *Kokumin no tomo* (to 1895) is published in the manner of a European review.

Hakubunkan publishers are founded.

1889   *Kokka* (Flower of the Nation, to present) art historical journal is started, with woodblock reproductions of famous artworks.

1891   *Waseda bungaku* (Waseda Literature, 1891–98 and 1906–27) is founded by literary naturalist Shimamura Hōgetsu (1871-1918).

1893   *Bungakukai* (Literary World, to 1898) is founded.

1894   *Taiyō* (The Sun), a major national journal for the new middle class, begins publication by Hakubunkan.

1894–95   Woodblock prints are able to meet demand for prints of the war between Japan and Qing China.

1895   Circulation of the daily newspapers *Ōsaka asahi shimbun* and *Hōchi shimbun* reaches 400,000.

Newspaper income comes to depend greatly on advertising revenue.

1896   Mitsu Gofukuten (which from 1902 becomes the Mitsukoshi department store) begins to have designed posters for advertising, separate from picture leaflets (*ebira*).

Railway-side poster sites also begin to appear

Tokyo School of Fine Arts opens a design section, as does Tokyo Industrial High School in 1901.

1897   *Hototogisu* (Little Cuckoo, to 1902) magazine is founded by Masaoka Shiki (1867–1902), a poet. Appears with lithographic illustrations by Kuroda Seiki and others.

1900   *Myōjō* (The Daystar, 1900–08 and 1921–27) magazine begins publication. It is associated with the introduction of *Art Nouveau*, particularly through the illustrations of Fujishima Takeji, and writers such as Mori Ōgai (1862-1922), Ishii Hakutei, Takamura Kōtarō (1883–1956), Ishikawa Takuboku (1885–1912), Kitahara Hakushū (1885–1942) and Kinoshita Mokutarō (Ōta Masao, 1886–1945). Alphonse Mucha's 1896 design of *Sarah Bernhardt* is published in issue 6 of 1900.

Hakubakai (White Horse Society, founded 1896, art school from 1898), exhibits prints of Emil Orlik (later a teacher of Georg Grosz). He is introduced in a *Taiyō* article in July 1901.

1901   Fujishima Takeji is responsible for the cover of *Myōjō* until late 1905.

1902   *Bijutsu shinpō* (Art News, to 1920) begins publishing from Gahōsha, the company of Kunikida Doppō.

The journal *Jitsugyō no Nihon* is founded by Masuda Giichi, who later publishes *Yōnen no tomo*, (The Friend of Youth), *Fujinsekai* (Women's World, until 1933), and *Nihon shōnen* (Japan Youth) in 1904.

Ōsaka mainichi shimbun starts a design department, and in 1904 its rival, the *Ōsaka asahi shimbun*, starts a Design Prize for Advertising.

1903   *Tokyo Puck* is founded by Kitazawa Rakuten as a humorous magazine and includes independent illustrations by Yamamoto Kanae, Morita Tsunetomo, and Kawabata Ryūsui.

Heimin Shinbun (Common People's Newspaper, a socialist weekly, banned 1907) begins and publishes illustrations by Hirafuku Hyakusui, Takehisa Yumeji, and later by Ogawa Usen, Tobari Kogan, Kosugi Misei, and Takehisa Yumeji.

Kajita Hankō (1870–1917)and Kaburagi Kiyokata do illustrations for popular novel *Konjiki yaksha* (The Demon Gold) by Ozaki Kōyō.

November: The French illustrator Bigot leaves Japan, his press being acquired by the academic painter Okada Saburōsuke, who begins etching.

First chromolithographed poster made for Kirin Beer.

1904   April: *Myōjō* publishes an article by Ishikawa Toraji on Alphonse Mucha, illustrating the latter's work from the July 1, 1897 issue of *La Plume*.

July: *Myōjō*, edited by Ishii Hakutei, publishes an end grain woodblock engraving of *Fisherman* by Yamamoto Kanae. This work is usually taken as the first *sōsaku hanga*, or creative print, where the artist not only makes the image, but also cuts the block or prepares the plate and prints it, instead of leaving these two processes to a print craftsman as is the case earlier.

The literary journal *Shinchō* first appears.

1904–1905 Woodblock prints cannot meet the demand for illustrations of the war between Japan and Tsarist Russia. By 1910 woodblock publishing has almost ended.

1905   *Heitan* magazine produces five issues in a group around Yamamoto Kanae, Ishii Hakutei, and Morita Tsunetomo.

February: Hashiguchi Goyō does illustrations for the second part of Natsume Sōseki's *Wagahai wa neko de aru*.

1907   May: *Hōsun* begins publishing the first *Creative Print* magazine (to July 1911). The group again consists of Yamamoto Kanae, Ishii Hakutei, and Morita Tsunetomo, to whom are added Oda Kazuma, Igami Bonkotsu (1875–1933, a blockcutter who works on *Tokyo Jūnikei* (Twelve Views of Tokyo, 1910–14)) by Ishii Hakutei and Nishimura Kumakichi (printer). Igami later works on *Nihon Fūkei Hanga* (Landscape prints of Japan, 1917–20) a series by Ishii Hakutei, Ishii Tsuruzō, Morita, Hirafuku Hyakusui, Sakamoto Hanjirō, and Kosugi Misei. His students later include Fritz Rumpf, Helen Lam, Hiratsuka Un'ichi, and Nishimura Kumakichi (printer).

1908   The "bohemian" group *Pan no kai* is formed, being named after the god Pan.

1909   January: *Subaru* (Pleiades, 1909–13, run by virtually the same group as *Myōjō*) is published. In April 1910 it brings out Takamura Kōtarō's Expressionist manifesto *A Green Sun*.

April: Bernard Leach comes to Japan and in October opens courses in etching for the *Shirakaba* group.

1910   April, literary and artistic review *Shirakaba* begins publishing under the editorship of novelist Mushanokōji Sanneatsu.

Takamura's gallery holds a one-man print exhibition of work by Minami Kunzō, who had trained at the Royal Academy in London.

1911   February: Hashiguchi Goyō gains first selection in a poster competition for Mitsukoshi department store.

Hakubakai dissolved.

Taishō

1912   The earliest Fauvist group, *La Société du Fusain*, is founded by Saitō Yori, Kishida Ryūsei, Kiyomiya Akira, and also includes Yorozu Tetsugorō.

July: painters Okada Saburōsuke and Fujishima Takeji found the Hongō Painting Institute which will prepare students for entrance to the Tokyo School of Fine Arts and also educate many others who later become active as illustrators and printmakers.

1913	*Kamen* (Mask) magazine holds a print exhibition including work of Hasegawa Kiyoshi (later resident in France).
1914	*Tsukuhae* (Moonlight Reflections, to 7th issue in 1915) begins publication. The journal illustrations are drawn by Onchi Kōshirō, Tanaka Kyōkichi (d. 1915), and Fujimori Shizuo, and published by Rakuyōdō, the publishers of *Shirakaba*.
	There are 3000 retail bookstores in Japan, a figure which rises to 10,000 in 1927.
1915	Watanabe Shōzaburō asks Hashiguchi Goyō to supply a design for blockcutting and printing. Hashiguchi forms his own atelier thereafter.
1916	January: *Fujin kōron,* a women's magazine begins publication.
	Itō Shinsui does his first print for Watanabe, entitled *Looking into the Mirror.* Others later working for Watanabe include Kawase Hasui, Yamamura Kōka, Natori Shunsen, and Yoshida Hiroshi. The type of print will generally be known as *Shinhanga* (New Print).
	Takahashi Yumeji begins doing song-sheet covers for the Senow Company.
1917	February: The important early modernist poetry collection *Tsuki ni hoeru* (Crying at the Moon) by Hagiwara Sakutarō is published with prints by Tanaka Kyōkichi. Tanaka's work is taken over after his illness and completed by Onchi Kōshirō, who also does the cover.
	February: *Shufu no tomo,* a women's magazine, begins publication.
	March: Ishikawa Takemi first publishes what is to become Japan's largest-selling women's magazine, *Shufu no tomo,* usually selling 800,000–900,000 copies a month.
	Oda Kazuma publishes his twenty lithograph series *Tokyo fūkei* (Tokyo Landscapes), which marks a re-insertion into the modernist print movement of the "Famous Places" landscape prints pioneered as woodblocks in the 1820s to 1850s by Hokusai and Hiroshige, but this time with a modern, studio-based "Western-style" print technique.
1918	Nihon Sōsaku Hanga Kyōkai (Japan Creative Print Association) founded, with Yamamoto Kanae as President.
	April: the general intellectual magazine *Kaizō* (Reform) is founded.
1919	April: Yamamoto Kanae holds an exhibition of Children's Free Painting, and in October opens his Institute for Farmers' Art in Ueda, Nagano.
1920	The number of newspapers circulating is 1100, with a combined circulation of 6–7 million.
1923	September: Tobari Kogan publishes his *Sōsaku hanga to hanga no tsukurikata* (Creative Prints and Printmaking).
1924	Fourth Kokuga Sōsaku Kyōkai (National Painting Creative Association) exhibits prints. 1925 January: *Kingu* mass-circulation magazine publishes, reputedly with 700,000 copies.
	May: Sugiura Hisui forms the designers' group Shichininsha.
	June: Oda Kazuma founds a Print Research Institute in Matsue.
	The trade journal *Kōkoku sekai* (Advertising World) commences publication.
1926	April: The industrial designers' association, Shōgyō bijutsu kyōkai, is formed.

Early Shōwa

1927	The annual official art salon, Teiten (Eighth Imperial Art Academy Exhibition), begins a print section.
1928	Onchi Kōshirō and Kawakami Sumio begin their series *ShinTokyo Hyakkei* (Hundred Views of New Tokyo).
	November: first Proletarian Fine Arts Exhibition is held.
	This year about 500,000 households own radio receivers.
1930, 1936	Overseas recognition of *Shinhanga* solidified with two exhibitions, both at Toledo, Ohio.
	December: Sixteen newspapers in Tokyo protest against restrictions on the press.
1931	January: Three modernist and Western-style print associations combine to form Nihon Hanga

Kyōkai (Japan Print Association). Its journal *Shinhanga* (New Print, not to be confused with neo-Japonaiserie *Shinhanga* publishes by Watanabe) puts forward a new kind of realism and humanism but which is somewhat distanced from that of Proletarian Art.

1933   October: Hirafuku Hyakusui dies, thus marking one end to artistic links between new print-makers and the late Meiji illustrators.

1934   January: The print run of *Fujin no tomo* reaches a peak of 1,200,000. To print this magazine requires 512 pages for the main magazine and 766 pages when there is a supplement. These includes a print run of 1,650,000 for the half-tone, three-colored plates, and 600,000 for the monochrome plates.

April: Under extreme pressure from the police and with declining popular participation, ten groups dissolve the Proletarian Cultural League, marking the end of cultural activity by the political left until after the defeat in 1945.

October: Yamana Ayao and Kōno Takashi are involved in illustrations for the first issue of *NIPPON*, an offcial Japanese propaganda magazine directed at overseas readers, and luxury printed in gravure.

1935   May: Tokyo School of Fine Arts set up a temporary printmaking atelier.

1939   April: One of the first modernist printmakers, Onchi Kōshirō, goes to China as a war artist for the Army. In May 1943 he becomes head of the Print Patriotic Society under the Imperial Rule Association.

Bibliography

Chapter 1: The Artists Start to Dance (Mizusawa)

Nabei Katsuyuki, *Kanchūbōjin*, Tokyo, Asahi Shimbunsha, 1953.

Ōshima Mikio, *Umi wo watattasākasu gēnin — Kosumoporitan Sawada Yutaka no shōgai*, Tokyo, Heibonsha, 1993.

Schubert, Dietrich, "Rezeptions-und Stilpluralismus in den frühen Selbstbildnissen von Otto Dix," in W. Hager and N. Knopp (eds), *Beiträge zum Problem des Stilpluralismus*, Munich, Prestel Verlag, 1977, pp. 203–24.

Unno Hiroshi, "Senkyūhyakunijūnendai no mōdo to butō," in *Senkyūhyakunijūnendai no Pari yori — Kawashima Riichirō, Goncharova, Larionov*, Tokyo, Shiseidō, 1995.

"Yorozu Tetsugorō 'Ratai bijin' no gendaisei," in *Jibun noshizen o motometa gaka Yorozu Tetsugorō*, Tokyo, Chōritsu.

Yorozu Tetsugorō, "Tetsujin dokugo," in *Tetsujin garon*, revised edition, Tokyo, Chūō Kōron Bijutsu Shuppan, 1985.

———, "Watashi no rirekisho," *Chūō bijutsu*, November 1925.

Chapter 2: Indices of Modernity (Clark)

Aoki Shigeru (ed.), *Meiji yōga shiryō, Kaisō hen*, Tokyo, Chūō Kōron Bijutsu Shuppan, 1985 (includes Yamamoto Kanae: "Hosun jidai"; Gōta Kiyoshi: "Seiyō mokuhan omoidebanashi"; "Watanabe Yūkō joshi to Meijishōnen no hanga").

——— (ed.), *Meiji yōga shiryō, Kiroku hen*, Tokyo, Chūō Kōron Bijutsu Shuppan, 1986 (includes "Dōban, Sekiban kankei shiryō").

——— (ed.), *Nihon no kindai bijutsu*, vol.12, *Hanga*, Tokyo, Ōtsuki Shoten, 1994.

Fletcher, Angus, *Allegory: The Theory of a Symbolic Mode*, Ithaca, Cornell University Press, 1964.

Fraser, James, Steven Hellwer, and Seymour Chwast, *Japanese Modern: Graphic Design Between the Wars*, San Francisco, Chronicle Books, 1996.

Karatani Kōjin, *Shūen wo megutte*, Tokyo, Fukutake Shoten, 1990.

Kawabata Naomichi, "Modanizumu to shōgyōbijutsu," in Mizusawa Tsutomu (ed.), *Mobo Moga, 1910–1935 Ten*, Kamakura, Kanagawa Kenritsu Kindai Bijutsukan, 1998.

Kayano Yatsuka, *Kindai Nihon dezain bunkashi, 1868–1926*, Tokyo, Firumu Aato Sha, 1992.

Kondō Fumie (ed.), *Taishō, Shōwa shōnen shōjo zasshi no meibamen-shū*, Tokyo, Gakken, 1992.

Kōriyama Sachio, *Insatsujutsu kōza*, Tokyo, Insatsu Zasshisha, 1927 (Zōfu Gohan), 1942.

Mie Kenritsu Bijutsukan (ed.), *20 seiki Nihon bijutsu saiken (I), 1910 nendai, hikari kagayaku inochi no nagare*, Tsū, Mie Kenritsu Bijutsukan Kyōryokukai, 1995.

——— (ed.), *20 seiki Nihon bijutsu saiken (II), 1920 nendai*, Tsū, Mie Kenritsu Bijutsukan Kyōryoku-kai, 1996.

Minami Hiroshi (ed.), "Nihon modanizumu: Ero, guro, nansensu," *Gendai no esupuri*, no. 188, March 1983.

———, *Taishō bunka*, Tokyo, Keisō Shobō, 1965.

Nagamine Shigetoshi, "Meijiki 'Taiyō' no jūyō kōzō," *Shuppan Kenkyū*, no. 21, [n.d.].

Najita, T. and H.D. Harootunian, "Japanese Revolt Against the West: Political and Cultural Criticism in the Twentieth Century," in P. Duus (ed.), *The Cambridge History of Japan*, vol. 6, *The Twentieth Century*, Cambridge, Cambridge University Press, 1988.

Ono Tadashige, *Hanga*, Tokyo, Iwanami Shoten, 1961, 1985.

_____, *Sekibanga*, Tokyo, Bijutsu Shuppansha, 1967, 1976.

Satō Akinobu, kanshū, *Hashiguchi Goyō-Ten*, Tokyo, Odakyū Bijutsukan and Tokyo Shimbun, 1995.

Senuma Shigeki, " 'Taiyō,'" *Bungaku*, vol. 23, no. 7, 1955.

Shikano Masanao, " 'Taiyō,' shu toshite Meijiki ni okeru," *Shisō*, no. 450, December 1961.

Shimaya Seiichi, *Nihon hanga hensenshi*, Ōsaka, Ōsaka Shuppansha, 1939.

_____, *Insatsu bunmeishi*, vols 4 and 5, Tokyo, Satsuki Shobō, 1980.

Shimonaka Kunihiko, *Meisaku Sashie zenshū*, 10 vols, Tokyo, Heibonsha, 1980.

Shōji Sensui, "*Hongo kappan i'nyū igo*," in *Shōji Sensui chosaku shū*, vol. 9, *Shoshi hen*, Tokyo, Shuppan Nyūsu, 1982.

Sōga Tetsuo (ed.), *Genshoku gendai Nihon no bijutsu*, vol. 11, *Hanga*, Tokyo, Shōgakkan, 1978.

Suzuki Masafushi, *Hakubunkan "Taiyō" no kenkyū* (Chūgoku Kankei, Shinbun Zasshi Kaidai, III), Tokyo, Ajia Keizai Kenkyūjo, 1979.

Suzuki Sadami, "Kyōdō kenkyū hōkoku sōgō zasshi 'Taiyō' no sōgōteki kenkyū' chūkan hōkoku – sono3 jo" (and papers by Oda Michiko, Barbara Satō, Mitani Toshimasa, Hayashi Masako), *Nihon kenkyū*, vol. 17, February 1998.

_____, *Modan toshi no hyōgen*, Tokyo, Shirojisha, 1992.

Takami Hideo, kanshū, *Nihon kindai hanga no ayumi-ten: Nagase Yoshirō to Taishō, Shōwa senzenki no sakkatachi*, Tsukuba, Ibaragi Tsukuba Bijutsukan, 1994.

Takemura Tamio, *Taishō bunka*, Tokyo, Kōdansha, 1980.

Tokyo-to Bijutsukan, Yamaguchi Kenritsu Bijutsukan, Hyōgo Kenritsu Kindai Bijutsukan, and Asahi Shimbun (ed.), *1920 Nendai Nihon-ten: Toshi to zōkei no montāji*, Tokyo, Asahi Shimbun, 1988.

Tsubotani Zenshirō, *Hakubunkan gojūnenshi*, Tokyo, Hakubunkan, 1937.

Uehara Iwao (ed.), *Taishō Shōwa josei no fūzoku rokujūnen-shi*, Tokyo, Shufu no Tomosha, 1977.

Yamaguchi Masao, "Meiji shuppankai no hikari to yami: Hakubunkan no kōbō," [n.p., n.d.].

Chapter 3: The Formation of the Audiences (Omuka)

B.K., "Sekisan Bekken," *Mizue*, no. 46, January 1909, pp. 25–6.

Banjii, untitled statement, *Chūō bijutsu*, vol. 2, no. 1, January 1915, p. 118.

Fujishima Shūka, untitled statement, *Chūō bijutsu*, vol. 2, no. 2, March 1916, p. 114.

Gotō Kogai, untitled correspondence, *Mizue*, no. 7, January 1905, p. 20.

Henja (the editor), untitled statement, *Mizue*, no. 57, December 1909, p. 20.

Iwamatsu Jun, "Nihon no manga," *Atorie*, vol. 4, no. 9, September 1927.

_____, "Tomicha no e," *Atorie*, vol. 4, no. 7, August 1927.

Jun [Iwamatsu Jun], "4 jōhan danpen go," *Atorie*, vol. 5, no. 5, May 1928.

"Kaikoku," *Mizue*, no. 1, July 1905, p. 18.

Kisha (a staff writer), "Dokusha no pēji ni tsuite," *Atorie*, vol. 3, no. 10, October 1926.

Kon Wajirō and Yoshida Kenkichi (eds), *Kōgengaku: Modernologio*, Tokyo, Shunyōdō, 1930.

Matsui Senoo, "12 gatsugō o mite," *Chūō bijutsu*, vol. 4, no. 3, March 1918.

Miki Sadao, "Gadan kyūshō-roku," *Atorie*, vol. 2, no. 1, January 1925, p. 147.

Mizu no awa, "Nōgyō ka geijutsu ka," *Mizue*, no. 150, August 1917, pp. 35–8.

Mizue, no. 31, December 1907, p. 13.

Nakai Shōji, "Mizue no kachi," *Mizue*, no. 214, December 1922, p. 34.

Nittenshi Hensan Iinkai (ed.), *Nittenshi*, vol. 11, Tokyo, Nitten, 1983.

_____, *Nittenshi*, vol. 5, Tokyo, Nitten, 1981.

Omuka Toshiharu, "The Non-Continuity of the Avant-Garde," trans. by Chiaki Ajioka, in ex. cat. *Modern Boy, Modern Girl*, Sydney, Art Gallery of New South Wales, 1998, pp. 137–43.

_____, " 'Ginzara' jidai no Tōgō Seiji," in ex. cat. *Tōgō Seiji ten*, Kagoshima City Museum of Art, 1994, unpaginated.

_____, "Hihan sareru ishi — Ei Kyū no geijutsu to shōgai," in Honma Masayoshi (ed.), *Ei Kyū sakuhinshū*, Tokyo, Nihon Keizai Shinbunsha, 1997, pp. 10–33.

Ōshita Tōjirō, "Mizue go shūnen shokan," *Mizue*, no. 64, July 1910, p. 39.

Ruskin in Japan, Kamakura, Museum of Modern Art, 1997.

Ryokuyō, "Akitaken no fūkei," *Mizue*, no. 57, December 1909, p. 19.

Sankyaku dōjin, "Yo wa naniyue ni e wo egakitsutsu ariya," *Mizue*, no. 105, November 1913, p. 29.

Shiroya sei, "Ane no moto e," *Mizue*, no. 73, March 1911, p. 34.

Shitsumon sei, *Mizue*, no. 157, March 1918, p. 41.

Starting Anew in the Meiji Period: A Retrospective Exhibition of Paintings from the Hakubakai Group 1896–1911, Tokyo, Bridgestone Museum of Art, and other museums, 1996–97.

Sugita Hideo (Ei Kyū), "Gaji zakkō," *Atorie*, vol. 4, no. 1, January 1927.

Sugita, "Shin," *Atorie*, vol. 4, no. 2, February 1927.

Taishō gajin netwâku: Taguchi Kikutei ga hiraita Chūō bijutsu, Akita, Akita Museum of Modern Art, 1996.

Takada Keichū, "Dokusharan no shinkō o nozomu," *Chūō bijutsu*, vol. 4, no. 3, March 1918.

Tōkyō Geijutsu Daigaku Hyakunenshi Henshū Iinkai (ed.), *Tōkyō Geijutsu Daigaku hyakuneshi*, Tokyo, Ongaku no Tomosha, 1987.

Tōkyō Kokuritsu Hakubutsukan, *Tōkyō Kokuritsu Hakubutsukan hyakunenshi*, Tokyo, Tōkyō Kokuritsu Hakubutsukan, 1973.

Tsubouchi Naoko, untitled statement, *Chūō bijutsu*, vol. 2, no. 2, February 1916, p. 115.

_____, untitled statement, *Chūō bijutsu*, vol. 2, no. 3, March 1916, p. 119.

Chapter 4: On Rationalization (Kashiwagi)

Catalog, Kinomesha Exhibition of 1927.

Hayden, Dolores, *The Grand Domestic Revolution: History of Feminist Design for American Homes, Neighborhoods and Cities*, Cambridge, Mass., MIT Press, 1981.

Keiji Kōbō (ed.), *Seisan kōgyōteki kagu*, Tokyo, Kōyōsha, 1935.

Kogure Joichi, "Jugo kokumin seikatsu no gōrika," in his collection of essays, *Watashi no kōgei seikatsu shōshi*.

_____, *Wagaya wo kairyō shite*, Tokyo, Hakubunkan, 1930.

Kōgyō Chōsakai (ed.), *Kōgei nyuusu*, 1944.

Matthews, Glenna, *Just a Housewife*, Oxford, Oxford University Press, 1987.

Nishikawa Tomotake, *Kōgei gairon*, Tokyo, Kōseikai, 1935.

Research Committee for Improved Housing (ed.), *Jūtaku kagu no kaizen*, Tokyo, Seikatsu Kaizen Dōmei, 1924.

The Alliance for Lifestyle Improvement (ed.), *Seikatsu Kaizen Dōmeikai no honryō, Seikatsu kaizen*, vol. 1, 1921.

Chapter 5: Japanese Modernism and Consumerism (Weisenfeld)

Bogart, Michelle, *Artists, Advertising, and the Borders of Art*, Chicago, University of Chicago Press, 1995.

Crawcour, Sydney, "Industrialization and Technological Change, 1885–1920," in Peter Duus (ed.), *The Cambridge History of Japan: The Twentieth Century*, Cambridge, Cambridge University Press, 1988.

Fraser, James, Steven Heller, and Seymour Chwast, *Japanese Modern: Graphic Design Between the Wars*, San Francisco, Chronicle Books, 1996.

Gossot, Anne, "L'affiche publicitaire et le *gurafikku dezain* au Japon (1854–1960)," *Histoire de l'art*, no. 24, December 1993, pp. 79–91.

Greenhalgh, Paul (ed.), *Modernism in Design*, London, Reaktion Books, 1990.

Hamada Masuji, "Shōgyō bijutsu sōron," in Kitazawa Yoshio (ed.), *Gendai shōgyō bijutsu zenshū*, vol. 24, Tokyo, Ars Shuppansha, 1930, pp. 1–92.

_____, "Uridashi gaitō sōshoku no gainen to shōgyō bijutsu," in Kitahara Yoshio (ed.), *Uridashi gaitō sōshokushū*, vol. 10, *Gendai shōgyō bijutsu zenshū*, Tokyo, Ars Shuppansha, 1928, pp. 3–7.

_____, "Shashin oyobi manga ouyō kōkoku no gainen," in Kitazawa Yoshio (ed.), *Shashin oyobi manga ouyō kōkokushū*, vol. 13, *Gendai shōgyō bijutsu zenshū*, Tokyo, Ars Shuppansha, 1928, pp. 3–8.

Hatsuda Tōru, *Hyakkaten no tanjō*, Sanseidō Sensho, no. 178, Tokyo, Sanseidō, 1993.

Ishikawa Hiroyoshi and Ozaki Hatsuki, *Shuppan kōkoku no rekishi*, Tokyo, Shuppan Nyūsusha, 1989.

Iizawa Kohtaro, "The Bauhaus and shinkō shashin," in *Bauhausu no shashin korokiumu*, Kawasaki, Kawasaki Shimin Myūjiamu, 1997, pp. 134–9.

Kashiwagi Hiroshi, "Nihon no kindai dezain," in *Kenchiku to dezain, Nihon bijutsu zenshū: kindai no bijutsu IV*, no. 24, Tokyo, Kōdansha, 1993, pp. 168–75.

Kawahata Naomichi, "Kokusaku senden ni okeru datsu shōgyō bijutsu no nagare," in Matsudō Kyoiku Iinkai, *Shikaku no Shōwa 1930–1940*, Matsudō, Matsudō Kyoiku Iinkai, 1998, pp. 143–9.

Kayano Yatsuka, *Kindai nihon no dezain bunkashi 1868–1926*, Tokyo, Fuirumu Âtosha, 1992.

Kinross, Robin, "Introduction to the English-Language Edition," in Jan Tschichold, *The New Typography*, xv–xliv, trans. by Ruari McLean, Berkeley, University of California Press, 1987.

Kitazawa Noriaki, *Me no shinden*, Tokyo, Bijutsu Shuppansha, 1989.

Kitazawa Yoshio (ed.), *Gendai shōgyō bijutsu zenshū*, vols 1–24, Tokyo, Ars Shuppansha, 1928–30.
_____, *Kakushu shō uindō sōchishū*, vol. 4, *Gendai shōgyō bijutsu zenshū*, Tokyo, Ars Shuppansha, 1928–30.
Marquet, Christophe, "Asai Chū to 'zuan'," in *Kenchiku to dezain, Nihon bijutsu zenshū: kindai no bijutsu IV*, no. 24, Tokyo, Kōdansha, 1993, pp. 176–82.
Minami Hiroshi and Shakai Shinri Kenkyūjo, *Taishō bunka*, Tokyo, Keisō Shobō, 1965.
Mori Hitoshi, "The 1930s of [sic] Tokyo Kōtō Kōgei Gakkō," in Matsudō Kyoiku Iinkai, *Shikaku no Shōwa 1930–1940*, Matsudō, Matsudō Kyoiku Iinkai, 1998, pp. 23–31.
Murayama Tomoyoshi, *Kōseiha kenkyū*, Tokyo, Chōryūsha, 1926.
Nakai Kōichi, *Komasharu foto*, vol. 11, *Nihon shashin zenshū*, Tokyo, Shohan, 1986.
Phillips, Christopher, "Introduction," in *Montage and Modern Life: 1919–1942*, Cambridge, Mass., MIT Press, 1992, pp. 21–35.
Rubinfien, Louisa, "Commodity to National Brand: Manufacturers, Merchants, and the Development of the Consumer Market in Interwar Japan," Harvard University, PhD Dissertation, 1995.
Sugiura Hisui: Nihon modan dezain no kishu, Tokyo, Tabako to Shio no Hakubutsukan, 1994.
Tatsuke Yoichirō, *Oubei shōgyō posutā*, Tokyo, Nihon Kōkoku Gakkai Shuppan, 1926.

Chapter 6: The Cultured Life as Contested Space (Sand)

"Anka de tateta benri na ie," *Shufu no tomo*, vol. 1, no. 1, March 1917, p. 36.
Ambaras, David, "Social Knowledge, Cultural Capital, and the New Middle Class in Japan, 1895–1912," *Journal of Japanese Studies*, vol. 2, no. 1, 1998, pp. 1–33.
Bourdieu, Pierre, *Distinction: A Social Critique of the Judgement of Taste*, trans. by Richard Nice, Cambridge, Mass., Harvard University Press, 1984.
Chino Yōichi, *Kindai Nihon fujin kyōiku shi: taisei nai fujin dantai no keisei katei o chūshin ni*, Tokyo, Domesu Shuppan, 1979.
Fujiya Yōetsu, "Heiwahaku bunka mura shuppin jūtaku no sehyō ni tsuite," *Nihon kenchiku gakkai taikai gaku-jutsu kōen kōgaishū*, October 1982, pp. 2363–4.
_____, "Mejiro bunka mura," in Yamaguchi Hiroshi (ed.), *Kōgai jūtakuchi no keifu: Tōkyō no den'en yūtopia*, Tokyo, Kajima Shuppankai, 1988.
Garon, Sheldon, *Molding Japanese Minds: The State in Everyday Life*, Princeton, NJ, Princeton University Press, 1997.
Harootunian, Harry, "Introduction: A Sense of an Ending and the Problem of Taishō," in H.D. Harootunian and Bernard Silberman (eds), *Japan in Crisis: Essays in Taishō Democracy*, Princeton, NJ, Princeton University Press, 1974, pp. 3–28.
Huyssen, Andreas, *After the Great Divide: Modernism, Mass Culture, Postmodernism*, Bloomington, Ind., Indiana University Press, 1986.
Inaba Keiko, "Abe-sama no tsukutta gakusha machi Nishikatachō," in Yamaguchi (ed.), *Kōgai jūtakuchi no keifu*, pp. 48–60.
"Ippen shita natsu no shitsunai sōshoku," *Shufu no tomo*, vol. 10, no. 6, June 1926, p. 33.
Ishizuka Hiromichi and Narita Ryūichi, *Tōkyōto no hyakunen*, Tokyo, Yamakawa Shuppan, 1986.
Kinmonth, Earl, *The Selfmade Man in Meiji Japanese Thought: From Samurai to Salaryman*, Berkeley, Calif., University of California Press, 1981.
Kon Wajirō, "Kōgai fūzoku zakkei," reprinted in Kon Wajirō and Yoshida Kenkichi, *Moderunorojio "Kōgengaku,"* 1930 (facsimile edition, Gakuyō Shobō, 1986).
_____, "Shin katei no shinamono chōsa" (1926), reprinted in Kon Wajirō and Yoshida Kenkichi, *Moderunorojio "Kōgengaku,"* 1930 (facsimile edition, Gakuyō Shobō, 1986), pp. 164–5.
Maeda Ai, "Taishō kōki tsūzoku shōsetsu no tenkai, fujin zasshi no dokusha sō," in *Kindai dokusha no seiritsu*, Tokyo, Iwanami Dōjidai Raiburarii, 1993, pp. 211–83.
Minami Hiroshi, *Taishō bunka*, Tokyo, Keisō Shobō, 1965.
Nishikawa, Yūko, "Otoko no ie, onna no ie, seibetsu no nai heya: zoku sumai no hensen to 'katei' no seiritsu," in Wakita Haruko and Susan Hanley (eds), *Jendaa no Nihonshi 2: shutai to hyōgen, shigoto to seikatsu*, Tokyo, Tōkyō Daigaku Shuppankai, 1995.
Nishimura Isaku, *Sōshoku no enryō*, Tokyo, Bunka Seikatsu Kenkyūkai, 1922.
Nishiyama Uzō, *Nihon no sumai*, vol. 2, Tokyo, Keisō Shobō, 1976.
Ōkuma Yoshikuni, "Sōsetsu," in Jiji shinpō kateibu (eds), *Ie o sumiyoku suru hō*, Tokyo, Bunka Seikatsu Kenkyūkai, 1927.

Radway, Janice, "On the Gender of the Middlebrow Consumer and the Threat of the Culturally Fraudulent Female," *South Atlantic Quarterly*, vol. 93, no. 4, Fall 1994, pp. 871–93.

Shinbun shūroku Taishōshi dai 10 kan, Tokyo, Taishō Shuppan Kabushiki Kaisha, 1978.

Shufu no Tomosha (ed.), *Shufu no Tomosha no gojūnen*, Tokyo, Shufu no Tomosha, 1969.

Terade Kōji, *Seikatsu bunkaron e no shōtai*, Tokyo, Kōbundō, 1995.

Tōkyō Asahi shinbun, December 21, 1921, p. 5.

Tōkyōfu Shakaika, *Tōkyōshi oyobi kinsetsu chōson chūtō kaikyū jūtaku chōsa*, Tokyo, Tōkyōfu Shakaika, 1923.

Tsuruko, "Shumi to jitsuyō o kaneru chiisana yōkan," *Shufu no tomo*, December 1920, pp. 126–7.

Yumeno Kyūsaku, "Gaitō kara mita Tōkyō no rimen" (1924), reprinted in *Yumeno Kyūsaku zenshū*, vol. 2, Tokyo, Chikuma Bunko, 1992.

Chapter 7: The Café (Tipton)

Andō Kōsei, "Ginza jidai" (originally 1930) in Minami Hiroshi (ed.), *Gendai no esupuri*, no. 188, March 1983, pp. 131–4.

Asahi Shinbunsha (ed.), *Tōkyō no uta*, Tokyo, Asahi Shinbunsha, 1968.

Bradshaw Steve, *Café Society: Bohemian Life from Swift to Bob Dylan*, London, Weidenfeld & Nicolson, 1978.

Dōke Saiichirō, "Baishunfu ronkō" (originally 1928), in Minami Hiroshi (ed.), *Kindai shomin seikatsushi*, vol. 10, pp. 195–282.

Fujimori Terunobu, Hatsuda Tōru, and Fujioka Hiroyasu, *Ushinawareta teito Tōkyō: Taishō Shōwa no machi to sumai*, Tokyo, Kashiwa Shobō, 1991.

Garon, Sheldon, *Molding Japanese Minds*, Princeton, NJ, Princeton University Press, 1997.

Gonda Yasunosuke, "Modan seikatsu to hentai shikōsei," *Kaizō*, vol. 11, no. 6, June 1929, pp. 32–6.

Hatsuda Tōru, *Kafē to kissaten*, INAX Album 18, Tokyo, INAX Shuppan, 1993.

Hayashi Fumiko, *Hayashi Fumiko zenshū*, vols 1–3, Tokyo, Bunsendō, 1977.

Hibi Shigejirō, "Dōtonbori dōri" (originally 1930), in Minami Hiroshi (ed.), *Kindai shomin seikatsushi*, vol. 2, pp. 185–240.

Hori Makoto, "Gendai jokyūron" (originally 1931), in Minami (ed.), *Gendai no esupuri*, pp. 184–90.

Ishikado Harunosuke, *Ginza kaibōzu: Dai 1-pen Ginza hensenshi* (originally 1934), in Minami (ed.), *Kindai shomin seikatsushi*, vol. 2, pp. 286–332.

Katō Hidetoshi, "Service-Industry Business Complexes — The Growth and Development of 'Terminal Culture'," *The Japan Interpreter*, vol. 7, no. 3–4 (Summer–Autumn 1972), pp. 376–82.

Kusama Yasō, *Jokyū to baishōfu*, in the series *Kindai fujin mondai meicho senshū zoku hen*, vol. 9, Tokyo, Nihon Tosho Sentā, 1982.

Matsuzaki Tenmin, "Shinjuku inshōki, 2" (originally 1930), in Minami (ed.), *Kindai shomin seikatsushi*, vol. 2, pp. 349–51.

Minami Hiroshi (ed.), *Gendai no esupuri — Nihon modanizumu*, no. 188, March 1983.

——— (ed.), *Kindai shomin seikatsushi*, vol. 2, *Sakariba to uramachi*, Tokyo, San'ichi Shobō, 1984.

——— (ed.), *Kindai shomin seikatsushi*, vol. 10, *Kyōraku to sei*, Tokyo, San'ichi Shobō, 1988.

Mori Hideto, *Taishū bunkashi*, Tokyo, Kabushiki Kaisha Sanpō, 1964.

Murashima Yoriyuki, "Kanraku no ōkyū — kafe" (originally 1929), in Minami (ed.), *Kindai shomin seikatsushi*, vol. 10, pp. 317–79.

———, "Osaka kafē dan'atsushi" (originally 1929), in Minami (ed.), *Gendai no esupuri*, pp. 171–83.

Murobushi Kōshin (Takanobu), "Kafe shakaigaku," *Chūō kōron*, September 1929, pp. 188–91.

Nagy, Margit, "Middle-Class Working Women During the Interwar Years," in Gail Bernstein (ed.), *Recreating Japanese Women*, Berkeley and Los Angeles, University of California Press, 1991, pp. 199–216.

Newell, Susan, "Women Primary School Teachers and the State in Interwar Japan," in Elise K. Tipton (ed.), *Society and the State in Interwar Japan*, London, Routledge, 1997, pp. 17–41.

Ōbayashi Munetsugu, *Jokyū seikatsu no shin kenkyū*, in the series *Kindai fujin mondai meicho senshū, Shakai mondai hen*, vol. 3, Tokyo, Nihon Tosho Sentā, 1983.

Seidensticker, Edward, *Low City, High City*, Cambridge, Mass., Harvard University Press, 1983.

———, *Tokyo Rising*, Cambridge, Mass., Harvard University Press, 1991.

Shōwa Day by Day — Shōwa nimannichi no zenkiroku, vol. 1, Tokyo, Kōdansha, 1989.

Shunya Yoshimi, *Toshi no doramaturugi — Tōkyō, sakariba no shakaishi*, Tokyo, Kōbundō, 1987.

Silverberg, Miriam, "The Café Waitress Serving Modern Japan," in Stephen Vlastos (ed.), *Mirror of Modernity*, Berkeley and Los Angeles, University of California Press, 1998, pp. 208–25.

Takada Tamotsu, "Kafe, chian Nihon" (originally 1929), in Minami (ed.), *Gendai no esupuri*, pp. 167–9.

Tōkyō Hyakunenshi Henshū Iinkai (ed.), *Tōkyō hyakunenshi*, vol. 5, Tokyo, Gyōsei, 1979.

Uchida Roan, "Modan o kataru" (originally 1928), in Minami (ed.), *Gendai no esupuri*, pp. 16–24.

Watanabe, Shun'ichi, "Metropolitanism as a Way of Life: The Case of Tokyo, 1868–1930," in Anthony Sutcliffe (ed.), *Metropolis 1890–1940*, London, Mansell, 1984, pp. 403–29.

Chapter 8: An Alternate Informant (Sato)

Adorno, Theodor W. (with George Simpson), "On Popular Music", *Studies in Philosophy and Social Science* (Zeitschrift für Sozialforschung), vol. 9, 1941.

Beetham, Margaret, *A Magazine of HER OWN?: Domesticity and Desire in the Woman's Magazine, 1800–1914*, London and New York, Routledge, 1996.

Bobcock, Robert, *Consumption*, London and New York, Routledge, 1993.

Bungei shunjū, January 1928.

Chimoto Akiko, "Nihon ni okeru seibetsu yakuwari bungyō no keisei," in Ogino Miho et al., *Seido toshite no onna — sei, san, kazoku no hikaku shakaishi*, Heibonsha, 1990.

Fujin kōron, March, May, and July 1920.

Fujitake Akira, "Taishō bunka no seiritsu," in *Kōza gendai jānarizumu*, vol. 1, Tokyo, Jiji Tsūshinsha, 1981.

Fujokai (Seikatsu kairyō), May 1918.

Fukuda Sumiko et al., *Kōtō jogakkō shiryō shūsei — kōto jogakkō no kenkyū*, vol. 2, Tokyo, Ōzorasha, 1990.

Gluck, Carol, *Japan's Modern Myths: Ideology in the Late Meiji Period*, Princeton, NJ, Princeton University Press, 1985.

Grossman, Atina, "The New Woman and the Rationalization of Sexuality in Weimar Germany," in Ann Snitow, Christine Stansell, and Sharon Thompson (eds), *Powers of Desire: The Politics of Sexuality*, New York, Monthly Review Press, 1983.

Harrington, Ann M., "Women and Higher Education in the Japanese Empire (1869–1945)," *Journal of Asian History*, vol. 21, no. 2, 1987.

Hatsuda Tōru, *Hyakkaten no tanjō*, Tokyo, Sanseidō, 1993.

Hermes, Joke, *Reading Women's Magazines*, London, Polity Press, 1995.

Hirabayashi Hatsunosuke, "Fujin zasshi kanken," *Kaizō*, March 1927.

Iwasaki Jirō, *Bukka no sesō hen*, Tokyo, Yomiuri Shinbunsha, 1982.

Kimura Ryūko, "Fujin zasshi no jōhō kūkan to josei taishū dokushasō no seiritsu," *Shisō*, 812, February 1992.

Koyama Shizuko, *Ryōsai kenbo to iu kihan*, Tokyo, Keisō Shobō, 1991.

Maeda Ai, *Maeda Ai chosakushū*, vol. 2, Tokyo, Chikuma Shobō, 1989.

Matsushita Keiichi, "Taishū kokka no seiritsu to sono mondaisei," *Shisō*, no. 389, November 1956.

Mitsuda Kiyoko, "Kindaiteki boseikan no juyō to henka — 'kyōiku suru hahaoya' kara 'ryōsai kenbo' e," in Wakita Haruko (ed.), *Bosei o tou — rekishiteki hensen*, vol. 2, Tokyo, Jinbun Shoin, 1985.

Miyake Yasuko, *Gozen kuji*, Tokyo, Jitsugyō no Nihonsha, 1928.

Mott, Frank Luther, *A History of American Magazines, 1741–1930*, vols 1–5, Cambridge, Mass., Harvard University Press, 1938–39.

Murakami Nobuhiko, *Nihon no fujin mondai*, Tokyo, Iwanami Shinsho, 1978.

Nedan no Meiji, Taishō, Shōwa fūzoku shi, Tokyo, Asahi Shinbunsha, 1981.

Nishikawa Junsei, *Fujin shin undō*, Tokyo, Kōkyō Shoin, 1920.

Ogi Shinzō, Kumakura Isao, and Ueno Chizuko (eds), *Nihon kindai shisō taikei — fūzoku, sei*, Tokyo, Iwanami Shoten, 1990.

_____, Haga Tōru, and Maeda Ai, *Tōkyō kūkan — 1868–1930*, vol. 3, *Modan Tōkyō*, Tokyo, Chikuma Shobō, 1986.

Ōhama Tetsuya and Kumakura Isao, *Kindai Nihon no seikatsu to shakai*, Tokyo, Hōsō Daigaku, 1989.

Oka Mitsuo, *Fujin zasshi jānarizumu*, Tokyo, Gendai Jānarizumu Shuppankai, 1981.

Okano Takeo, *Nihon shuppan bunka shi*, Tokyo, Hara Shobō, 1981.

Shufu no tomo, July 1918.

Shufu no Tomosha no gojūnen, Tokyo, Shufu no Tomosha, 1967.

Sōgō jānarizumu kōza, vols 5, 7, 10, and 12, Tokyo, Naigai Shuppansha, 1931.

Sukemori Kinji, *Joshi shinsahō*, Tokyo, Kinkōdō, 1928.

Uchida Roan, *Uchida Roan zenshū*, vol. 3, Tokyo, Yamani Shobō, 1987.

Uno, Kathleen, "The Origins of 'Good Wife, Wise Mother' in Modern Japan," in Erich Pauer and Regine Mathias (eds), *Japanische Frauengeschichte(n)*, Marburg, Forderverein Marburger Japan-Reihe, 1995.

Wright, Gwendolyn, "Prescribing the Model Home," in Arien Mack (ed.), *Home: A Place in the World*, New York, New York University Press, 1993.

Yamakawa Kikue, *Yamakawa Kikue shū*, vol. 5, Tokyo, Iwanami Shoten, 1982.

Yosano Akiko, "Fujin zasshi no dakyōteki keikō" (1919), in *Teihon Yosano Akiko zenshū*, vol. 11, Tokyo, Kōdansha, 1980.

Chapter 9: The Divided Appetite (Aoyama)

Akutagawa Ryūnosuke, *Akutagawa Ryūnosuke zenshū*, vol. 3, Tokyo, Iwanami Shoten, 1977.

Aoyama, Tomoko, "Cannibalism, Gastronomy, and Anorexia: A Short History of Eating in Modern Japanese Literature," paper presented at the 19th Biennial Conference of the Japanese Studies Association of Australia, July 1997, to be included in the forthcoming proceedings.

Arashiyama Kōzaburō, *Bunjin akujiki*, Tokyo, Magajin Hausu, 1997.

Barthes Roland, *Elements of Semiology*, trans. by Annette Lavers and Colin Smith, New York, Hill & Wang, 1967.

———, *Empire of Signs*, trans. by Richard Howard, New York, Hill & Wang, 1982.

———, *Monogatari no kōzō bunseki*, trans. by Hanawa Hikaru, Tokyo, Misuzu Shobō, 1979.

———, *The Rustle of Language*, trans. by Richard Howard, New York, Hill & Wang, 1986.

Chiba Sen'ichi, *Gendai bungaku no hikaku bungakuteki kenkyū, modanizumu no shiteki dōtai*, Tokyo, Yagi Shoten, 1978.

Davis, A.R. (ed.), *Modern Japanese Poetry*, trans. by James Kirkup, St Lucia, University of Queensland Press, 1978.

Edogawa Ranpo, *Ankokusei, Yami ni ugomeku*, Tokyo, Shunyōsha, Edogawa Ranpo Bunko, 1988.

Fowler, Edward, *The Rhetoric of Confessions: Shishōsetsu in Early Twentieth-Century Japanese Fiction*, Berkeley and London, University of California Press, 1988.

Hagiwara Sakutarō, *Hagiwara Sakutarō*, Itō Shinkichi et al. (eds), *Nihon no shiika*, vol. 14, Tokyo, Chūō Kōronsha, 1968.

———, *Hagiwara Sakutarō shū*, *Nihon kindai bungaku taikei*, vol. 37, Tokyo, Kadokawa Shoten, 1971.

Hayama Yoshiki, Kobayashi Takiji, and Nakano Shigeharu, *Hayama Yoshiki, Kobayashi Takiji, Nakano Shigeharu shū, Gendai nihon bungaku zenshū*, vol. 67, Tokyo, Chikuma Shobō, 1967.

Hayashi Fumiko, *Hayashi Fumiko shū, Shōwa bungaku zenshū*, vol. 19, Tokyo, Kadokawa Shoten, 1953.

Hijiya-Kirschnereit, Irmela, *Rituals of Self-revelation: Shishosetsu as Literary Genre and Socio-cultural Phenomenon*, Cambridge, Mass., Harvard University Press, 1996.

Hirabayashi Taiko, *Hirabayashi Taiko shū, Shinsen gendai nihon bungaku zenshū*, vol. 18, Tokyo, Chikuma Shobō, 1959.

Ishige Naomichi, *Shokuji no bunmei ron*, Tokyo, Chūō Kōronsha, Chūkō Shinsho, 1982.

———, *Shoku no bunka chiri, shita no firudo wāku*, Tokyo, Asahi Shinbunsha, Asahi Sensho, 1995.

Itō Shinkichi et al. (eds), *Nihon no shiika*, vols 14, 16, 20, and 26, Tokyo, Chūō Kōronsha, 1967–70.

Kaikō Takeshi, *Saigo no bansan*, Tokyo, Bungei Shunjūsha, Bunshun Bunko, 1982.

Kajii Motojirō, Miyoshi Tatsuji, and Hori Tatsuo, *Gendai nihon bungaku zenshū*, vol. 43, Tokyo, Chikuma Shobō, 1954.

Karatani Kōjin, *Nihon kindai bungaku no kigen*, Tokyo, Kōdansha Bunko, 1988.

Kawabata Yasunari, *Kawabata Yasunari shū, Gendai nihon bungaku zenshū*, vol. 66, Tokyo, Chikuma Shobō, 1967.

Kawamoto Saburō, *Taishō gen'ei*, Tokyo, Chikuma Bunko, 1997.

Keene, Donald, *Dawn to the West: Japanese Literature in the Modern Era*, vol. 1, New York, Henry Holt & Company, 1987.

Kitaōji Rosanjin, *Rosanjin midō*, Tokyo, Chūkō Bunko, revised edition, 1995.

Lévi-Strauss, Claude, *The Raw and the Cooked: Introduction to a Science of Mythology, I*, trans. by John and Doreen Weightman, New York and Evanston, Harper & Row, 1969.

Miyamoto Yuriko, *Gendai nihon bungaku zenshū*, vol. 64, Tokyo, Chikuma Shobō, 1967.

Miyazawa Kenji, *Kōhon Miyazawa Kenji zenshū*, vol. 11, Tokyo, Chikuma Shobō, 1974.

Nakano Miyoko, *Kanibarizumu ron*, Tokyo, Fukutake Bunko, 1987.

Ogi Masahiro, *Rekishi wa gurume*, Tokyo, Chūkō Bunko, 1986.

Ogino Anna, *Watashi no aidokusho*, Tokyo, Fukutake Shoten, 1991.

Sata Ineko and Tsuboi Sake, *Sata Ineko Tsuboi Sakae shū, Nihon gendai bungaku zenshū*, vol. 83, Tokyo, Kōdansha, 1964.

Shea, G.T., *Leftwing Literature in Japan: A Brief History of the Proletarian Literary Movement*, Tokyo, The Hosei University Press, 1964.

Shiga Naoya, *Shiga Naoya shū, Gendai bungaku taikei*, vol. 21, Tokyo, Chikuma Shobō, 1963.

Suzuki Sadami, *Nihon no "bungaku" o kangaeru*, Tokyo, Kadokawa Sensho, 1994.

Suzuki, Tomi, *Narrating the Self: Fictions of Japanese Modernity*, Stanford, Stanford University Press, 1996.

Takahashi Gen'ichirō, *Bungakuō*, Tokyo, Kadokawa Bunko, 1996.

Takamura Kōtarō, *Takamura Kōtarō zenshū*, vol. 1, Tokyo, Chikuma Shobō, 1957.

Tanaka, Yukiko (ed. and trans.), *To Live and to Write*, Seattle, Wash., The Seal Press, 1987.

Tanizaki Jun'ichirō, *Tanizaki Jun'ichirō zenshū*, vols 6 and 10, Tokyo, Chūō Kōronsha, 1973.

Toda Tatsuo, "Shokuyoku," *Mavo*, no. 2, July 1924, [n.p.].

Washburn, Dennis C., *The Dilemma of the Modern in Japanese Fiction*, New Haven and London, Yale University Press, 1995.

" 'Watashigatari' no gensetsu ni tsuite," *zadankai* with Hijiya-Kirschnereit, Kamei Hideo, Suzuki Tomi, Fujii Sadakazu, and Munakata Kazushige, *Bungaku*, vol. 9, no. 2, Spring 1998, pp. 2–26.

Chapter 10: The Past in the Present (Wilson)

Anderson, Benedict, *Imagined Communities: Reflections on the Origin and Spread of Nationalism*, London and New York, Verso, revised edition, 1991.

Berger, Peter L., *Facing up to Modernity: Excursions in Society, Politics, and Religion*, Harmondsworth, Penguin Books, 1979.

Clement, Ernest W., *A Handbook of Modern Japan*, Chicago, A.C. McClurg & Co., 4th edition, 1904.

"Eiga monogatari: Dōinrei," *Ie no hikari*, December 1931, pp. 67–71.

Fritzsche, Peter, *A Nation of Fliers: German Aviation and the Popular Imagination*, Cambridge, Mass., Harvard University Press, 1992.

Gluck, Carol, *Japan's Modern Myths: Ideology in the Late Meiji Period*, Princeton, NJ, Princeton University Press, 1985.

Halstead, Murat, *The War Between Russia and Japan, Containing Thrilling Accounts of Fierce Battles by Sea and Land*, Sydney and Melbourne, Walter R. Hayes & Co., c. 1906.

Hara Kei, "Sekai ni gokai saretaru Nihon no kokuminsei (Nihon wa hatashite gunbatsukuni nari ya)," October 1920, in *Hara Kei zenshū*, vol. 1, Tokyo, Hara Kei Zenshū Kankōkai, 1929, pp. 1128–36.

Hatoyama Ichirō, "Kenkoku no seishin ni tsuite," *Fujo shinbun*, February 14, 1932, p. 4.

"Heiki to gunkan," *Ie no hikari*, January 1933, pp. 16–18.

Iwasaki Sakae, "Hikō shōshi buyūden," *Ie no hikari*, June 1933, pp. 43–7.

Kajima, Morinosuke, *The Diplomacy of Japan 1894–1922*, Vol. II, *Anglo-Japanese Alliance and Russo-Japanese War*, Tokyo, Kajima Institute of International Peace, 1978.

Kamata Eikichi, "Sangyōteki aikokushin," *Ie no hikari*, October 1932, pp. 20–1.

Katsura Tarō, *Katsura Tarō jiden*, Tokyo, Heibonsha, 1993.

Keene, Donald, "The Sino-Japanese War of 1894–95 and its Cultural Effects in Japan," in Donald H. Shively (ed.), *Tradition and Modernization in Japanese Culture*, Princeton, NJ, Princeton University Press, 1971, pp. 121–75.

"Kōgun no iryoku atarashii heiki," *Ie no hikari*, June 1933, pp. 200–1.

"Kojin dōtoku to kokusai dōtoku," *Fujo shinbun*, March 13, 1932, p. 1.

"Kokoku Nihon no fukkō: daishinsai jūshūnen ni saishite," *Fujo shinbun*, August 27, 1933, p. 1.

"Kokumin undō," *Fujo shinbun*, December 13, 1931, p. 7.

Lone, Stewart, *Japan's First Modern War: Army and Society in the Conflict with China, 1894–95*, Basingstoke, Macmillan, 1994.

———, "Region and Nation in Wartime Japan, 1904–05," paper presented to Asian Studies Association of Australia Conference, Sydney, September–October 1998.

"Manshū gunji bidan," *Ie no hikari*, February 1932, Children's Section, pp. 172–8.

Matsumura Sazo and Akashi Hirotaka, *Shōwa tokkō dan'atsushi 5: shomin ni taisuru dan'atsu*, Tokyo, 1975.

Mineda Hiroshi, "Isho ga monogataru yamato damashii," *Ie no hikari*, February 1932, pp. 12–13.

Noma, Seiji, *The Nine Magazines of Kodansha: The Autobiography of a Japanese Publisher*, London, Methuen & Co., 1934.

Oakley, Jane H., *A Russo-Japanese War Poem*, Brighton, Standard Press, 1905.

Ôe Shinobu, *Nichiro sensô to Nihon guntai*, Tokyo, Tachikaze Shobô, 1987.

Ôe Soten, "Manshû kôshinkyoku," *Ie no hikari*, March 1932, pp. 182–3.

Pierson, John D., *Tokutomi Soho, 1863–1957: A Journalist for Modern Japan*, Princeton, NJ, Princeton University Press, 1980.

"Senran no Shina de iryoku o hakkisuru shinheiki no hanashi," *Fujo shinbun*, February 21, 1932, Girls' Section, p. 4.

Tan'o Yasunori and Kawada Akihisa, *Imeeji no naka no sensô* (*Kindai Nihon no bijutsu 1*), Tokyo, Iwanami Shoten, 1996.

Trefalt, Beatrice, "War Monuments, War Memories and Nationalism," paper presented at the Asian Studies Association of Australia Conference, Sydney, September–October 1998.

Van Alstyne, Richard W., *The United States and East Asia*, London, Thames & Hudson, 1973.

Wilson, Sandra, "Bureaucrats and Villagers in Japan: *Shimin* and the Crisis of the Early 1930s," *Social Science Japan Journal*, vol. 1, no. 1, April 1998, pp. 121–40.

_____, "The Russo-Japanese War and Japan: Politics, Nationalism and Historical Memory," in David Wells and Sandra Wilson (eds), *The Russo-Japanese War in Cultural Perspective*, Basingstoke, Macmillan, 1999, pp. 160–93.

Yamawaki Fusako, "Taibô no 1932 nen," *Fujo shinbun*, January 1, 1932, Girls' Section, p. 1.

Chapter 11: Modern Selves and Modern Spaces (Mackie)

Anderson, Benedict, *Imagined Communities: Reflections on the Origins and Spread of Nationalism*, London, Verso, 1983.

Aoyama, Tomoko, "The Divided Appetite: 'Eating' in the Literature of the 1920s," this volume.

Barlow, Tani E. (ed.), *Formations of Colonial Modernity in East Asia*, Durham, Duke University Press, 1997.

_____, "Introduction: On 'Colonial Modernity'," in Tani Barlow (ed.), *Formations of Colonial Modernity in East Asia*, Durham, Duke University Press, 1997, pp. 1–20.

Berman, Marshall, "The Signs in the Street," *New Left Review*, 1984.

Chakrabarty, Dipesh, "Afterword: Revisiting the Tradition/Modernity Binary," in Stephen Vlastos (ed.), *Mirror of Modernity: Invented Traditions of Modern Japan*, Berkeley, University of California Press, 1998.

Chimoto Akiko, "The Birth of the Full-Time Housewife in the Japanese Worker's Household as Seen through Family Budget Surveys," *US–Japan Women's Journal*, English Supplement, no. 8, 1995.

Clark, John, "Indices of Modernity: Changes in Popular Reprographic Representation," this volume.

Damousi, Joy, *Women Come Rally: Socialism, Communism and Gender in Australia, 1890–1955*, Melbourne, Oxford University Press, 1994.

Fujii Tadatoshi, *Kokubô Fujinkai*, Tokyo, Iwanami Shoten, 1985.

Fujime Yuki, *Sei no Rekishigaku*, Tokyo, Fuji Shuppan, 1997.

_____, "The Licensed Prostitution System and the Prostitution Abolition Movement in Modern Japan," *positions: east asia cultures critique*, vol. 3, no. 1, Spring 1997, pp. 135–70.

Garon, Sheldon, *Molding Japanese Minds: The State in Everyday Life*, Princeton, NJ, Princeton University Press, 1997.

_____, "The World's Oldest Debate? Prostitution and the State in Imperial Japan, 1900–1945," *American Historical Review*, June 1993, pp. 710–32.

Gordon, Andrew, *Labor and Imperial Democracy in Prewar Japan*, Berkeley, University of California Press, 1991.

Grewal, Inderpal, *Home and Harem: Nation, Gender and the Cultures of Travel*, Durham and London, Duke University Press, 1996.

Hosoi Wakizô, *Jokô aishi*, Tokyo, Kaizôsha, 1925.

Inoue, Mariko, "The Gaze of the Café Waitress: From Selling Eroticism to Constructing Autonomy," *US–Japan Women's Journal*, English Supplement, no. 15, 1998.

Ishimoto Shidzue, *Facing Two Ways: The Story of My Life*, New York, Farrar & Rinehart, 1935 (reprint: Stanford, Stanford University Press, 1986).

Kashiwagi Hiroshi, "On Rationalization and the National Lifestyle: Japanese Design of the 1920s and 1930s," this volume.

Koschmann, J. Victor (ed.), *Total War and "Modernization,"* Ithaca, Cornell University Press, 1998.

Mackie, Vera, "Liberation and Light: The Language of Opposition in Imperial Japan," *East Asian History*, no. 9, 1995, pp. 99–115.

_____, *Creating Socialist Women in Japan: Gender, Labour and Activism, 1900–1937*, Cambridge, Cambridge University Press, 1997.

Matsumoto Katsuhira, *Nihon shakaishugi engeki shi: Meiji Taishō hen*, Tokyo, Chikuma Shobō, 1975.

Menzies, Jackie (ed.), *Modern Boy, Modern Girl: Modernity in Japanese Art 1910–1935*, Sydney, Art Gallery of New South Wales, 1998.

Mizusawa Tsutomu, "The Artists Start to Dance: The Changing Image of the Body in Art of the Taishō Period," this volume.

Murobushi Kōshin (Takanobu), "Kafe shakaigaku," *Chūō kōron*, September 1929.

Muta Kazue, "Images of the Family in Meiji Periodicals: The Paradox Underlying the Emergence of the 'Home'," *US–Japan Women's Journal*, English Supplement, no. 7, 1994, pp. 53–71.

Nakazawa Yōko, "Katei, uchi, kanai, hōmu," in Satō Kiyoji (ed.), *Kōza Nihongo no goi*, vol. 9, Part 1, Tokyo, Meiji Shoin, 1983, pp. 222–7.

Narita Ryūichi, "Women in the Motherland: Oku Mumeo through Wartime and Postwar," in J. Victor Koschmann (ed.), *Total War and "Modernization,"* Ithaca, Cornell University Press, 1998.

Nava, Mica and A. O'Shea (eds), *Modern Times: Reflections on a Century of English Modernity*, London, Routledge, 1996.

Nishikawa Yūko, "The Changing Form of Dwellings and the Establishment of the *Katei* (Home) in Modern Japan," *US–Japan Women's Journal*, English Supplement, no. 8, 1995, pp. 3–36.

Omuka Toshiharu, "The Formation of the Audiences for Modern Art in Japan," this volume.

Robertson, Jennifer, *Takarazuka*, Berkeley, University of California Press, 1998.

Sand, Jordan, "At Home in the Meiji Period: Inventing Japanese Domesticity," in Stephen Vlastos (ed.), *Mirror of Modernity: Invented Traditions of Modern Japan*, Berkeley, University of California Press, 1998, pp. 191–207.

_____, "The Cultured Life as Contested Space: Dwelling and Discourse in the 1920s," this volume.

Sato, Barbara Hamill, "An Alternate Informant: Middle-Class Women and Mass Magazines in 1920s Japan," this volume.

Silverberg, Miriam, "The Café Waitress Serving Modern Japan," in Stephen Vlastos (ed.), *Mirror of Modernity: Invented Traditions of Modern Japan*, Berkeley, University of California Press, 1998.

_____, "Advertising Every Body," in S.L. Foster (ed.), *Choreographing History*, Bloomington, Ind., Indiana University Press, 1995.

_____, "Remembering Pearl Harbor, Forgetting Charlie Chaplin, and the Case of the Disappearing Western Woman: A Picture Story," in Tani Barlow (ed.), *Formations of Colonial Modernity in East Asia*, Durham, Duke University Press, 1997.

_____, "The Modern Girl as Militant," in Gail Lee Bernstein (ed.), *Recreating Japanese Women: 1600–1945*, Berkeley, University of California Press, 1991, pp. 239–66.

Stoler, Ann Laura, "Educating Desire in Colonial Southeast Asia: Foucault, Freud, and Imperial Sexualities," in Lenore Manderson and Margaret Jolly (eds), *Sites of Desire, Economies of Pleasure: Sexualities in Asia and the Pacific*, Chicago, University of Chicago Press, 1997, pp. 27–47.

_____, *Race and the Education of Desire: Foucault's History of Sexuality and the Colonial Order of Things*, Durham, Duke University Press, 1995.

Summers, Anne, *Damned Whores and God's Police: The Colonization of Women in Australia*, Harmondsworth, Penguin Books, 1975.

Suzuki Sumuko, "Jūgun kangofu," *Jūgoshi nōto*, no. 3, 1979, pp. 1–8.

Suzuki Yūko, *Jokō to rōdō sōgi*, Tokyo, Renga Shobō, 1989.

Tipton, Elise, "The Café: Contested Space of Modernity in Interwar Japan," this volume.

Vlastos, Stephen (ed.), *Mirror of Modernity: Invented Traditions of Modern Japan*, Berkeley, University of California Press, 1998.

Weisenfeld, Gennifer, "Imaging Calamity: Artists in the Capital after the Great Kantō Earthquake," in Jackie Menzies (ed.), *Modern Boy, Modern Girl: Modernity in Japanese Art 1910–1935*, Sydney, Art Gallery of New South Wales, 1998.

_____, "Japanese Modernism and Consumerism: Forging the New Artistic Field of '*Shōgyō Bijutsu*' (Commercial Art)," this volume.

Wilson, Sandra, "The Past in the Present: War in Narratives of Modernity in the 1920s and 1930s," this volume.

Notes on Contributors

Tomoko Aoyama is a senior lecturer in the Department of Japanese at the University of Queensland, Brisbane, Queensland, Australia.

John Clark is an associate professor in the School of Asian Studies and Department of Art History and Theory at the University of Sydney, Sydney, New South Wales, Australia.

Kashiwagi Hiroshi is Professor of Design at Musashino Fine Arts University in Tokyo, Japan.

Vera Mackie is the Foundation Professor of Japanese Studies at Curtin University of Technology in Perth, Western Australia, Australia.

Mizusawa Tsutomu is the Head Curator at the Museum of Modern Art, Kamakura in Kanagawa Prefecture, Japan.

Omuka Toshiharu is a professor in the Institute of Art and Design at the University of Tsukuba, Ibaraki Prefecture, Japan.

Jordan Sand is an assistant professor in the Department of East Asian Languages and Cultures at Georgetown University, Washington, DC, USA.

Barbara Hamill Sato is a professor at Seikei University in Tokyo, Japan.

Elise K. Tipton is a senior lecturer in Japanese Studies in the School of Asian Studies at the University of Sydney, Sydney, New South Wales, Australia.

Gennifer Weisenfeld is an assistant professor in the Department of Art History at Duke University, North Carolina, USA.

Sandra Wilson is a senior lecturer in Asian Studies at Murdoch University, Murdoch, Western Australia, Australia.

Index

Page numbers in bold type (e.g. **15–24**) refer to the major discussion of a topic.
Page numbers in italics (e.g. *15*) refer to illustrations.